WILFRID SHEED

Wilfrid Sheed was born in London on 27 December 1930. His parents were the writers and publishers Frank Sheed and Maisie Ward Sheed, founders of the publishing firm Sheed and Ward.

He was educated at Downside Academy and Oxford. In the late 1950s he began writing about movies for *Jubilee* in New York, and later was the drama critic and book editor for *Commonweal*. His reviews and essays have appeared in many magazines and newspapers, including *The Atlantic, Esquire, GQ, Life, The New York Times Book Review*, and *Sports Illustrated*.

His novels *Office Politics* (1966), *Max Jamison* (1970) and *People Will Always Be Kind* (1973) were nominated for National Book Awards; he has also been nominated for the National Book Critics' Circle Award in criticism.

His other novels are: *A Middle Class Education* (1960); *The Hack* (1963); *Square's Progress* (1965); *The Blacking Factory & Pennsylvania Gothic: A Short Novel and a Long Story* (1968); *Transatlantic Blues* (1978); and *The Boys of Winter* (1987).

His essays, articles, and reviews have been collected in several volumes: *The Morning After* (1971), *The Good Word & Other Words* (1978); *Essays in Disguise* (1990). Among his other works of non-fiction are *Muhammad Ali: A Portrait in Words and Photographs* (1975); *Clare Booth Luce* (1982); *Frank & Maisie: A Memoir with Parents* (1985); *Baseball and Lesser Sports* (1991); and *My Life as a Fan* (1993). His "memoir of recovery," *In Love with Daylight* (1995), is available in A COMMON READER EDITION.

He has received a Guggenheim fellowship, an award in literature from the National Institute and American Academy, and a Grammy Award for his liner notes to *The Voice: Frank Sinatra, The Columbia Years 1943–52*. From 1972 until 1988 he was a member of the Book-of-the-Month Club editorial board.

Wilfrid Sheed and his wife, the writer Miriam Ungerer, live in Sag Harbor, New York.

SO-BFA-505

By the same author in
COMMON READER EDITIONS:

Max Jamison

In Love with Daylight: A Memoir of Recovery

The Morning After
. . . and Long After

SELECTED ESSAYS AND REVIEWS

Wilfrid Sheed

A COMMON READER EDITION
THE AKADINE PRESS
2001

To Liz, Frank and Marion

*Wasted hours
that could have been spent
practicing the uke,
the bank shot, laughing.*

Acknowledgments

All the reviews in Part Four and two pieces in Part Three: "Theater Revisited" and "Theater 1980 (as seen by *The New York Times*)," were first published in *Esquire*. The articles "The Politician as Professor" and "The Writing Condition" first appeared in *New American Review*. The other essays and reviews (some in slightly different form and under different titles) appeared in: *The New York Times Book Review, Encounter, The Atlantic, Commonweal, The New York Review of Books, Life, The Critic, Book World* and *Sports Illustrated*. The author wishes to thank the editors of these publications for permission to reprint.

The Akadine Press thanks *Commonweal* ("William Buckley: The Killer with a Heart of Gold") and *The Yale Review* ("There Goes the Judge") for permission to reprint.

Contents

Introduction   xiii

PART ONE

1 / *The Politics of Reviewing*   3
2 / NORMAN MAILER: *Genius or Nothing*   9
3 / WALKER PERCY: *The Last Gentleman*   18
4 / JAMES JONES: *Go to the Widow Maker*   22
5 / JOHN UPDIKE: *Couples*   36
6 / GORE VIDAL: *Reflections upon a Sinking Ship*   43
7 / *Orchids for Miss Hightower*   48
8 / *Collected Short Prose* of JAMES AGEE   52
9 / BERNARD MALAMUD: *Pictures of Fidelman*   59
10 / *The Artist as Blimp*   62
11 / *Racing the Clock with* GREENE & PRITCHETT   66
12 / JAMES BALDWIN: *Tell Me How Long the Train's Been Gone*   76
13 / ROBERT COOVER: *The Universal Baseball Association*   79
14 / WILLIAM STYRON: *The Confessions of Nat Turner*   83

ix

CONTENTS

PART TWO

Superb → 1 / *Confessions of a Sports Nut* 93
2 / *The Good Old Days in California* 105
3 / EUGENE MCCARTHY: *The Politician as Professor* 121

PART THREE

1 / *The Kitchen* 135
2 / *An Evening's* FROST 138
3 / *Marat/Sade* 142
4 / *The Glass Menagerie* 147
5 / *The Seven Descents of Myrtle* 151
6 / *Inadmissible Evidence* 154
7 / *Hughie* 157
8 / *Baker Street* 161
9 / *A Delicate Balance* 165
10 / *A View from the Bridge* 168
11 / *Theater Revisited* 172
12 / *Theater 1980 (as seen by The New York Times)* 180

PART FOUR

1 / *Blow-Up* 185
2 / *La Guerre est Finie* 189
3 / *Persona* 191
4 / *On Violence* 195
5 / *Les Carabiniers/ How I Won the War/
Cinéma Vérité* 202
6 / *In Cold Blood* 209
7 / *The Hippie Revolt/ 491/ The Stranger* 212

Contents

8 / *The Hour of the Wolf* 216

9 / *Thérèse and Isabelle/ Young Törless* 219

10 / *Chicago/ Weekend* 222

11 / *The Birthday Party* 227

12 / *The Fixer/ The Charge of the Light Brigade/ Greetings* 230

PART FIVE

1 / *The Minor Novelist* 237

2 / *Private* CHAMBERS *v. Public* CHAMBERS 243

3 / ALBERTO MORAVIA: *The Lie* 253

4 / S. J. PERELMAN: *Baby, It's Cold Inside* 256

5 / CHESTERBELLOC 259

6 / KURT VONNEGUT: *Slaughterhouse-Five* 276

7 / WILLIAM GOLDING: *The Pyramid* 280

8 / NORMAN PODHORETZ: *Making It* 283

9 / GIUSEPPE BERTO: *Incubus* 293

10 / IRIS MURDOCH: *The Red and the Green* 296

11 / *The Writing Condition* 299

. . . AND LONG AFTER

1 / WILLIAM BUCKLEY: *The Killer with a Heart of Gold* 307

2 / *There Goes the Judge* 318

Introduction

"WHO IS MAX JAMISON?" THIS PECULIAR question has followed me ever since I wrote a novel of that name about a critic who couldn't turn off his engine, but kept on reviewing everything in sight from his furniture to his family to, most brilliantly and brutally, himself. Max was nothing if not fair.

Since readers seem to prefer true stories to made-up ones, and since I was getting kind of curious myself, I tried for a while actually answering the question, in hopes of surprising myself with the truth. But none of the names I came up with, from Alexander Woollcott to Pauline Kael to Flaubert's ever-popular "Jamison, *c'est moi*" quite seemed to fit, including, thank God, my own, as was proved once and for all, I trust, by my first collection of reviews and stuff called *The Morning After*, which came out not long after Max, and which the Akadine Press is now obligingly reissuing alongside it. Max most decidedly did not write "stuff" and would not have approved a single word of mine, even if I'd stayed with my working title of *Kiss the Blood Off My Typewriter*, which he had perhaps inspired himself.

"So Max Jamison is a composite, right?" For a piece that may possibly run, space allowing, on the last page of next month's Arts roundup, this discussion has probably gone on quite long enough, and the above sentence seems to be universal interview-speak for "time's up!" Now if you'll just agree to this obvious proposition . . .

But to an unknown writer (as which writer is not these days?), one more line in the *Podunk Picayune* is always worth shooting for. So one day, I finally decided to answer this question too. "No, he's not a composite," I said, "he's an essence."

Eureka! "Max Jamison is a composite," the man wrote anyway, but I *had* surprised myself after all with the whole secret of writing novels, my novels anyhow. You just hang around a subject, professional, political, domestic, for a few years or minutes until you suddenly get the gist of it and then without consciously thinking about it again, you turn on the dream machine and start taking notes. And pretty soon a voice will come in. Who *is* this and what does he want? Never mind. Keep him talking and maybe he'll give himself away, plus possibly the person he's talking to, and, if you're really hot today, maybe some décor and an indefinable smell. And by the time you're done, someone will tell you that you have just written a perfect description of a person you've never met and a place you've never been.

Thus, after the inevitable treading of water and crossing of burning sand for the usual 100 years or so, one arrives at a complete Max Jamison; and once he's on the page, he's also on his own. Your guess about him by now is at least as good as mine—and maybe as good as his too. Because although Max much prefers to talk for himself and have the last word, I'm not sure he ever gets himself quite right. People seldom do.

My own reviewing life is quite another story. In fact, I myself might very well be a composite. My first reviewing self was simply a common-or-garden kibitzer trolling for laughs. A friend named Ed Rice had asked me to cover movies for his highbrow Catholic picture magazine, if you can imagine such a thing, called *Jubilee*, and I told him I hadn't seen a movie in three years. "That's great," he said. "Just make some jokes." And, he added reassuringly, "They don't even have to be about movies."

That was simply what you did with movies in the late 1950s. *Jubilee* could be deadly serious about the other arts, as I learned when I tried cracking some jokes about Giacometti as well. But when it came to Hollywood, you were expected to smirk and roll your eyes to heaven; it was a proof of your own seriousness—until, that is, the mid-1960s, when the movies themselves suddenly became a very serious subject, and my jokes, which by then I was making for *Esquire*, seemed as dated as an old grad with a funny hat and a noisemaker. ("You have the finest mind in the 18th century," snarled one reader. "You're too kind," I answered. "I'm not that good.")

But meanwhile, I had found a much more congenial form of criticism, to wit theater reviewing, which is far and away the most exacting and exciting kind of criticism there is. You can doze off at a film, and fall dead asleep over a book, and no one need ever know; but one lapse of attention at a play can snap the thread and cost you the whole evening. A play is a single experience that has to be taken at a single sitting. And if you miss a line, it's no use asking someone else to tell you about it. The whole carpet has unraveled and you just have to go back and start over again.

Each time you see a play is a distinct experience too. The cast is in a different phase and so are you. A play doesn't just sit there like a book, but comes to unpredictable life again and again. And, as at sports events, you, the spectator, feel like part of what's happening. Actors know within moments what kind of audience they're working with tonight, even before it has uttered a sound, while the first misplaced cough probably sounds like a tray of glasses crashing.

So there you sit, straining every capillary not to cough, sneeze, or daydream—above all, not to snore—all of which can seem sinfully tempting in the greenhouse air of Broadway theater. And, you're expected to *write* about this? Never mind. Just often enough a great production will come along and turn the whole nerve-wracking procedure to a pure excitement that you can ride home on like surf, as if your review too were now part of the event.

After that, movie reviewing seems like a vacation in, well, would you believe Perth Amboy, New Jersey? While doing it perfectly is probably out of the question because there is too much to talk about, doing it adequately is a snap for the same reason. Nobody seems to care which ball of wool you chase. Critics who decide to devote their entire space to the art of Bugs Bunny or Hitchcock's use of the close-up are probably doing their job as well as anyone else, for at least two good reasons. (1) Movies are modernist despite themselves and no matter how conventional they try to be, plot summaries and cast roundups will always seem to miss the point. The key *has* to be somewhere else, and maybe Hitchcock's close-ups are exactly the place to look. And (2) people go to the movies to see Tom Hanks and Julia Roberts, period. They read you to rap, or be rapped at, about movies. There is little or no connection.

Not so with books. For several years I had been reviewing these too, without considering this a serious occupation. Reviewing each other is the jury duty of the literary life: we simply pass the pencil round and round, drawing a wobbly line each time between the appearance of log-rolling and the real possibilities of envy or contempt. But things get tenser as you approach the top, and as my own assignments became more important, I suddenly found myself making friends and enemies for life with people who might, among other things, someday be reviewing *me*, with either transparent flattery or heart-felt hatred, a bad bet either way. Although one author, whose book I liked, jocularly offered me a free heart transplant, something every critic could use, the death threats sounded much more believable.

It was never like this at the movies. In fact, it is probably impossible to hurt a movie's feelings—where do you begin? With the assistant sound coordinator? And it's not all that easy with a play either, unless you write for the next day's newspaper. By the time most magazine reviews appear, the play has either closed, or is so drunk with success that it can't hear you anymore.

But book authors are always tender, even when they're out of print, and success only makes them more so. And no review turns out to be too insignificant to get under their skins and stay there forever. *The Morning After* actually kicks off with a lighthearted piece on this subject, and it certainly does have its comic side. But making enemies is seldom totally funny and as one gets to know one's targets as real people—something academic critics seldom do, which is why they're such killers—one may be subject to regrets and reconsiderations, and here are a couple of mine.

To begin with the easiest, Gore Vidal wrote one of his trademark sniffy notes to the *Times* after my piece came out, but I assumed this was just *pro forma*, like Norman Mailer's genial offer to push me down stairs after some forgotten review of some forgotten book. Vidal's whole style seems to invite and defy attack. Like Muhammad Ali sticking out his chin and pointing to it, Vidal knows he's too fast to get hit, and on a platform I expect he's right. But in print, even the slowest moving battleships must land one occasionally. And whether I did so or not (I'd be the last to know), Gore had no business getting sore about it. He *started* it, by throwing out the first smirk.

My only regret about the piece is my callow view of homosexuality at the time. Of course (a phrase I should perhaps use more carefully) homosexuality is genetic, not chosen; and no, it doesn't always show. Since the great Closet Exodus a few years back, the most amazing people have turned out to be gay, and to use the simile in my original piece—Brooklyn Dodger fans were usually *much* easier to spot.

My other Vidal-related fibrillation, not big enough to call a regret, is that he hadn't yet written, so I hadn't yet read, the best of his historical American novels, *Burr, Lincoln*, and *1876*. If I had, I might not only have been a touch more respectful, but might also have recused myself from reviewing William Styron's *Nat Turner*, and spared everyone some grief. When I finally read

Henry James's opinion that all historical fiction is more or less humbug, I understood both my Nat Turner problem and my Vidal non-problem perfectly. No one can ever quite recapture the feel and sound of another period. A young writer setting a story as recently as World War II will still get it slightly wrong. So what chance does one have when there's no living memory left to check with? Charles Dickens's version of the cockney dialect in *Pickwick Papers* is totally at odds with Bernard Shaw's in *Pygmalion*, which again is quite unlike anything going around London today. So how can one put words into mouths that made such different sounds? Or even know what the same words meant to them? Garry Wills has shown that practically every phrase in the Declaration of Independence had a slightly different value then than now. So—a whole book?

The Vidal solution, and incidentally that of Robert Graves and a few other English fictorians, is simply to get it as right as one can by steeping oneself in whatever is timeless about one's subjects—Vidal *knows* Washington, Graves knew the Mediterranean—but then, to use the unknowable part as a private playground for one's wit, imagination, and craft to romp around in. Vidal's presidents and congressmen are like Madame Tussaud's waxworks, who come to life every hundred years or so in the *real* twilight zone which *is* history, while *I, Claudius* could pass for an ingenious after-dinner charade devised by scholars. "Okay, you be Livia and I'll be Tiberius and let's see what happens." Sometimes, by a process similar to simultaneous equations in math, some truths may actually be arrived at; but if not, you'll have had and conveyed some fun, and maybe taught somebody something.

However, *Nat Turner* is much too serious to be a game, or have a playground attached to it. The author bets his whole bankroll on getting everything right the first time. And if you can do this with *any* time-place, the old South might very well be it. If, as Faulkner says, "the past isn't even the past" down there, why *shouldn't* Styron have heard what he needed as it hung there in the still air?

And if, to cut to the point, he indeed had, who the hell was I, a New Yorker from London and Sydney, to say he hadn't? Or so at least the author's friends, of which he has an enviable number, argued every time I ran into one for the next few years, until I didn't know what to think, except that the front page of *The New York Times Book Review* is, or was, a sensitive place to try out one's theories of historical fiction, and that the author's own reported rage at my review (which he denied when we met) might have been more than justified by the venue: I'd have been pretty burned up too, although as it turned out, I had done Styron a super-small favor by giving him a white enemy to snarl at to balance all the black ones he may have felt he had to be more polite to.

The matter of venue probably also made some difference to my, I like to believe, genuine post-review friendship with James Jones. The gremlins who attend to these things had contrived for Jim and his jolly wife Gloria to move into my neighborhood not long after *The Morning After* came out, so I decided to get this thing over with right away by confronting the man and taking my medicine. But all he said was, "Well, I was sore as hell at first—but at least you took me seriously as a wrahter [that's how he said it]. And besides, I thought *your* last novel lost its nerve someplace in there."

Well, okay. After mumbling something about maybe my nerves weren't as strong as his, I returned happily to my fence-mending, pointing out that at least I'd given him credit for two good books, to which he quickly added "I think that should be three" and if by this he meant the one he was currently working on, he might well have proved right, if only he'd lived long enough to finish it. As it is, the posthumous remains of his putative third good book, published under the name of *Whistle*, constitute one of those tantalizing fragments like Fitzgerald's *The Last Tycoon* that might or might not have hit the moon.

Anyhow, the bottom line, friendship-wise, may be that I'd reviewed Jim's book in *The Atlantic Monthly*, not the *Times*, and he'd probably been in Paris when it had come out, so who cared?

But appearing in *The Atlantic* did not spare me from my last and most curious specimen. Not so long ago, at a book party for William F. Buckley, Jr., I was accosted by a man I didn't recognize anymore who said, or rather sneered, "I guess there's a statute of limitations, you son-of-a-bitch" and turned on his heel. "Who *was* that?" I asked someone. "Don't you *know*?" someone piped back.

Welcome to the world of Norman Podhoretz, where there obviously *is* no statute of limitations, even after thirty years, and where enemies are forever. In fact, Podhoretz had written a book around then called *Ex-Friends* in which ancient feuds still sound as fresh as this morning's razor cuts. In his own defense, he says this is what happens automatically to anyone who moves politically from left to right. But surely friends so easy to lose are just as easy to forget, and besides can always be replaced by equally superficial ones from the new neighborhood. So why does Podhoretz keep glancing over his shoulder? Nobody is looking back at him anymore. Several of his ex-friends are actually dead by now, and presumably past caring, while the most voluble of the survivors, Norman Mailer, has since diversified in such sedulously up-to-date directions as moon landings, Marilyn Monroe, and Madonna, leaving the old New York cultural wars, if not in the dust bin, at least in the filing cabinet, of history. So what makes Podhoretz think that anyone under 70, or living outside New York, still cares?

And the answer, which seems clear from this sad later book, is that the late '60s must truly have been a traumatic time for him, and that losing all those friends probably hurt like hell, politics or no politics. In which case, I wish I'd kept out of it. Reviewing is not that important. At least mine isn't. Max Jamison may have other views.

Indeed, I began to have qualms about my piece almost before it appeared. *The Atlantic* had a long lead time back then and all I knew about *Making It* so far was that two hyper-ambitious friends of mine told me it might be an important book—and if it *was* important, it was a menace.

Soon after that, though, the assault began, and no human

should have to put up with the amount of bile that poured like lava onto Podhoretz's head over the next few weeks. Book reviewing should enact some equivalent to the technical knockout in boxing and simply call such massacres off. And the pain must have been all the worse because to a bizarre extent, Norman *was* his book, so that all the criticism was perforce personal. He had laid himself on the line and lost.

In the weeks after my review appeared, I received a charming letter from Philip Rahv, the king of the New York intellectuals, inviting me to write some more essays just like it for *his* magazine, *Modern Occasions*, and this combined with other small signs of approval from the unofficial New York Family of Ideas and Letters enforced the impression that Podhoretz had made a massive miscalculation and laid an egg with the very people he most admired and had most wanted to impress.

But if so, his comeback would show breathtaking brio and heart-stopping chutzpah. Who *were* these people anyway, except a bunch of knee-jerk liberals? The next year or two would witness a total revision of Podhoretz's cosmology, complete with brand new allies and a spanking new philosophy that one can only call paleo-neo-conservatism, into which he flung himself with zestful rage. He had not really lost friends at all, but had made political enemies, a much more dignified thing to do. As I recall, one also heard the perhaps inevitable rumors of a nervous breakdown around then, but Norman assures us that he had never felt saner than he did at that moment. And while a cynic might be tempted to say "that's great—and how is *Mrs.* Napoleon?," there's a ruefulness about this book that suggests a possible layer of self-awareness and of conscious decision-making that may have been underneath the rubble all along. And a more recent debate between him and Victor Navasky of *The Nation* in *The New York Times* shows him all the way out of his bomb shelter and talking to his enemies again the way a good intellectual should.

Nevertheless, after mulling over Max and pondering Podhoretz, I decided there must be a less morbid and, dare one say, less constipated way of "doing" both Arts and Letters. And in no time, I found myself riffling through the names of old friends whom it would be a pleasure to write about in this vague connection: Stanley Kauffmann, for instance, the gentleman film critic who only turns nasty in print; and the noisy Dwight MacDonald, who bellowed like a bull when he thought you were wrong, but could turn on a dime and start agreeing with you vigorously if you made your point. "And don't let anyone talk you out of it," he might add; and the two almost diametrically opposite drama critics John Simon and Robert Brustein, who, if you could somehow pool their strengths, might make the ideal critic, and who in their quite different ways can both manage to get a positive charge out of negative feedback. Brustein once suggested that Lillian Hellman was actually kept alive by feuds. But one doesn't need to gorge on the things like Hellman to find that an occasional fight can tone up the system wonderfully while keeping one's aesthetic ideas on a war footing where they belong.

But then I remembered a piece I had already published about someone quite different again who made a perfect stage villain, and who has enjoyed both the steamiest of confrontations and the pleasantest of lives by simply scrubbing off his war paint between numbers and wiping away the savage leer and literally sailing away on a literal boat: in short, the complete anti-Jamison and anti-Podhoretz.

No one has ever accused Bill Buckley of taking his ideas any less seriously than Podhoretz takes his, or of not hitting just as hard in argument. Yet he wears his many enemies lightly—*they* may stop talking, but he doesn't—and has even been known to make friends with some of them. Anyway, ideology is no barrier. As the great (what? liberal is too tame a word, radical too programmatic) journalist Murray Kempton lay dying, Buckley, his long-time friend and sparring partner, visited him every day, bearing, among other things, facetious messages from Kempton's friends, including me, who was also hospitalized just then, but mercifully not dying, and receiving things like life-quickening Godiva chocolates from this same Buckley.

So my liking for the man does not mean that I've gone over to his side; it means that I don't have to. You don't need to pass an entrance exam to become Buckley's friend, but if you did, I suspect that the highest marks might go to those of us who disagree with him the most. What fun are people you can't fight with?

Clare Boothe Luce once said that the worst thing about growing old was that she didn't have any "warm, personal enemies" left. I have at least one, and Buckley has dozens, and I'm including him here just for that, as an end piece for both Max and Podhoretz and in memory of Kempton too who was the patron saint of every young journalist who wants to know just how much he can get away with in terms both of prose and sheer orneriness.

If Buckley makes one kind of ending, the next piece "There Goes the Judge" makes a second one that could actually double as a beginning. The very title *The Morning After* had presupposed a world in which reviewers always have precious time to think, and preferably to dream, before talking. As Rilke says, one must open oneself completely to art, which means for critics staying open very late indeed some nights, absorbing the after-tastes and shocks, or the absence of them, and keeping one's opinions at bay until the experience has sunk in as deep as it's going to. *Then* you can talk.

This world seemed to end abruptly for me one day in September of 1988 when the lunch dishes at the Book-of-the-Month Club where I'd been judging books for 15 years, were dramatically cleared away and we were told in effect that we'd been taking too long. The war against Time to Think was underway not just at the Club but all over town. The chain stores suddenly seemed to be sending their new books back the day before they got them, and the publishers were firing them off equally fast to the second-hand bookstores and oblivion, which meant that the only successes now were the instant successes. And just like that, browsing was out, along with talking to the store owner about his favorite poet, and just plain wallowing in the funky miasma of dust and pipe smoke that told you what kind of store you were in, and that time had stopped.

So now it's up to the public to sit down on the tracks and let progress spin its wheels for a while, and there are signs it is doing so by such simple moves as supporting the classic bookstores that do remain so enthusiastically that an author can feel like a rock star in some of them and cruising for old books online and apparently even by leaning on the Book-of-the-Month Club a little. At any rate, the Club has recently responded by announcing the restoration of the judge system, though without the power and without the lunch. Which, of course, misses the point completely, because Time to Think preeminently implies time to eat lunch, and take meaningless strolls and long thoughtful naps as well.

Once these essential preparations are done with, get ready to rumble! Like the sovereign sport of cricket, the old Book Club lunches only looked genteel from a distance—just a group of old-timers sipping sherry by the hour, what harm could they do? Up close, it could actually get so politely intense that occasional executives who dropped by looked as if they'd strayed into midtown traffic at rush hour. The speed of thought practically knocked them over, as would the alleged sherry if they'd tried some (to settle this libel once and for all, I never saw a single drop of sherry the whole time I was at the Club, although they may have used it in cooking).

It wasn't just the lunch that did it, though, but the power to decide things. The late J. Anthony Lukas, who was in on the second and final kill, used to tell me how flat it felt every month to crank up all that machinery just to deliver an opinion. It was like asking a pitcher to go into his full wind-up to throw a cornflake. We needed real stakes out there, real money, for the table to move and the spirits to start talking. And although I never touch the stuff myself, I actually believe that the next big adventure of this sort will occur on the Internet, which already shows all the symptoms of a great bookstore, including lower back pain, mild astigmatism and a compulsion to share your discoveries with strangers. And you can drink, smoke and eat to your heart's content throughout, and even enjoy that most basic of pleasures, the one that makes the whole thing work, reading the same sentence over and over and rolling it on your tongue like wine and absorbing it into your soul. "Shall I compare thee to a summer's day?" "She walks in beauty, like the night." A whole world awaits.

So is Max Jamison online by now? It's a pleasure to say that I haven't the faintest idea.

W. S.
May 2001

The Morning After
. . . and Long After

SELECTED ESSAYS AND REVIEWS

PART ONE

I / The Politics of Reviewing

You laughed when the *Times Book Review* said, "Mr. Bagbalm has always had a special interest in history books"—announcing its reviewers as it might be Evelyn Waugh introducing an idiot nephew. But did you ever stop to think what editorial desperation this might speak for? how awesomely little there is to say about the average reviewer? or how even those cautious tags often overstated his qualifications wildly? Did you stop at all to think about those things?

No occupation designed for dim younger sons was ever easier to enter than book reviewing; or, once entered, easier to rise in. You go immediately to the top, it is the least you can ask, and stay there as long as that taste for history books holds out. Mr. Bagbalm becomes a leading critic with his third solo hour and remains one until he rots.

So whatever politics a microscope may turn up in this game can have little to do with upward mobility. Since there is absolutely no way of not reaching the top—and since the top proves to be so close to the bottom—the satisfaction must be sought crabwise, foraging side to side, magazine to magazine; passing on the way other reviewers of similar, sometimes almost interchangable sensibility, who are lurching counterclockwise.

One minnow, or toe of swimmer, that comes one's way

immediately is finding one's name in the full-page ads. Well, God knows, it isn't much: they usually put you between Bruce Ace of King Kong Features and the author's best friend. Still it can brighten a Tuesday morning, and all it takes is one pimping little adjective. The publisher will pluck it from a forest of sneers— O.K., the King Crab rejects this one. After all, if he squanders himself on the Susann, they won't use him for the Bellow. Cynical little fellow, but there he is. At those prices, you're probably lucky to get him.

Next comes the real, high-class bait: the chance of having a famous author for a chum. Well, maybe not a complete chum, but you'll get a nice postcard and a "Why, it's Bagbalm!" when he comes to town hawking his latest. No, please don't try to visit him on the Cape.

This, like the name in the paper, is a temptation easily rejected in its grosser forms, although who knows what scurvy deals the subconscious cooks up? Speaking for myself, I am quite happy with my little collection of postcards—including one from a novelist whose book hadn't even come out yet, but who was covering every conceivable base in advance. I also got one after the only downright dishonest review I can remember writing, saying that I was the only man who had ever understood this particular writer. It was like biting into a worm.

So much for log-rolling by anticipation: this stuff, a worn dime under the plate, hardly enough for even lovelorn reviewers who entered the game to meet people. As for log-rolling proper, the heavy work must be left to amateurs and one-shot hustlers who don't have to cruise this particular bar again. One regular will usually do it for another (bite or stroke, it's all we know): but otherwise, the soupiest encomiums are siphoned into harmless blurb quotes. And anyone who believes those deserves (reviewer's malediction) to pay for his own books.

However, even if you don't need a friend, you may not feel like taking on a new enemy at this particular time. Authors are ferocious haters with a rotten sense of proportion. (I know, because I happen to be a typical example.) Receiving a bad review is like being spat on by a complete stranger in Times Square; and nothing can convince these people that it's just a job, spitting on people, like any other.

Perhaps you can woo back the author eventually—a wailing public retraction is one way, a large gift of money might be another—but you will never get his wife. She, along with a chattering network of friends and publishers, have long since worked out a case against you that will last a lifetime. You maliciously asked for the book so that you could pan it and destroy the author's earning capacity; you are gangrenous with jealousy because you can't get published yourself; you are a racist, a sexist, and either a fag or a fag-baiter (an honest reviewer can expect both of these)—and on and on, into the paranoid night.

When the reviewer, who is, almost by definition, a man of rather pale motivation, gets wind of these charges, he feels like a parking offender on Death Row. To find some lady deep in the bag at a P.E.N. Club social, glaring at you venomously for a review you barely remember writing, calls for a special kind of temperament. I do know one critic who rings up just to say, "Guess who glared at me venomously last night?"—living, as it were, on the feedback of his own venom. But he might be called a natural critic; the rest of us are drifters, who stumbled into reviewing one cold, hungry night and swore we'd be gone the next day. So—whether it is our own pain or the author's that hurts the more, we incline to soften as we go along and get found out. We ask for books we expect to like, and by George, we usually like them.

Several magazines are all too happy to oblige; and here, I suppose, real politics as opposed to private crotchets comes in. On the small magazines, the lower rungs of vaudeville where most of us got our small break, sadism is still good copy. As anyone knows who has tried it, growing up highbrow in Anglo-America is the toughest childhood left; and the people who have made it constitute the meanest, most competitive audience around. (Businessmen are softies by comparison.) Dishonesty on a small magazine usually means acting tougher than you are, trying to write like Bogart.

When we take our Dead End Kids manners to the large circulation magazines, we find the air softer by half. Middle-brow insecurity cannot endure for long these killer doses of mental cruelty. The readers, who are presumably either groaning in Dr. Fang's office or fighting off plane-sickness, tend to identify with the victim rather than the executioner; and anyway, since they probably haven't heard of either of you, your rages are wasted on them. At *Life* and even *The New Yorker*, one is advised not to waste good space on trivial demolition work—a reasonable policy on the face of it, but one which has a slow draining effect on flawed characters, i.e., ours. Having read the damnfool book (the hard part), one is reluctant not to commit the review; so one reads into *Twilight Dawn* or *Fifty Years at the Embassy* a pinch more significance than is, strictly speaking, there: which nets you in one go a place in the ad, a chum, and a slight reputation for sluttishness.

The *Times Book Review* I have found to be more honest than people suppose—at least, once the book has been assigned: assignation is a separate branch of diplomacy, which I won't go into here. The friends-publishers network watches it especially closely for grudges and payoffs. A pan will send them into a witches' dance; a puff has eyebrows shooting up all over town.

Yet, despite its twin burdens of fatty circulation and advertising gold, the *Time* lets it reviewers go to hell in pretty much their own way. Only once did I ever experience, or hear tell of, the slightest good gray pressure: and perhaps the incident helps locate the precise snapping point, at least for that month of that year. In the instance, a fortune was riding on a book I didn't much care for, and the Famous Publisher later gave off some menacing growls on the strength of that, at the Publishers Ad Club. Yet such pressure as there was did not reach me in commercial terms, though one heard rumblings and rumors of rumblings off-stage.

It just so happened that the editor here genuinely admired the book and thought we might be blowing a classic; he suggested I might like to change my mind; to which I could only say that any change would be for the worse. My word order was finally juggled slightly, so that the sting was moved all the way back to the tail (see page 83), but the editor grimly allowed the verdict to stand, whoever might have been pushing *him*. The book did show up in the New and Recommended column next week, which took some doing; and I assumed I would never again be trusted with a big-budget book. But I was, and I was the only one in the country who liked it, too (a classic subconscious sellout).

The story shows the full span of one's travels, from small magazines to larger ones. For a circulation under 100,000 my review would have seemed insipid. In fact, an old colleague was kind enough to tell me so. My respect for the author's previous work had caused me to pull punches until my back hurt. Yet, in the *Times*, it still looked like a bloodbath.

Some reviewers claim to enjoy power, even on this miniature scale. But if it depresses you and makes you want supper sent up to your room, you find yourself wishing that the *Times* had less of it. Sensing the lonely importance of your review, you may lapse into muddleheaded kindness and a groping for middle positions that don't exist. When this happens, no bribe has changed hands, no paper crown for Mr. Nice; you have sold out simply to your own weakness and the fundamental thinness of your vocation.

Letters that follow logically from this piece.

One from Mr. Bagbalm whinnying that it isn't all that easy to get into reviewing, and you know it. Right you are, Otis. But there is always some journal somewhere—is there not?—that will catch your droppings; save these and send them to a slightly more important paper. In six months you will be absolutely at the top, unless you are simply too good for them. Every failed reviewer knows this to be so. Incidentally, for the slicks you do need certain rudimentary entertainment skills—a comic use of the first person, a bag of shiny phrases. For the rest, simple waltz steps will do.

The second letter I expect to get is more serious. "Maybe a reviewer cannot advance himself much in his own profession, but surely he can in the one next to it: specifically, might not a novelist or scholar grease or obstruct his own path by greasing or obstructing the paths of others?" Certainly the obstruction part is true. A novelist I know cannot get his books reviewed in two national magazines because he rapped one of our local Napoleons—a stiff price to pay for sadism, even if I'd enjoyed it that much. Of course, for every powerful enemy, there is a friend with his hands tied. "Confidentially, you were absolutely right about so-and-so," whispers one of so-and-so's pals at the publication party. But this is strictly under the table stuff. Writers love to see each other pummeled; but they vanish like Good Germans if you need public corroboration from them.

A novelist can probably only hurt himself by reviewing other novelists. He looks ugly stalking a lodge brother; and uglier still, fawning on one. Flattery is pathetically easy to spot, however sly you may think you're being about it. Sometimes a kindly old reviewer will let slip a book of his own and will collect his I O U's; but they will look like I O U's, with the thumbprints still on them—"warm, wonderfully human," phrases like that. The ideal reviewer, in a political sense, writes no books at all, lives outside New York but doesn't *resent* New York, has no credentials—because every credential is a trap. He simply— well, how to put it?—has an interest in history books.

1971

8

2 / NORMAN MAILER:

Genius or Nothing

People who have written about norman Mailer tend to feel that once is enough. Especially around New York, the Cult of Personality is so dense that you usually wind up with armfuls of cloud. Mailer himself has talked about the Public Self that obscures his daily self from view. But the Public Self follows him home and climbs into his books and obscures his literary self too, and the result is that he just doesn't get written about the way other writers do.

Having reviewed him three times myself, and having come up with three different answers, I had decided to give the whole thing up. But recently I was asked to do a piece for a German magazine, far off the Mailer beat, and it seemed like a chance to clarify my thoughts. For once, one wouldn't feel that one was either abetting a promotion machine or flinging oneself in front of it. Now that the piece is back in New York, I am assailed with the usual doubts. Anyway, this is how it went.

Norman Mailer's use of the word "existentialist" has become by now something of a running joke, or owlish put-on. Since he has coupled it with every conceivable school of noun, it is impossible to tell precisely what he means by it. But if it has something to do with making yourself up as you go along, then it may be the right word for him after all.

Until recently, I had supposed that the one link between his various identities was the wish to be a genius in each. "Genius or nothing" has been his proposition—the greatest whatever, novelist, playwright, moviemaker of his generation, nation, universe (depending on his *afflatus* that day): not simply the most talented, although he uses the word a lot, but something beyond talent. In his acting roles, he has used the names Pope and King; but transparently, the one he was groping for shyly was God.

But then I saw him campaigning in East Harlem, for Mayor of New York, and I was forced to reconsider. Here he was humbly shaking hands with bar-flies and street Arabs, who patently hadn't heard of him, solemnly introducing the wife, and playing the hack politician without winks or flourishes. For once, he was settling for much less than genius: settling for simple competence and accuracy of impersonation. The new existential Mailer had thrown off his last link with his old selves. In the course of his self-creation, he was even willing to be commonplace. (In a Nixon year, it was possibly the only game left.)

These changes are not capricious. To survive in the American limelight, it is advisable to change your act not once but often. And Mailer understands the American limelight as well as anybody alive (with the possible exception of Allen Ginsberg, who crawled alone from the wreckage of the Beat Generation). Before he became a writer, Mailer considered going into advertising; as, of course, he did. *Advertisements for Myself* is not just a cute title but a statement of what Mailer believes the writing trade to be all about. When his friend Norman Podhoretz wrote a clumsy piece of self-promotion called *Making It*, Mailer came roaring to its defense. He is, among other things, as loyal as a Mafia chief; and he was not going to desert a disciple just because the latter had botched an assignment.

It is thus no great accusation of Mailer to say that he has caught every fashion at its crest. He has never, to the best of my knowledge, denied it. Rolling with the times is part of what being a genius is all about. American writers are especially prone to think of themselves as spokesmen for their generations, so that the line between prophet and journalist is a blurry one at all times.

Thus it is no accident that Mailer wrote the first big war novel, subsequently managed to hook himself onto both the Beat Generation and the French Existentialists, jumped off in time to catch the Negro express, elbowed briefly to the front of the Peace Movement, worked Vietnam into a novel title (an almost infallible sign of charlatanry), and caught up with the movie fad, all in the course of no time at all. And who is the first writer to tell us about the moon? This is just an abridged survey. In between he wrote a play, which he considered the most exciting theatrical event since World War II; then having established his genius one more time, he left the form behind. Who goes to plays anyway?

An opportunist? Of course. Prove to him that there's anything wrong with that. In personal style, he is the greatest of the businessmen-adventurer writers. I have seen him pull out a wad of notes to bet on some trifle, then plunge the notes into a wine glass to prove his ascendancy over money. Mailer is not a primitive in this respect but a conscious follower of tradition. His old crony, Seymour Krim, recently accused him of introducing crassness and success-worship to American letters. But in fact Scott Fitzgerald could have written the same about Hemingway, and Edith Wharton could have written the same about Scott Fitzgerald. Here as elsewhere, Mailer is not always the innovator he appears.

It seems on balance priggish to resent Mailer, the celebrity. He has been a good conscientious one, always providing the best copy he can, and putting on a spirited show even when he can't feel much like it. He is notably patient and courteous with most strangers most of the time. Carpers are disarmed by his excellent manners and his evident eagerness to be liked. If you are a writer yourself, you may find yourself being joshed and flattered into Mailer's army. He understands that you want to be a genius too, and shows every consideration.

Hence, everything written about him in the New York area tends to be either sycophantic or disproportionately surly. It goes without saying that he is resented by writers who won't or can't exploit their personalities as artfully and unflaggingly as he does. Yet he has made it better to be a writer in America; he has made the career seem exciting at a time when it threatens to sink from sight. If one must have a celebrity culture, let us by all means stuff some literary men into it.

The question for us is not why Mailer keeps shedding his skin but whether it has been good for him. In terms of artistic production, his career is a disappointment so enormous that it almost begins to look impressive. He had the makings of a first-rate naturalistic novelist but veered from that, either because it was too easy or because the jig was up with naturalistic novels; and he has not lingered long enough in any other form to master it. When he does do something outstanding now, as in parts of *Armies of the Night*, it will usually be found to be in the old naturalistic mode. His descriptions of persons and places are demoniacally acute. But he gains no help from the forms themselves. His movies are just like his speeches, his play was just like his novels; the necessity of being a genius flattens them all out indiscriminately.

Mailer rejects like Lucifer the principle that to be great you must first be good. In his famous novel, *The Naked and the Dead*, he did try simply to be better than his rivals, to win within the rules. But he has not allowed that to happen lately. He has produced work for which words like "good" or "bad" are simply irrelevant. Mailer has some intelligent ideas about art, yet artistically his later work is slapdash and even amateurish. His novel *An American Dream* is gawky and improvised; his play *The Deer Park*, hard-breathing and stilted. Submission to form requires some minimal self-effacement, and Mailer can see no point in writing if not to advertise. It is inconceivable that he would ever write something anonymously—or write a single page without announcing his presence. Naturalistic novels were too anonymous and he dropped them. Good movies are anonymous too, so he makes bad ones. Good actors are anonymous, so he comes on as a ham. "Greatness," as Orson Welles has shown, can actually war with goodness; genius can obliterate talent.

It was not always so. Mailer has written a harrowing account of a nervous semi-collapse around the time when he was finishing *The Deer Park*, his third published novel, and that would seem as likely a turning point as any. Having tasted fame with *The Naked and the Dead*, he had flopped comparatively with the more experimental *Barbary Shore;* and it now looked as if his new book mightn't get published at all. He was learning a lesson familiar to Americans and perhaps to others: that simply being a good writer isn't enough.

No one gives up fame without a struggle, least of all a man whose favorite metaphor is his fists. His first reaction was to divide the non-stop showing off, which celebrity seems to require, from his serious work. He wrote the pieces which later made up *Advertisements for Myself*—rampant ego displays to keep the public alert while he worked on the big novel. But the strain proved too much. The energy kept flowing into the advertisements and would not go into the sustained work. Until, to produce any sustained work at all, he had to *include* the advertisements in it. And even this must be done quickly. His writing became, and remains, hasty and manic.

To justify this transfer of energy, he resolved at least to be an interesting subject. And he succeeded. The advertisements got better, and so did the product. His feats of introspection began to treat wider and wider sectors of experience. His strategy was to become the subject he wanted to write about—a cop, a politician, a burned-out romantic—and then simply to write about himself. Without taking his eye off Mailer for a minute, he became a first-rate reporter.

This imaginative projection requires colossal nervous exertion. And Mailer seldom cheats. He may be a chameleon, but he is a sincere one. He really *does* turn into those things. To do so, he surrenders trappings of Self that other writers cling to; although he talks about himself relentlessly, he is quiet about his origins, his parents, his childhood, anything that would nail his ego down to specifics and keep it from reincarnating. He has passed the ultimate test of sincerity. Lots of bright well-behaved boys have toyed with romantic insanity, but Mailer actually got there. It cannot have been easy for a mathematics prodigy and "nice little Jewish boy from Brooklyn" to turn into an authentic wild man, but he did it—up to a point. That is, he takes turns being crazy and being sane.

The sane Mailer directs him toward the hot subject matter— whether it be a Peace March, a political convention, or the drug scene. He makes an intelligent survey of what's happening: Professor Mailer is one of our shrewdest, most level-headed analysts. Then at some point he allows the devil to take over, to find the things that only a devil can find. Sometimes he descends into gibberish. Sometimes he finds nothing, and fakes it. But madness, edited by intelligence, pays off often enough. Whether dealing with yippies or small-town Republicans, Mailer follows the Chestertonian principle of exploring the psychosis proper to the group, the identifying madness, and letting it enter him, like an exorcist opening himself to a devil. (I mention Chesterton not just to startle the Germans but because I find some bizarre affinities between these two dazzling, slovenly mystics.)

Rhythm, grace, courage play a part in this process, and he exalts these qualities at length. But ultimate accuracy depends on how well his head is working at the moment. Intelligence, in fact, leads the list of both his assets and his liabilities. Because he is so clearly intelligent, people pay close heed to his gibberish.

A wild man who is also smart is the kind of wild man for us. If he can (and he does just often enough) write some of the best book criticism around, then his stuff about cancer and bowel movements can't be as silly as it sounds. Professor Mailer earns credit to pay for self-made wild man Mailer's sprees.

These latter can be nerve-racking affairs, facetious, badly written, a compulsive pouring of brain onto page. Yet he turns them finally to some sort of account. His plastic and cancer demonology is full of illuminating metaphors. I have discussed these elsewhere in terms of LSD and the drugged consciousness, the sense of magic powers residing in objects, which obliges one to make moral distinctions between, say, telephones and air conditioners. The Jewish moralist in Mailer follows him everywhere, even into sleep and hallucination. (Otherwise, the only effect of his Jewishness is his determination not to be typed by it.)

Mailer has made much of his association with marijuana and booze. But his hallucinatory intuition that everything must be watched carefully brings to mind another period in Mailer's life—his days as an infantryman in World War II. His fear of plastics and bad buildings is of a piece with his alertness to personal threat. Environment *as such* is menacing, like a South Pacific jungle, where trees move, and insects, mud, Japs form a single enemy. His rightly famous powers of observation have a firm base of suspicion. And when they go wrong (as when he sees Mafiosi glaring at him in Chicago restaurants), it is like a war veteran's fever, turning mosquitoes into dive bombers.

His intelligence hurts when it takes the form of facetious ingenuity. Mailer lunges at a lot of cute theories, bowling over facts and contradictions on the way. During his mayoralty campaign he wrote an essay, full of trumped-up indignation, blaming the general hostility in New York entirely on air pollution. This was interesting, except that, as every New Yorker knows, the town was hostile long before air pollution had been heard of. This was not a trivial slip; it meant that he hadn't thought out the nature of the city but had stopped at the first catchy explanation he came to.

And this could be multiplied many times over. As a journalist, he tries to master his subjects too quickly, relying on intuition to get it right. Mailer would rather be far-fetched than dull—for which we thank him—but it means that you have to decide which category of statement to trust. When the wild man bursts in too soon on the sane one, watch out. (*Why we are in Vietnam*, indeed.) Or when the sane man is being too clever to be true. Or when, like the rest of us, Mailer is writing for the sake of writing.

This leaves a lot of other times, and a prophet should not be scored on his mistakes. *Armies of the Night* is full of blinding hits and misses. But it tells a good novelist's lode about the relation of town and country, new and old in America. On this subject, Mailer is close to pitch-perfect. Ever since, or perhaps even before, he joined the army and found out what it meant to be an urban Jewish boy in a redneck barracks, he has been uncannily alert to social style and the reasons for it. Mailer the brawler, Mailer the club fighter, is his personal response. But when he describes the enemy, the marshals and assorted goons, it is still with an edge of fear that makes them live. Otherwise, his paranoia is for entertainment now, not use. Outside of the odd burst of rage, he is a startlingly kind man.

What does the existential future hold for him? Who knows? With his vitality, he could make the return to Art, which is barred to most who leave it. He has formidable equipment, though not limitless. Humor is outside his range, is in fact basically inimical to his drastic thrusting temperament. But his simple outrageousness gets laughs (as William Buckley's does) and this may mislead him. In his movies particularly, he resorts to comedy to get him out of artistic corners: a windy blustering comedy, consonant with greatness, but an evasion all the same. If Mailer's fierce competitiveness damps down with middle age, and he sticks to what he does best, his masterworks may lie ahead.

His gravest handicap is that his worst moments are often his most genius-y, and he sometimes seems to cultivate them for just that reason, though the critic in him must know better. His foolishness can seem, at times, too calculated, a sane man trying his damndest to be crazy. (Everybody knows that geniuses are crazy, don't they?) In my darker moments, I sometimes wonder whether Mailer is crazy at all. His clipped speech and watchful eyes suggest that the frenzy may have started out as some kind of bet with himself. But even if so, he has been true to its demands, has laid the pressure of occasional madness on his brain and has got some fine writing moments out of it, as well as some passing bad ones.

If he just forgets about masterworks and sticks to the rather special art of direct self-promotion, his future will still be interesting. Because he gives himself unstintingly, opening his lungs to experience with a romantic willingness that comes close to being noble. Also, from our less exalted point of view, a weather vane with that kind of accuracy is something to prize. Watch Mailer: if he turns to contemplation, buy a prayer mat; if he stays with politics, expect huge voter turnouts. As Mailer goes, so goes the nation. That is the form his genius takes.

1971

3 / WALKER PERCY:

The Last Gentleman

Lᴇᴛ's ᴄʜʀɪsᴛᴇɴ ᴛʜɪs ᴛʜɪɴɢ ʀɪɢʜᴛ, ᴡɪᴛʜ ᴀ quote from the panjandrum, Edmund Wilson: "The Northerner is apt to underestimate the degree to which the Southern writer —however intuitive, intelligent, imaginative, well-traveled, well-read—may fail to accept our assumptions or to sympathize with our aims. We do not realize that he lives in a world in which planning, reform, progress, making the world safe for democracy, laying the foundations of a classless society, promoting the American way of life do not really mean anything at all."

This lack of concern is not necessarily villainous. Mr. Percy, for one, is not the kind of Southerner who sets his face against the great Yankee abstractions (you might as well battle the wind), any more than he minds their overgrown children—psychiatry, sociology, high-level ecumenism. What puzzles him is a world in which the abstraction comes first: the conceptualized Yankee world where plans are always proceeding for this and that but where nobody asks the serious questions such as what does the neighborhood feel like, how does it sound in the afternoons, can you get a decent nap, how do the children look, etc.—the questions that the poet puts to the schoolman concerning the texture of life.

Mr. Percy is above all a student of textures (even his lovers "rub dorsal surfaces") and *The Last Gentleman* is a fantastically intuitive report on how America feels to the touch. He uses for probe a Southern Gulliver named Williston Bibb Barrett, who for some years has been trying to suck nourishment out of the thin Northern air. Barrett has no objection to joining groups and interrelating with his peers, if those are the things one does (this is the sense of the word "gentleman"); but he regards them mainly as cultural pastimes, like attending games or sitting on the porch with his aunts. To worry first about their intellectual validity would be to approach life backwards.

Unfortunately, Barrett's psyche tends to collapse on this diet. He learns group therapy like a young gentleman learning to dance, but he might as well be chewing on air. It does nothing for the sense of emptiness and obliteration in New York, the awareness that the Great Disaster has already occurred. The important landmarks of the imagination, i.e., the sense of time and place, have become so pale in the North that at moments they wash away completely, and Barrett forgets who he is and wanders off arbitrarily to Ohio or Virginia. (In Mississippi you can tell a Tuesday afternoon from a Thursday; here he is always forgetting what month it is.) Other times he finds himself being bombarded by "ravening particles" of collective anxiety which obstruct vision, and which Barrett can only fend off by straining everything through a giant telescope.

The answer would seem to be to return to the South, and this in a roundabout way he does. But all is not well here either. For he finds that in some ways he now prefers the sad self-consciousness of the North to the pointless good cheer of the South. He catches himself saying "hi" to people before they are in earshot. His trick knee jumps so often that he has to hold it down and hobble like a spastic. When he discovers his uncle and colored servant cackling over Cap'n Kangaroo he realizes that time and place are being washed away here too, that the Madison Avenue bulldozer has already begun to work. And beyond all this, the unsolved question of race has left the South a blank, a fixed grin at an old joke. So Barrett lights out West where the air is empty of both memory *and* ravening particles.

Mr. Percy looks at Barrett through both ends of Barrett's own telescope. Through the small, comic end he is the last of a line of Southern gentlemen who have passed from bravery through irony to ironic helplessness—culminating, in Barrett's case, in a sensibility so fine that you can't use it any more: a perfect instrument that snaps in your fingers. Through the other end, he looks rather different. There he becomes the robust American naïf, a little like George Brush in *Heaven's My Destination*—the gypsy missionary on pilgrimage through America. Oddly enough, the two halves match: one of several truths that Mr. Percy is on to. It is all a question of context.

Mr. Percy in fact does so many things so well that he managed to accordion several types of novel into one. There are semi-parodies of the hectic on-the-road novel (where the hero keeps waking with mysterious bumps on the back of his neck), of the mysterious-gothic-family novel (this he has more trouble with, and small wonder), and of the novel of galloping disaster (models: *Candide, A Cool Million*). He even manages to pull off a deathbed baptism scene exactly the way Evelyn Waugh should have done it in *Brideshead Revisited*.

This fiendish dexterity has annoyed a critic or two, who feel that too much cleverness can be a formal defect. But on the whole the book is seamlessly designed. The set-pieces are knitted from the same material as the others, and come in the right places. The only jarring note is a casebook kept by one of the characters in which ideas are discussed explicitly. This offends against one's Northern taste for smoothness and technical efficiency; worse, it substitutes for the rendering of an important character, and this hurts.

But it is gentlemanly to make at least one mistake, and Mr. Percy doesn't make many others. Page-for-page and line-for-line this is certainly one of the best-written books in recent memory. As a Southern writer, Percy inherits the remains of a sonorous musical language. But beyond that, his unique point of view forms beautiful sentences like a diamond cutting glass.

Most writers nowadays are like the advertisers who have to stress marginal differences to conceal basic similarities. But with Percy, the problem would seem to be the reverse. He must make concessions in order to sound even a little like the others. As a Southern Catholic and as a comparatively late-blooming novelist, he sees everything his own way. Like his hero, who feels at his best in thunderstorms, his reactions are bizarre and effortlessly unexpected. By a constant play of metaphor and acute literalness —seeing the thing as something else, seeing it as precisely itself, a whipsaw arrangement—he re-creates the world, and gives the readers the run of a brand-new sensibility. His humor, which is considerable, consists largely of this breaking down of received categories. (E.g., the old Chestertonian question: If you saw a man eating and didn't know what eating was, what would you suppose he was up to? Percy sees things that way all the time.)

A review can only touch on one or two aspects of this remarkable book. To use Henry James's simile: Mr. Percy has woven too rich a rug for the pattern to be easily detached; the figure must remain in the carpet. If things seem to go a little awry toward the end, it may be that the reader has taken his eye off the thread for a moment. The riddles are not meant to be solved in one sitting.

One of them, for reasons of complexity and difficulty of paraphrase, has not been mentioned at all; so let's use it to end the ceremony. On top of its other distinctions, *The Last Gentleman* is one of the few serious religious novels of recent years. The question, among others, that concerns Mr. Percy is the one that fretted Albert Camus—why do we not commit suicide? But Percy, characteristically, does not answer the question with a formula. Like a good Christian, he writes a novel instead.

1966

4 / JAMES JONES:

Go to the Widow Maker

With most writers, once you've said the book is bad you've said all there is to say; but with James Jones, you have barely begun at that point. For Jones is the king of the good-bad writers, those writers who seem to be interesting by mistake and in spite of themselves, and whose motto might well be E. B. White's advice to James Thurber concerning his drawings—to wit: "If you become any good, you'll be mediocre."

Technically, there is little danger of Jones's ever becoming any good. His prose, struggle manfully with it as he may, remains a sneer-and-grin, pulp-fiction prose. His philosophical disquisitions sound like second-drawer reform-school bull sessions. His dialogue is wooden and undifferentiated, to the point where you can scarcely tell the girls from the boys. And to make assurance doubly sure, he seems to have passed beyond the reach of normal editorial protection against himself.

His new book, *Go to the Widow Maker*, contains easily his worst writing to date. "He listened to the radio picking his teeth" might happen to anybody. But how about three "agitatedlys" and one "agitated" in the course of a page and a half? ("Agitatedly, Bonham motioned . . . agitatedly he motioned . . . motioned Grant violently . . . agitated finger.") Or the four "roars" in a space of eleven lines? His people are never allowed to laugh, they must always "roar with laughter." And—sure sign of second-class matter—each must carry an identifying phrase wherever he goes, like dog tags: the girl with the "champagne-colored hair," the man with the "dirty cop's grin," etc. One poor wight, clearly in the author's bad books, is forever saying things "in his brutal fashion," even when he is only asking for the salt. And so on—enough to make any agitated reader roar violently. Or, to use another Jonesism, "the irrationality of it was insane."

It has always been easy to make fun of Jones on this level, especially when his publisher allows him to go out with his buttons undone like this. Jones is a real literary primitive (unlike Norman Mailer, who can turn it on and off) and, as such, a natural butt for the smoothies; he has also made a rather tasteless amount of money, which is an offense to all pious people.

Yet the body of his work amounts to something, and this very fact thrusts him ahead of his betters and earns him at least some of that money. Even his new book amounts to something, within this corpus (by itself it is almost worthless). His vulnerability includes a vulnerability to experience which many of his tight-faced competitors lack, but that by itself would not be enough—we have had our fill of absorbent writers over the years. What Jones adds to it (besides impressive and easy-to-miss gifts for construction and process descriptions) is that rarest of blessings or curses, a private obsession that picks up echoes elsewhere, an obsession of public value.

This quasi-prophetic gift enabled him to write a first-rate book about World War II which was not even about World War II: *From Here to Eternity* was concerned with small-time brutality in the peacetime army, yet it said more about the war than all the painstaking combat novels put together. Then when Jones got on to the war itself, in *The Thin Red Line*, his crazy gift produced a universal book about the texture of war everywhere.

Thus, any book he writes, even an apparently trashy one, must be approached with respectful caution. We want to know if his obsession is still in working order, and whether it can ever be harnessed to peaceful use. So far, his peace writing has kept one foot stubbornly in the war—but in this perhaps he still carries his generation with him. In any event, his books must be read all of a piece.

Go to the Widow Maker makes sense only if we read it as the further adventures of the Jones enlisted man who began life in *From Here to Eternity* and was forged and twisted into adulthood in *The Thin Red Line*. Let us suppose that one of these worthies, sprawled on his bunk at Pearl, has just been handed his discharge papers and a check for a million dollars—possibly for a best-selling novel that he has pecked out in his spare time.

What does he do first? Well, he drinks and screws himself insensible, of course, this being his profession's reaction to money. But when he comes to, there is the million dollars still standing there with hardly a dent in it. In the song "Reenlistment Blues" in *From Here to Eternity*, the happy solution to this problem is to get rolled and have your money taken away: and even, for good measure, to wind up in the can, with no freedom at all. But this money is banked, he is chained to it. So the Jones man starts on his travels. Hung-over and neurasthenic from combat, he makes a stern effort to pull himself together. What do you *do* with civilian life anyway? What is it for? The trouble is that his chief experience of it up to now has been in the form of military leave—anonymous hell-raising with faceless girls in nameless hotels. This he will keep slipping back into with relief, treating whatever town he happens to be in like occupied territory; but there is no army to return to now, no frame to his debauchery, and no justification for it. An endless shore leave is a pretty fair version of hell. But what else is there to do?

The Jones man is essentially a vagrant, which means that his life has been a compound of freedom and feckless dependency. The army is the ideal nest for him, a place where he can wave his finger at authority and lean on it at the same time. In civilian life, he can still wave a finger at "them," and there is a lot of vague talk in the later Jones about statesmen and politicians and the people who are running everything, but it is just talk now. His problem is too much freedom, not too little, and how to get through the day on his own devices.

In the turgid pages of *Some Came Running*, he manages to find fault with every segment of society that might possibly help him to pass the time, including the writing fraternity and the returned-enlisted-man fraternity—his two natural sanctuaries. He also despises the bourgeois ascendancy, which leaves him no place much to go except the local saloon. He doesn't need a job, and for reasons which may become clear as we go along, he isn't looking for a wife and family. So those obvious points of connection are also bypassed.

In fact, the only social unit of any use to him is the local school teacher, Miss Guinevere French, a thirty-five-year-old virgin, whom he characteristically takes for a nymphomaniac. Guinevere represents "class" and authority and it becomes his ambition to debauch her and master the civilian community that way; rather like Sergeant Warden evening scores with the officer class via cuckoldry in *From Here to Eternity*.

In the end, the mother-virgin eludes him and his problem goes unsolved. He doesn't get rolled, he gets himself arbitrarily shot—a classic release from the toils of freedom. But the Jones man doesn't really die; the death is a fake, a stage shooting. He turns up again immediately in the form of one of Guinevere's pupils named Wally Dennis, who finds his way into a Korean foxhole. Yet even this doesn't quite satisfy: because we sense that with a million dollars in his pocket the Jones man wasn't going to join no war and have his ass shot off.

Go to the Widow Maker, his second civilian novel, offers a more likely solution. In this, the Jones man has reconstructed a military situation for himself which permits him to remain a vagrant. He has put himself in the hands of a patroness called Carol Abernathy, who runs his life for him, browbeating him like a sergeant and permitting him the occasional severely limited spree, or leave: performing, by the by, the part of the traditional American wife and mother, steering her boy through the complexities of civilian life and giving him something to rail at impotently.

As the novel opens, the Jones man is attempting to get his discharge from this woman, and thus indirectly to rid himself of the last vestiges of the war, for which Carol Abernathy has been surrogate. He is now Ron Grant, America's greatest living playwright, but he has never engaged society first-hand. Mrs. Abernathy runs a tight little seminary for celebrity writers, celebrity clerics, and Ron Grant has been a model pupil. Mrs. Abernathy's hold on Grant would be quite incomprehensible if we had nothing to go on but this book. She is presented as a hysterical shrew with failing powers, too repulsive even for pity. After fourteen years, Grant has found nothing to like about her; in fact, he has found out nothing about her at all. For a great playwright, his reading of this woman's character is astonishingly superficial.

Hence, the drama of his break with her is no drama at all. He seems to be writhing in invisible chains—why doesn't he just walk out? Jones throws in some movie-nightmare stuff about Carol Abernathy dressed as death, visiting him in sleep, but this doesn't seem to help; like so much in the book, it is half-baked, arbitrary. Or, Jones's new vice—literary.

The real bones of the novel must be dug for in the earlier books. Grant doesn't just walk out on his patroness any more than Prewitt just walked out on the army. One of the dominant themes in *From Here to Eternity* is the horrid fascination with reenlistment, with becoming a twenty-year man. The characters hate the army with every ounce of their strength, and yet contrive ways to be trapped by it—like Grant tying up his money with Mrs. Abernathy. The Jones man does not change his style easily.

And was Carol Abernathy, the authority-woman, always such a bitch? There is reason to guess that she once showed a fair face like a recruiting poster; for surely she is related to Gwen French, the virginal school teacher in *Some Came Running* who attracted the Jones man so powerfully when he first got back to America. Carol Abernathy has gone the Fiedler route from virgin to bitch, and Grant can, of course, no longer remember the virgin part at all. Yet even here he shows his old tendency to reenlist: for his escape from Carol Abernathy is taken in the *Widow Maker* by way of a new girl who shows, by her moodiness and incipient hysteria, every sign of becoming another Carol Abernathy later on.

If there were any sign at all that Jones knew what he was doing, this might be quite a useful theme. But the book is written in a spirit of misguided triumphalism, as if the Jones man had really come to the end of his travels. The new girl, one Lucky Vivendi, is apotheosized in the text as something between Joan of Arc and Bernard Shaw—her "sophisticated wit" always has the table in a roar (although the few samples sound more like Marjorie Main than G.B.S.); her beauty is inventoried endlessly and everyone she meets is reduced to a simpering pulp by it; she is not a virgin but a highly romanticized semi-pro as sexually compliant and rewarding as a Hemingway heroine.

Jones says in an introductory note that he is trying to tell a beautiful love story. But the Jones man has as much trouble with women as with any aspect of civilian life. Outside of an ecstatic enumeration of ruttings, and hoarse exclamations of pride over her peerless beauty, he doesn't know what to do with his prize. As in *A Farewell to Arms*, the love affair is essentially static, as far advanced on the first page as the last. It can only progress, like a P. G. Wodehouse romance, by way of outer mechanisms—the most obvious being jealousy, of which there is a surfeit. The Jones man must always be fretting about whether he has got hold of a whore, partly because, as a foreign soldier on leave, he simply doesn't know and partly because he hasn't learned anything else to judge a woman by. Does she or doesn't she? is the only question you learn in the barracks, or have time to apply outside. And we know that the void between them will be filled with trouble when, fourteen years on, he understands his new woman as little as he understood his old one.

Part of Lucky's attractiveness to him is an indefinable "classiness" (totally indefinable to the reader) and this is another old theme of Jones's which emerges more muddled than ever in this book. Ron Grant is variously described as coming from a good old family and as being a coarse-grained oaf. But what significance Jones attaches to these revelations it is hard to say. A vague and meaningless note of snobbery is struck from time to time as the author addresses himself to the cruder characters. But with what object? In *The Thin Red Line* one character breaks off a friendship forever because his pronunciation has been corrected: but there is no such clean dramatic use of the social-inferiority question in the new book. The Jones man is now presented as an aristocratic plebeian who has it both ways and neither way. Class is another aspect of the civilian scene that the Jones man doesn't know what to do with—though, as with marriage and work, he feels he ought to do *something*.

Again, all this is meaningless outside the larger context. But if we remember that the Jones man was lowered a class by being a soldier and then raised a class by being a celebrity (as it were, by joining the clergy), we understand his concern with the question. One day a bum, the next a lord: but both the demotion and the promotion have occurred outside the normal social structure, so he never really knows what has happened. He only knows that it seems to be important.

To gauge the hero's complete alienation from social forms, meditate on the following passage. The setting is a party of allegedly sophisticated people which the sophisticated Lucky has graced with her regal attendance: "Now dressed to the teeth with full make-up and a simple sheath dress, and those magnificent tits and that high, back-switching ass below the champagne hair, Lucky had every man in the house breathing hot through his nose and with one hand in his pocket to finger himself tentatively through the cloth." That must have been some fancy party, boss.

The truth is that the Jones man never stays in one place long enough to get the customs down right. His nonexistent regiment is always leaving: and besides, it always turns out he was too drunk to notice much. To make matters worse, he now goes everywhere as a celebrity, and has grown inured to rather special treatment. When his diving instructor (the occasion for the book is skin diving and we'll get round to that in a moment) tells him what a superb brave pupil he is, he accepts it as his simple due, as might the Emperor Nero taking bows at the Olympic Games. When he stays at a hotel whose owner caters only to celebrities, he becomes swiftly smitten by this sleazy little sycophant and regards him at once as a deep true friend. It is not for nothing that Jones is called the Hemingway of the fifties and sixties. In this world of the phony compliment and the padded bill, it would take a sharper or colder eye than the Jones man's to discern reality. Even the incomparable Lucky is not proof against celebrity fever. She jokingly tells of a club she used to belong to whose object it was to have sex relations with authors. Jokingly she tells him. Of course, all that is behind her, now that she has found true love with Grant. Still, it may strike slow-thinking Ron as a funny coincidence one of these days that an old club member finally got what she wanted.

The parasitic celebrity-world might have made a good theme too (though we've been there before) if Jones had known that that was his subject. But as Buckminster Fuller says, a fish is the last one to notice water, and most of these revelations are inadvertent.

What Jones apparently thinks he is writing about is a man's search for courage in the blue waters of the Caribbean. And this is where the book goes really seriously wrong. Not simply because the courage business is once again "literary," a standard O.K. "theme," but because it leads him at last to a false and uncharacteristic position vis-à-vis his own material.

That Grant is a coward, in the first place, is something we simply have to take on faith. The author keeps telling us that he is one, but is so loath to admit anything really bad about his hero that the cowardice has no moral soil to grow in: it is an isolated freak. Once again, Jones tries to get by with that creaking device, the bad dream: in this case a dream about a *big fish!* —which he exorcises, of course, by going fishing.

To find what is really eating Grant, we must return one last time to *The Thin Red Line*, where he catalogued every last variety of fear, possibly before closing the book on it forever. Grant's special brand no doubt reposes there. In that novel we also get clues to the great conundrum: why it is that certain men who have proved their courage definitively on the battlefield feel compelled to prove it again and again, ritualistically, in later life.

We get certain clues, but Ron doesn't. His theory about courage, which forms a climax to the book, is the most dishearteningly flimsy thing in it. Everything the Jones man had learned on Guadalcanal—that courage is accidental, circumstantial, glandular; that you may have it in the morning and lose it in the afternoon; that it may share all the same symptoms as fear, and the same neurotic base—all this exquisite sophistication in the field has been planed down to a simple pop-psychology assertion. Why does a man have to prove his courage? A) Because as a boy he was impressed by the size of his father's mem-

ber. That, for a 600-page book about courage, would have to
be called a pretty flat conclusion.

But Grant is beside himself about his discovery and carries
on as follows: "I think the whole world is all like that. Russians,
Chinese, Americans; Presidents, Prime Ministers, everybody. All
of them trying so hard to grow up to Dad's, Dad's thing." So
far, no harm—simple barrack-room spitballing about what ails
the world. You know what's wrong with them Chinese? Penurse
envy. Fact. But things get out of hand after that. "So they take
refuge in bravery. It becomes important to be brave. It is more
important to them to be brave than to be anything. Only by
being brave can they be what they think—hope—is manly, a
man. *No other way*. Bravery. That proves they're men. [Got
that?] So they make up games . . . Politics, war, football, polo,
explorers. Skin diving. Shark-shooting. All to be brave. All to
be men." Over and out.

As a survey of world events, this pretty much defies comment. As I get it, if Daddy had only looked more shrewdly to
his buttons, we wouldn't need politics, exploration, or even polo.
Well, O.K. You don't argue with a man like that, you just find
another bar.

What is serious in terms of Jones's development is this sud-
den about-face regarding the active life in general. The lumping
together of war and skin diving might be acceptable from a city-
bred intellectual who can't see without his glasses. But Jones is
a sportsman who understands and enjoys the world of violence.
He would not write about it so well otherwise. And he knows
enough to make distinctions. He knows, for openers, the difference between war and skin diving. He knows in his bones that
it is no bad thing for a man to test his courage against nature.
He knows also that the pleasure of danger sports, from skin diving to mountain climbing, is much more subtle than a simple
testing and retesting of manhood. One might add that the desire
to prove one's courage is far from the universal phenomenon

that Jones suggests—most of us would be delighted to escape such tests indefinitely, and can only be forced or goaded into them: Jones knew this when he wrote *The Thin Red Line.* What would he, in his heart of hearts, make of John Berryman's assertion that America is the one country where it is possible to grow up without discovering that you are a coward? The new Jones would approve of such a country, I suppose. But the old Jones, who wrote the good books, would know it was no country for him.

"It's like they're [the skin divers] not men. *Any* of them. They're small boys playing that they're men." This is the schoolmarm talking, not the real Jones man. He has been sold a bill of goods about sports, maturity, etc., but it sits ill with him. After all, his creator has just written a long book glorifying the hunting of fish, and it is morally phony for him to disown this pastime completely on the last few pages. Jones himself must know that he doesn't write so well about gentler pursuits: he owes some loyalty to his best material. So he just mumbles this stuff about polo—it isn't a Jones truth and there isn't much he can do with it, but he does the best he can.

Actually, the healthiest things that happen in the book are the ones that take place under water. Jones draws a hamhanded parallel between the killing of fish and the predatoriness of people on land, but it doesn't work. The sea behavior may be disapproved on principle, but in execution it is brave, cooperative, a full use of one's powers; the land behavior is idle, mischievous, degenerative.

The trouble is that Lucky Vivendi disapproves of the sea behavior: and in submitting his soul to a new authority the Jones man has no recourse but to bend his will on the point—for the time being, at least. Lucky, however, is not altogether a real person; she is also a well-thumbed copy of *Love and Death in the American Novel* by Leslie Fiedler, or some other psycho-literary text.

For Jones has always been the quintessential specimen of

Fiedler's thesis: he is lyrical about male companionship and always sourly grateful to escape to it; his women are whores or saints, and in neither case is a real relationship with them possible; and violence and death still constitute the best lay of all. The suspended sexuality of the soldier and the banked-up sadism make the perfect paradigm to Fiedler's American novelist. In *Go to the Widow Maker*, Jones is trying most energetically to shake this role.

Jones may or may not have read Fiedler's intimidating book; but he can hardly have escaped its influence, any more than any other American novelist can. At least Lucky Vivendi seems to have read it, for she calls Grant a half-fag every time he goes out with the boys, until she has him saying it too, and she is suitably baleful about violence and death as rivals.

Jones does his best to save Lucky from Fiedler's net by making her neither a virgin nor a whore but a good-bad girl, or adult. Jones seems unaware as yet that an adult relationship can transcend these categories altogether. But he is aware of too many other things. Jones is what Fiedler calls a mythopoeic writer, and the era of self-consciousness has played hob with mythopoeic writers. Jones cannot be himself right now. His natural story, the one that he tells in spite of himself, would play right into the Fiedlerians' hands: so he has to tell it "knowingly" and twist it when necessary.

Essentially, Carol Abernathy is the virgin gone rancid on a pedestal, and Lucky Vivendi is her replacement. The Jones man is more at home with the boys, and he does equate sex with death. Jones knows this—he even has Grant's courage increase after a sexual falling out with Lucky—but he keeps trying to manipulate his story to make it look like a cure. He makes Lucky into a grownup woman who will rescue Grant; he turns "the boys" into bisexual birds of prey, the easier for Grant to become disenchanted with them; and finally, falsest note of all, he has Grant himself denounce fishing, war, and polo!

In all this, the Jones man is trying to accommodate himself

to alien values, and to ignore his own insights into things like courage and violence, concerning which he probably still has something to tell us—although possibly not in the role of celebrity skin diver. It would help if he would learn to be less suggestible. The things that he learned in his earlier adventures are not without value, and should not be overturned by every schoolmarm, real or imaginary, who comes along. We certainly don't look to him for a rehash of popular Freudianism.

It is tempting to equate Jones himself with the Jones man, and his slovenliness in leaving similarities lying about adds to the temptation. But there is no law against making metaphors out of your own experience to see how they work, and there is also no reason to suppose that Jones hasn't done just this. At the moment, though, he seems to have lost a grip on what is really happening to his hero, seems not to realize the implications of what he is saying. The result is a noxious kind of wish thinking which, combined with that prose and his embryonic powers of social observation, makes a pretty rich mess.

With any other writer, such a book would constitute an unpromising set of entrails for next time. But with Jones, who knows? It seems a miracle any time he writes a good book: and yet, he has already written two of them, and how many postwar writers can match that? The Jones man remains a valid creation, a child of the thirties and of the war fumbling through the fifties and sixties, and Jones can't help telling a certain amount of truth about him. A great playwright he isn't (his next play is going to be all about skin diving!), but his other hang-ups sound real enough. At the moment he seems played out, too pooped to go have a look at Vietnam, say, or even to travel third-class incognito. Jones places him in his thirties, but he sounds older than that—sounds as if he is coping with the onset of middle age, another phenomenon he seems totally unprepared for.

The danger right now is that he finds himself with less to say and to fewer people. His vagrant romanticism and his bulging wallet make him rather a special case anyway, but not without interest: what hurts is that his roots in World War II are beginning to look quaint. His abstention from regular civil life, from child rearing and job promotions on the one hand or relevant opposition to these on the other, has kept him stuck in the past, and this cuts him off finally even from his own generation.

He doesn't belong in the American sixties in the role either of parent or of rebel. Readers cannot be asked to trace his behavior to the battlefield indefinitely or to mope around the Caribbean with him solving problems that they themselves don't have the time to cultivate. Those fourteen arrested years in Carol Abernathy's seminary have made him something of a museum piece, a Pierce-Arrow among contemporary novelists. So unless James Jones wants to go back to straight war novels (and I can't see his ambition settling for that), his present task must be to drag his boy all the way into the postwar world and find him something useful, or usefully useless, to do.

1967

5 / JOHN UPDIKE:

Couples

A FEW YEARS AGO, NORMAN MAILER THE CRITIC publicly advised John Updike to keep his foot in the whorehouse door and forget about his damn prose style. At the time this sounded typically elfin, the kind of advice that Norman peddles by the yard or the bucket, but Updike took it anyway, with rather startling results. As occasionally happens, Mailer's opinion turned out to be a little more sober than it looked.

Updike does, to be sure, take the famous style for several lengthy airings in this new novel, but he keeps it on a strong chain the rest of the time. Also, his whorehouse is some distance from Mailer's, at times more ethereal, at other times more like the inside of a lab. But such as it is, he undoubtedly keeps his foot in it. This question should probably be gotten over with quickly, because rumor has it that *Couples* is a dirty book. But although Updike does call all the parts and attachments by name, so does the Encyclopaedia Brittanica. And if this is a dirty book, I don't see how sex can be written about at all.

Anyhow, Updike's treatment of sex is central to his method, which is that of a fictional biochemist approaching mankind with a tray of hypersensitive gadgets. One pictures him starting his inquiry somewhere down on the beach, where the bivalves cluster and separate for reasons best known to themselves; proceeding cautiously inland to queer, box-like habitations, feats of engineering, man's ingenious nesting habits; and finally to man himself, clustering and separating, sure enough, forming couples and dissolving them, accreting whole communities, and smashing them up, for reasons every bit as obscure as the bivalves'.

The community of *Couples* is a peculiar sub-group, spawned by World War II and already half extinct. They are the people who wanted to get away from the staleness of the Old America and the vulgarity of the new; who wanted to live beautifully in beautiful surroundings; to raise intelligent children in renovated houses in absolutely authentic rural centers. Eventually, they brewed up their own kind of staleness and vulgarity; the children were left to shift for themselves, and were lucky to grow up no worse than square; the beautiful surroundings became overbuilt; the wrong people moved in; America caught up with them. Updike's slide lecture on this crowd skewers them better than any sociological study has done, or could do.

We meet them the way we meet actual people, that is, vaguely. Updike does the introductions like a preoccupied host —that's Frank Appleby over there, does something in stocks, I believe; that's his wife Janet or Marcia (you didn't catch which). For pages we flounder like new people in town. Is Appleby the one who dances badly, or is he the professor at M.I.T.? We hear the noise they make together, see the group-face, but still can't make out which is which.

This means that later, as we follow their more specific doings, their adulteries and their basketball games, we can always pick up the dull, meaningless roar of the first cocktail party. Bit by bit, the gossip comes in. Appleby is having a thing with Marcia little-Smith (that's how we got that bit confused), and Janet Appleby is returning the compliment with Harold little-Smith. Eddie Constantine and Roger Guerin are working out a homosexual attraction through wife-swapping. And so on. Updike's master subject is the relation of individual to collective decadence, and he tackles it with the distancing irony of a white-coated Edward Gibbon, checking out a small branch of civilization.

To complete the analogy, there are also barbarians pressing the couples from without—dull new parents at the P.T.A., stupid suggestions at the Town Meeting. At the zenith of their powers, the couples had routed the original bores from Tarbox (the name of their ex-urban Utopia). But now they are harassed themselves by a new wave of young, vigorous bores. Thus, threatened from without, decaying from within, perish all human communities. An old story, but Updike has added enough scorching new observation to save it from formula.

But the process of decay also has a more intimate side: even amoebas have their private crotchets. What is wrong with these particular people? Where is that death rattle coming from? Having been chastised for explaining his symbols in *The Centaur*, Updike has buried them a little deeper this time and isn't saying a word. The jacket blurb concedes that one character is meant to be a priest and one is a scapegoat, but this is a tease, because that was one of the few symbols the reader would have got on his own.

However, when an author leaks a clue, it is probably an important one, so let us see how the religious metaphor works out. The couples of Tarbox have fallen into a simple religious or cultic alignment: another of those biological phenomena that interest Updike. The rituals are things like touch football, sacrificial party games, and ceremonial bibulations. The priest doubles as the buffoon—a clumsy, eloquent eunuch named Fred Thorne, who organized the games to "humanize" the others, and then, like some minor-league Alexander Woollcott, scourges things along until someone bursts into drunken tears. The scapegoat is a building contractor named Piet Hanema, who constitutes a running threat to everyone, by virtue of his honesty, total heterosexuality, and sense of death, all dangerous anti-social extremes.

Since Updike's theology is Christian, it is not surprising that the scapegoat also condemns the priest, becoming a priest himself in the process; while Thorne obligingly takes over as victim. But that is a private matter, a story within a story. What matters publicly is that Thorne is the one who speaks for the community; and this is because he believes that life is ultimately foul and malignant, and must be guarded against. The point of having a church at all is to keep out the dark.

It becomes clear that this is what the other couples felt, too, when they fled America to hole up in their quaint seaside retreat. Exurbanism usually contains more escape than quest even in the first year. The couples despise their priest Thorne as only a clergyman can be despised. But they also follow his lead faithfully, his sense of the spiritual. And when he points the sacred bone at Hanema, there is no question of who will leave the tribe.

But in banishing the scapegoat the priest also breaks up the tribe; in more humdrum terms, when group-man loses misfit-man, there is no one left to play with and the game is over. Every community, even the most enlightened, needs these two . . . Thorne, the fearer of life and organizer of amnesiac activities; Hanema, the coward and the embracer of life (the Greek word means both); also, Hanema the builder whose new structures change the community, and challenge its commitment to death; Hanema the adulterer, who threatens dead marriages and builds rickety affairs over them; Hanema the freelance acrobat who makes up his own play without regard to the priest. When Thorne rejects Hanema, life leaves the community, and the dead hand of organized religion remains. The hard core of couples still meet, still play, but less often, and with less enthusiasm. When the organizer drives out the prophet, even the organization suffers.

Ingenious—and if that were all there was to the book, possibly too ingenious. But Updike has built around this main theme not only many lesser ones (Hanema's love life is so full of them I lost count), but also a girding of literal truth that stands up on its own. This is an authentically decadent community; the dry rot is everywhere; and if the priest and scapegoat were to stop flailing each other, it would fall apart all the sooner. The tension between these two has been one of the few life-giving elements.

Unfortunately, the other actors seem to exist somewhere lower down on the scale of nature than the two principals. They are treated as flat characters, identifiable only by their mannerisms. One of them talks in French tags, another burps a lot. And when for a moment they fail to do their thing, they become almost interchangeable.

But I don't think this is an oversight on the author's part. Biochemist Updike probably believes wholeheartedly in the existence of flat characters: flatness, that is, deliberately chosen and cultivated. Repeated mannerisms like repeated touch football are mummy's bandages, keeping out the corrupting air of life. They do not preclude some limited movement, some wit— on the contrary, the couples maintain quite high standards of mental agility, and Updike has a chance to reveal a first-rate talent for this kind of dialogue.

The success of his social comedy comes, however, at a slight cost in psychological precision. Updike lays on the comic flatness, the inability of the minor characters to feel, a little too heavily at times, in order to make a point. This point comes out clearly in a scene that takes place the evening of Kennedy's assassination. Fred Thorne, cruise organizer, goes ahead with a party he was planning, because he had already bought the booze; but everyone will behave seriously for once, show that other side of their characters. Of course, they don't; the party turns into the usual fatuous revel, half-drunken and furtively lecherous; wisecracks are made about Kennedy; seriousness is simply beyond them at this stage. Their rituals have left them with a compulsive reflex of Fun.

Updike has used a quote from Paul Tillich as the book's frontispiece, to the effect that when citizens believe they have no effect on the life of society, the result is favorable to religion but bad for democracy. So this is one of the things the book is about. The death of a President means nothing to these people, locked as they are in their religion of Play. They have been too individualistic in terms of Society and not enough in terms of themselves: an epitaph to the Eisenhower years. Connections are even hinted between Kennedy and Piet Hanema—two men who offer Life and surprise to these dead cells of American life, these play-churches, and are rejected. Two scapegoats.

But enough meaning is enough. The book can also be read simply as a fiendish compendium of exurban manners—the dinner-party scenes, the protocol of adultery, the care and neglect of children. The games are described with loving horror. The incidents of wife swapping are a nice blend of Noel Coward and Krafft-Ebing. As to that style—it is there in set-pieces, which can almost be read separately. It is most in evidence when the subject is things and processes: building and construction lore, home furnishing, etc., reminding one that Updike's weakness is not too much beauty but too much precision; he tells you more than you want to know, in words as arcane and exact as old legal language. Yet this does help to establish the "thingness" of his world, the complex mineral and vegetable terrain through which his people must crawl and mate and expire.

Tragedy is not really possible in this world, although suffering may be constant. Updike is not a humanist. Man is too small to fuss over inordinately. In a thousand years, the village of Tarbox will be gone, and the waves will still be pounding along; but as far as the stars are concerned, the waves don't matter either. The only question that counts is whether God exists and whether His intentions are friendly—for us, and for our brothers the rocks.

This kind of stoicism is easy enough to fake. And Updike

can be quite the virtuoso. But with each book, his position seems a little less flashy and more solid. In *Couples* he has written a painful natural history of Man, and it would have been in his interests to make it big with personal tragedy. But this goes against his religion. So instead, it trails off on a note of irony, like *Tender Is the Night*. Existence is tragedy enough for a Calvinist temperament like his own: and nothing that happens to anyone in particular can add very much to that.

1968

6 / GORE VIDAL:

Reflections upon a Sinking Ship

THERE ARE SOME PEOPLE TO WHOM ALL SELF-revelation is contemptible." *Scott Fitzgerald.* "The subject (as I shall now be known for modesty's sake) does not extend confidences to biographers." *Gore Vidal.*

The writing game has always been divided between the strippers and the hiders. Traditionally, straight confessional writing is the form for outsiders and minorities: Alexander Portnoy, James Baldwin, Wilde, Rousseau, even St. Augustine of Hippo, whose Roman friends laughed at his African accent—a motley group of immigrants and spiritual carpetbaggers. Obvious motives (excepting the good bishop for now) are to ingratiate, by admitting you are as weak and perhaps as comic as They said you were; and simultaneously to parade the one thing you have that They don't have: precisely, the freedom to confess.

Conversely, the hider is likely to be an aristocrat or a snob or both, a Waugh, a James, an old *New Yorker* writer. Motives: delicacy, taste, panic. "Never apologize, never explain" is a slogan for lords and confidence men alike. An insider cannot afford to confess or the game is up. And where an Alexander Portnoy can roll on the floor like a Catskills *tumler* for a laugh, the Subject (as we shall modestly call Mr. Vidal) cannot even let on that he *wants* a laugh. Like Lord Chesterfield, he keeps his lips firmly over his teeth.

43

What makes the Subject interesting is that, although the very model of a Wasp establishment writer at most times, he makes occasional forays into the gypsy camp. His second novel, *The City and the Pillar*, was confessional writing in the broadest sense: that is, it tore off a strip of the author's psyche, if not necessarily of his personal experience, and damn the consequences. Yet subsequent fictions have been so cool and bland that one wonders where he finds the energy to write so many of them. *Myra Breckenridge* plunged us once more into the dark corners; but now this latest collection of essays has us right back at the porter's lodge, staring into the fishy eye of the butler.

It seems the non-fiction is invariably more cautious than the fiction. It is when the Subject talks in his own voice that his tone is most impersonal. He discusses *The City and the Pillar* here as if it were written by some other fellow. Fiction was invented partly to allow the middle classes to disown their own dreams; and an essay detaching oneself from one's fiction is like a double safety lock.

The author's tone also seems to distance him at times from his own opinions. He defends various causes, sexual and political, that hardly seem worth defending unless with passion, in a tone of amused exasperation, like a don writing about faulty drains. An insider's manner applied to outsider's material. Why? Perhaps because, as a sometime politician, he knows that the light, dry tone will calm the swing reader, the one who may actually make a difference. Like the master, Bernard Shaw, who also learned persuasion on a lecture platform, he understands that rhetoric can make pornography as trivial as drains, and drains as portentous as pornography, as the need dictates.

Several essays indulge this kind of low-pressure pamphleteering for high-pressure causes. The favorite note is one of personal indifference. In the preface, after more or less predicting the total collapse of America, he finds "a somber satisfaction in knowing that the race as a whole is in quite as much trouble as the American empire." This lofty cynicism keeps him from sounding stuffy or earnest. It is a pure convention. What the somber satisfaction is about is actually a situation which he describes elsewhere as millions living at "famine level," "collective madness" in the cities, "man-made waste" everywhere; and a possible short and bloody end to even this. Satisfaction, my foot.

In his pet causes, Vidal is at least as stuffy and earnest as the next fellow. And perhaps more so. For instance, he returns to this matter of world population at least three different times, although once would have done it, and although he has nothing to say about it that hasn't been said by a thousand plodding letters to the *Times*. So far is he from being the dandy he lets on, that he is quite willing to write unoriginal and sub-literary essays in a cause that could be championed just as well by a man with half his gifts.

He pays the price, of course, in some poor essays. As a pamphleteer, he is obliged either to misrepresent the opposition or else to ignore it altogether. If the reader doesn't know the difficult questions, you'd be a damn fool to answer them for him. So Vidal's polemics are on the simple side. For instance, one of his major points, which turns up in various guises, is the necessity for tolerating homosexuality, and it goes something like this: (1) There is no such thing as a homosexual. (Basic liberal position: there is no such thing as race, no such thing as instinct, etc. This is known as blinding with Science. By redefining the phenomenon and saying it isn't what the reader thought it was, you make it disappear.) (2) There are only homosexualists ("I'm not a Jew, I'm Jew*ish*": *Beyond the Fringe*), i.e., those who by taste and habit march to a different drum.

Now pausing here. Most of the people likely to be reading Vidal had never supposed otherwise about homosexuals. The question that might interest them is not whether homosexuality is inherent (of course it isn't) but whether "taste and habit" are as trivial as all that, and whether the choice, however arrived at, has no important effects on other aspects of personality. Is being a homosexual really on the same level as being a Democrat or a Dodger fan? (And do not even these affect one's manner and appearance eventually?)

Just because a characteristic is not God-given, in the old sense, it does not automatically become arbitrary. Vidal seems to assume a psychology in which cultural conditioning is quite incidental and reversible. He dismisses received tribal customs, etc., as if these were a head cold that could be cured with a little common sense, rather than the very stuff of our characters, to be changed only slowly and painfully. He may even be right, but we can't have him tiptoeing past the difficulties like that. And even if he *is* right, one would still want to know whether there would be no significant difference between a homosexualist society (again, however arrived at) and a heterosexualist one.

One answer to this is suggested indirectly by the author himself, in a Manifesto at the end of the book. He suggests an Authority to control the number of births on the planet: a dreary but not illogical proposition. But he doesn't stop with that. The problem of who has the children can be eliminated by "anonymous matching in laboratories of sperm and ova," i.e., no more nasty procreation. The family can then be replaced by professional child-rearers. "The family is not a biological unit," he asserts (more blinding with Science: if it isn't a biological unit, it can go the way of tribal customs). He adds, without divulging his source, that many people would be happy not to have to raise their own children.

The interesting thing about the Authority is that it is not supposed to interfere in any other way with people's private lives. In other words, homosexualists are on their own, heterosexualists must restructure their lives entirely. It will be noted that this goes a bit beyond the demands of the population crisis. And one gets the uneasy feeling that the crisis is being used.

However, here as elsewhere, Vidal is a divided man. One

head says Progress, the other says traditionalist humanism, and the second head is not only the pleasanter but the more intelligent of the two. He argues much more rigorously against the new French novel (which significantly he accuses of smelling of the lab) than for his tiresome Authority. This long essay is written for a reader 180 degrees more sophisticated than the one the social pitches are aimed at, and one has to wonder what they are doing in the same book. Together with a review of Susan Sontag's *Death Kit*, they constitute a negative aesthetic worth arguing with.

Negative, because in shooting down the New Novel, he makes sure to shoot down all hope for any other kind of novel as well, with more of that gloomy relish of his. "The matter of fiction seems to be closed," he says, reverting to glibness. "Literature itself is on the verge of obsolescence." Delight in disaster is a constricting pose. It brings to mind Eeyore, the gloomy donkey in A. A. Milne. What, for instance, is the point of calling American literature "a strange list of minor provincial writers"? This is just more gloomy overstatement, as anyone knows who has encountered a real provincial literature.

This tone alternates with one of generous, even sentimental, appreciation as in excellent essays on E. Nesbit and John Horne Burns and even in an uproarious put-down of Henry Miller. At the end of an acute examination of Tarzan, he says that he finds the current popularity of escape fiction an "unbearably sad phenomenon." Really? Un*bear*able? Is this the same Mr. Cool speaking? These fluctuations define the book's emotional range: which is quick, slight, neither deep nor dull, as lively and superficial as a gavotte: the non-confessional book of the season.

1969

7 / *Orchids for Miss Hightower*

THE GREAT CRITIC SAINTE-BEUVE HELD, I BE-
lieve, a low opinion of Flaubert, Balzac, and Stendhal, his three
most gifted contemporaries. A ridiculous mistake for anyone to
make about three such famous men: and yet I sometimes wonder
whether masterpieces really are so easy to spot—supposing one
hadn't been told they *were* masterpieces, supposing they simply
arrived on the desk with inaccurate blurbs and unfortunate
jackets, like all the other novels.

The following weekly roundup, written in the style of one
of our more spinsterish reviewers, illustrates perhaps the worst
that could happen.

The Brothers Karamazov by Fyodor Dostoevsky proves
that the "unedited generation" is not confined to this country.
This sprawling, shapeless affair runs to some nine hundred and
forty pages, of which perhaps two hundred are actually connected with the plot: the rest vapor off into amateur philosophy,
mysticism, and anything else that happens to come into the
author's head. (It looks, from his religious preoccupations, as
though Mr. Dostoevsky rather wants to be another Graham
Greene—but he hasn't bothered to learn any of Greene's crafts-
manship. So sloppy is he that he begins the story in the first
person and then abandons the device without explanation.)

Mr. Dostoevsky also overwrites atrociously. His characters

are constantly breaking into sweats, turning green, and embracing each other quite regardless of sex. This may be meant as a commentary on post-Crimean War youth; or it may simply come from a callow desire to shock. In any case, American readers will find it incredible and not a little unpleasant.

Whether these rather tawdry, hysterical characters are worth writing a nine-hundred-page book about is the kind of question publishers should be asking themselves seriously these days. More and more of these plotless monsters have been appearing lately, many of them from the direction of Russia, while supposedly responsible editors are content to look the other way. This one has a plot of sorts, but it seems to have been tucked in at the last minute; what there is of it is melodramatic, improbable, and drowned in verbiage. The author does seem to have a certain crude power which might be put to some use by a really good editor, like Max Perkins; but we are shocked to hear that he is already sixty-seven years old.

Going from bad to worse, we come to a native American author every bit as undisciplined as Mr. Dostoevsky and a good deal more pretentious. *Moby Dick* by one Herman Melville seems to have just about every fault a novel can contain. It is written in dense, pseudo-biblical English (the author seems to be bucking for the title of the "new James Gould Cozzens"); nothing happens for hundreds of pages; the characters are quite unreal, especially the one called Captain Ahab, who is a stage villain of the rankest kind; and finally the use of symbols is embarrassingly broad and overdone.

I can't pretend to know how the story finally comes out, it gets bogged down halfway in impenetrable whale-lore, at which point this reader simply tiptoed away. One begins to fear that these young authors honestly believe that everything that interests *them* will also interest *us;* that they hardly know the word "discipline"; that, in short, they are bores.

The Red and the Black by Stendhal is at least decently written. But it contains most of the flaws of a typical first novel.

We are getting a little tired by now of these sensitive young men who take themselves with such deadly seriousness. Will Julien Sorel seduce the girl—well, honestly, who cares, we want to shout after a few hundred pages.

Alas, there are no real heroes in our literature anymore. Mr. Melville's hero is a whale, Mr. Stendhal's is a rather foppish, humorless young man obviously written with the Hollywood actor Tony Perkins in mind, who thinks that the world circles around his own petty problems, and who displays none of the broad humanity of, say, Tom Jones, who at least had the courage to laugh at sex.

Young people today have taken most of the fun and zest out of sex. Julien Sorel makes solemn and self-conscious weather of it indeed: perhaps he is a commentary on post-Napoleonic youth; but more likely since *all* first novels are autobiographical, he is simply a projection of the author's own gropings. In either case, eight hundred pages is rather too much of him. The author seems to feel so too, and finishes him off in a most perfunctory manner. The non-hero Sorel suddenly takes on romantic stature and dies a noble death—role playing, of course; but would such a young man be willing to die for his role? I beg leave to doubt it. This climax is so far out of key as to be unintentionally humorous. Young Mr. Stendhal should spend at least ten years learning his craft, and then try again.

The young writers of today are obviously not willing to take the trouble that yields up masterpieces. They give us half-finished books, rough blueprints of books, which too often achieve a flashing, short-lived success. Mr. Charles Dickens, whose first book *Pickwick Papers* threatened (though grossly padded) to rank him with Evelyn Waugh, has decided instead to compete with James T. Farrell. His *Oliver Twist* is the kind of slice-of-life realism that makes us expostulate: photography is *not* art. Also, it is just as inartistic to make all your characters unpleasant as it is to make them all pleasant. Life isn't like that, Mr. Dickens.

Oliver Twist is a searing commentary on post-Catholic Emancipation youth, with rather unpleasant anti-Semitic overtones and a set of sentimental alternatives. The book is at times little more than a spluttering tract. Yes, Mr. Dickens, we know that orphans are sometimes treated badly and that a bad environment can lead to a life of crime; but we are a little tired of having our noses rubbed in the obvious; and we are more than a little tired of watching authors, who feel that their own childhoods were unhappy, parading their self-pity in thinly disguised fictional form. Get back to comedy, Mr. Dickens, and stop trying to write "great English novels."

Miss Jane Austen has taken to inflating her small, quite pleasant talent in much the same way. She was writing quite a bit like Nancy Mitford for a while there, but with her new book, *Emma*, she has plunged into Krafft-Ebing's territory, where she decidedly doesn't belong. Here we have a classic lesbian situation, dimly understood by our lightweight author. The heroine is a pathetic character who needs professional treatment; hardly a fit subject for lending-library irony. Miss Austen is primarily a woman's magazine writer: it is disheartening, then, to find her going in for amateur psychiatry, and bringing to it a certain tasteless humor.

All in all, it has been a discouraging week. However, there has been one bright spot. *Seeds of Glory* by Wanda Hightower is a beautifully written book, about a young soldier who marches with Napoleon's armies and has many intriguing adventures before becoming a priest. The author's sensitiveness to atmosphere, her ability to describe a battlefield so that "you are there" make her book a memorable experience. The whole thing is blessedly short (125 pp.), underivative, and craftsmanlike.

I venture to guess that *Seeds of Glory* will live when the other books reviewed this week have been forgotten.

1963

8 / *Collected Short Prose of*
JAMES AGEE

J AMES AGEE WAS SO MUCH THE AMERICAN IDEA
of a writer—wild, lunging, unfulfilled; boozy, self-destructive,
sufficiently Southern; a refined model from the Thomas Wolfe
prototype—that we still keep sniffing around his literary remains
for the one work that would clinch it, the missing sonnet.

It will not be found in this book, which is mainly a waste
basket job, and published to look like one. But there are some
clues and confirmations. The early stories are just early stories,
no better or worse than most people's early stories. Promising.
But not terribly promising. The romantic death of feeling is
much on hand. "Waning moons and the wind in the trees, etc.
[my etc.] . . . I could no longer get excited over these things;
I could no longer even think of them without a slight sickened
feeling of shame, without ending by laughing at them and
myself." Amory Blaine could not have put the problem more
poignantly.

There is also a burst of near-Benchley humor, suitable to a
Harvard man. "[Sex] is my hobby. Sex and Stamps. But Sex is
lots more fun. Where would we be without it? Probably off
shooting pool somewhere." Otherwise, the stories tell us mostly
what we already know about Agee; that his powers of observation were extraordinary, but with a tendency to float free from

his purpose, and that his prose was vivid but sometimes pretentious (e.g., pointless inversions: "I told of Maine a lie or two") and sometimes strangely harsh on the ear.

The two satires that follow are so bad that even a college magazine would hesitate to publish them (and the second has the added burden of being dated to the point of inscrutability). In his introduction, Robert Fitzgerald says "you do not hear much of his parodies" but fails to draw the correct conclusion from this. Agee's versatility has been much commended, but he was versatile chiefly in the sense of attempting a lot of things (remember Beachcomber's famous chess master, who played seventy-six games simultaneously and lost them all?). Agee's best work in one form is surprisingly like his best work in another. Two of the four short descriptive bits that follow the disastrous satires could easily be inserted into one of his movie scripts. Both are crowd scenes so painstakingly described that your eyes almost begin to hurt from reading them. One would not be surprised to see camera instructions inserted. And as Pauline Kael has said, his power of visual evocation was also his outstanding gift as a movie critic. So his versatility was different ways of doing the same thing.

What comes next is the book's principal excuse, probably the most revealing thing that has ever been written about Agee by anyone. It is his Guggenheim application for 1937, surely the strangest application ever compiled by a sane man. It lists no fewer than forty-seven projects, several of them multiple, covering practically the whole of human experience from sex to politics. The good judges must have thought he was mad. This kind of scatterbrained fertility is usually associated with the cracked men in the patent office. And a look at the projects themselves indicates that Agee belongs as much to the line of wild-eyed American boy inventors and tinkerers as to any line of writers.

Two themes recur in a number of places. One has to do with

experiments in mixed media—plays merged with film, music with photography, books with records; and along with these, audience participation à la (or perhaps not) the Living Theater, an assault on Art "in any of its contemporary meanings," and a return to "directness" and "organic necessity" in the arts. These proto-McLuhanisms are probably not too startling as prophecies, being, even then, the obvious next jumps for fashion to take. But they are interesting in view of Agee's own work and what he was trying to do with it.

The second theme is a kind of split-screen approach to psychology. He has a notion to make a triptych of people's portrait photographs: one with the left side duplicated on the right, one with the right duplicated on the left, and one in natural full face. This would give us the sitter's conscious, unconscious and workaday characters: and by extension, his whole biography. He also suggests a triptych of a different sort for people's relationships to be seen as through "mirrors set in a triangle"—"[the] interflections, as the mirrors shift [being] analogous to the structures of contrapuntal music." Fitzgerald mentions that Agee's obsession with different points of view could drive you crazy in conversation, too.

One gets the feeling as one lowers this brainstorm of an application that what Agee really wanted was to produce a complete history of human sensibility using all the art forms at once while simultaneously transcending them. Writing happened to be the thing he did, but you often sense his impatience with the written word, as if it can't do enough for him. Even in an application for money, he bolts his syntax to keep up with the rush of his thought. It seems automatic to call him a natural writer because that sprawling proliferation looks natural, yet here he says that "I am at least as interested in moving pictures as in writing." And it seems a good bet that had he gone on living, he would have done less and less writing, outside of movie scenarios.

The Guggenheim people turned down his application, no

doubt backing away gingerly, and the projects mostly came to nothing. Agee was a man of quick enthusiasms. And when I asked his old colleague Manny Farber to describe him, he used that single word "projects." It wasn't that magazine work had shortened his wind: he could pursue one of his projects into an enormous book. But there is something manic about this, as if it must be kept a white-hot project until completed. And the overwriting, the sentences all twisted and writhing for effect, the Mailer-like eagerness to define and redefine his task in *Let Us Now Praise Famous Men,* seems to be the result.

His magazine work may have helped him to keep his observation so fastidiously exact: although to judge from a few lines quoted by Fitzgerald, he seems to have had this conscience about getting things right, down to the color on the bird's left wing, from boyhood on. I can think of no recent writer except John Updike with so puritanical a sense of obligation to the small truths; to the point of occasional tedium. Still, his fact-pocked essay on Brooklyn, rejected by *Fortune* and printed here, possibly profits from having been written for *Fortune* and not for the ages: precisely because he was obliged to put in all the topological and architectural minutiae that constitute the essay's real poetry and to ration the "boozy pseudo-poetry" (to use E. Wilson's phrase about Chesterton). Agee is always at his best down among the facts; and I have often wondered whether the original version of *Let Us Now Praise Famous Men* (also unfavored by *Fortune*) was not better than the windy masterpiece he finally published.

Not that there was a lack of wind over at the *Time-Life* of the thirties. *Time* in particular was notorious for its bursts of portentous fine writing, and these played straight to Agee's weakness. Fitzgerald quotes with approval an editorial, or whatever they called those company croonings, that Agee wrote for *Time* after the first atom bombs had been dropped. Here is a whiff of it:

. . . in the dark depths of men's minds and hearts, huge forms moved and silently arrayed themselves. Titans, arranging out of the chaos an age in which victory was already only the shout of a child in the street . . . the promise of good and of evil bordered alike on the infinite . . . Man's fate has forever been shaped between the hands of reason and spirit, now in collaboration, again in conflict. Now reason and spirit meet on final ground. If either or anything is to survive, they must find a way to create an indissoluble partnership.

Leaving aside the merits of this as free verse (I had an English English teacher who said once, sighting me along the length of his nose, "This sort of thing is much easier to write than many people suppose"), it will be noted that its content can be paraphrased down to a Chinese fortune cookie. And this cranking up of the rhetorical machinery in the service of an unexceptionable platitude was something that a man of Agee's temperament should not have been asked to do.

The years of vassalage at Time Inc. lent a spurious slickness of style and emotion to a naturally rugged talent. Fitzgerald describes Agee's piano-playing as "battered conclamant notes, quite a few near misses, very little sweet shading or pianissimo," and the same could be said of his best prose. One talks lightly of sellouts, but a writer of Agee's vitality can survive a lot of cheap work—so long as it does not exaggerate some weakness already there. The balance sheet is hard to keep with Agee. Time Inc. did send him to Alabama and Brooklyn and it did put him onto movies, where his contribution was enormous (unfortunately, all his movie reviews have been previously collected, so there is no excuse to talk about them now). On the other hand, Fitzgerald says that after the war he "found Jim in a corduroy jacket, a subtle novelty, and in a mood far more independent of Left or 'Liberal' attitudes. He had become a trace more worldly." This was a period when *Time* was puffed up like a pouter pigeon, and Agee's alleged mood matched that of his masters to a nicety.

Fitzgerald briefly raises the question of why Agee entered that organization so quickly and stayed so long. He writes: "Was it weakness that kept James Agee at *Fortune*, or was it strategy and will, for the sake of the great use he would make of it? . . . When you reflect on it in this way, weakness and strategy, instinct and destiny seem all one thing." Foraging the text for our own clues, we find in one of the early stories "that mood of sustained callousness and irony which I thought one desert afternoon had perpetuated in me, still serves me well. Although it has achieved a few complexities of perception which may perhaps enrich it, it remains my habitual state of mind, it dilutes experience to a fairly palatable beverage of dubious concoction." More romantic death of feeling, perhaps. But it sounds like good equipment for working on the old Time Inc.

And one finds on the Guggenheim application a project on the pathology of laziness. "A story," he explains, "of cumulative horror." One doesn't write such stories from the outside. Laziness in a busy writer suggests that some call is going unheeded, that writing is being used as an evasion, like non-stop talking. His pious boyhood might have set him off in one direction, writing in some sense for the Glory of God; but then as that faded he seemed reluctant to take on another motive in case it might war too bitterly with his first one: a common problem with partially lapsed Christians. He fended off aesthetic and political allegiances, from left and right, looking for truth in his triple mirrors. It is typical of Agee that he never quite gave up religion but never reembraced it either. As with Time Inc., he just hung on and raged.

The refusal to become anything in particular—Christian or atheist, aesthete or philistine, husband or bachelor, North or South, hobo or Time-Lifer—explains the fascination with multiple points of view and with the noncommittal art of the camera: itself to be used multiply, so that one statement can contradict another. This produced admirable effects in the way of kinetic prose, verbal photographs. But, for creative purposes, it had the effect of a slightly arrested development. Whether one plays what Seymour Krim has called the Great American Postponement game out of cowardice or out of a greed to choose everything, it leaves one similarly unformed and psychically incomplete. Agee remained, even in his face, the quintessential promising young writer to the day of his death at forty-five. And the masterwork of his maturity (*A Death in the Family*) is not the first American masterwork to be told in the first person of a child.

1969

9 / BERNARD MALAMUD:

Pictures of Fidelman

For a sad song on a cracked lute, you can't beat the lonesome wail of the unrequited artist. Any fool can love a muse that returns his favors. But when the muse says, "Frankly, honey, you're not my type," then you have love in its purest, most heart-rending form.

Which is how it goes with Arthur Fidelman, who pursues painting with hopeless ardor, even though the lady keeps telling him to get lost. In the course of these six stories he lurches through a gruesome little life cycle, from art student to ex-artist. In fact, he doesn't even have enough talent to be a student: his monograph on Giotto lacks spirit. Yet he plunges recklessly on, exploiting others and being exploited, just like a real artist. Bad painters can be just as ruthless as good ones, and Fidelman makes a smoldering pyre of men, women, and landlords in the cause of his junk, using the same excuses available to Michelangelo.

"The *Ode on a Grecian Urn* is worth any number of old ladies," said William Faulkner, defining the artist's relation to mother and hence to society. But if this is true of Keats, where does it leave Fidelman? Has a schlemiel no rights? The least Arthur can do is live like an artist, half angel, half pig: maybe the painting will come.

So he solemnly caricatures the various basic roles—the artist as priest, the artist as pimp, the artist as rich man's plaything. In each instance, he sees an impossible beauty that will justify everything: one masterpiece that will canonize his latest dunghill. But, *oi vey*, the masterpiece doesn't come, and we are left with the mess.

No one, mind you, suffers worse than Fidelman himself. He asks no one to sink lower, not even the prostitute in the best story ("A Pimp's Revenge"), who starts out posing as his mother and winds up posing as herself. A comedown for a madonna—but Arthur as the child turns up in a painting as a fifteen-year-old procurer. When Fidelman hurts, everybody hurts. No one since Richard Wagner ever caused such widening circles of discontent.

Bernard Malamud (let's be shifty and just call him incomparable) does not scruple to monkey with Fidelman's personality. In some scenes, he is the familiar Malamud victim-figure, meek and resilient; in others he is harder and more brittle. In one story he actually appears to die, only to pop up hopeless as new in the next one. Resurrections are nothing special to Fidelman. The eternal bad artist has his own thing going with the gods. At one point, the devil actually knocks him on the head with a spade, into a perfectly square hole in the ground he has been sculpting, but bad art is not so easily disposed of. Fidelman lives.

Most writers faced with this subject would simply have to invent another writer to tell it about. But Malamud is able to conjure up a complete painter with a complete painter's sensibility: which gives him a brand-new bottle to pour his old themes into—defeat and rebirth ("A New Life") and the consolations of stoic humor. The latter sometimes turns off the pain almost too sharply. "Ah, *i poveri morti*, though that depends on how you look at it." It is hard to write tragedy in the Yiddish palms-up vein: precisely because it was invented to avert tragedy. But Malamud uses this mannerism, no doubt originally designed to make big things small, only to prepare his hero for more distress. The jokes do not, as they might in less certain hands, reduce the stories to minor.

Malamud has somehow, by art or nature, acquired a genuine painter's way of looking at things and people, at a time when most novelists are working the same movie camera, and also a painter's viewpoint about Art as such. He almost seems to have concocted Fidelman in order to translate writing problems into painting problems and get a fresh look at them. For instance, while Fidelman is gulling the public with his holes in the ground, the real Malamud is giving a speech at the National Book Awards denouncing silly innovations in fiction. And I daresay a close check of the dates would show that the stories are often working notes, meditations on the problems of craft and spirit that the author was facing in the novel of the moment.

In the final episode we find Fidelman down to his last art form. He has throughout the book been making a shambles of a Grand Tour from Rome to Florence to Venice, which serves as the only plot you're going to get, and has tried everything from expressionism to forgery. Now he is on his way home. "In America," goes the last sentence, "he worked as a craftsman in glass and loved men and women." Which is not a bad metaphor for Mr. Malamud's own crystalline, compassionate art.

1969

10 / *The Artist as Blimp*

MORLEY CALLAGHAN'S EXCELLENT MEMOIR
That Summer in Paris catches the peculiar flavor of expatriate
life better than most memoirs. Paris in the twenties must have
been a pretty good place to be stranded in, yet it seems to have
secreted essentially the same sournesses as a hundred other European towns where American artists still swarm and fester. Joyce
wasn't talking to McAlmon; McAlmon told nasty stories about
Hemingway; Hemingway feuded with Fitzgerald. There is often this claustrophobic pettiness in expatriate communities, a
compound of rivalry, scratchy nerves, and seeing the same people at parties: you could call it the "what am I doing here" syndrome, complete with *angst* and a perfectly splitting headache.

Callaghan found that by the end of one summer he was beginning to feel displaced. This is fast going, but no record. In
the south of Spain where we recently spent a year, alienation sets
in almost immediately if it's going to set in at all. The new man
may soon be disproportionately irked by the sloppiness and un-
productiveness of the other artists: there is something devitaliz-
ing about just being around such people. Then, as his own production drops slowly off and his own sloppiness waxes, he may
reverse himself and take a dislike to the two or three expatriates
who really work: the placid men in straw hats who keep going
to Gibraltar for more paint.

The discontent works itself off in different ways. If the visitor is a latter-day Fitzgerald (chances are fair on this), he suddenly finds himself wanting to wrestle all the people in the restaurant; plunging into an affair with a woman he doesn't even like; getting a little frightened at his loss of control. He knows that if he doesn't go home soon he'll be taking off his clothes at parties—and people will be saying, "That's just Fred, taking off his clothes."

Worse still, the more he behaves "like an artist," the less he seems to perform like one. His touch temporarily goes, and with it all sense of what he wants to do artistically. He begins to wonder why he bothers at all—well, he came here to paint, and he's known around town as Fred the painter, so he'd better keep on with it: but the creative impulse is down to a small twitch by now. The other painters come over and say, "Fred—do you mind if I'm perfectly honest with you?" The product of their combined self-disgust is the pettiness referred to above.

The other side of this caricature, living by now at "The Acacias, Torremolinos" because he can't stand what's happened to England, is the remains of Colonel Blimp, the stage-philistine backing onto the stage-artist. Their cases are not as dissimilar as they might look. For Blimp too has lost his bearings. He too has spent his life billeted in countries that he has no feeling for and that he has adapted to his own convenience. While this was going on, his own country was growing away from him, so that when he finally got back to it, he was out of place there too and even laughed at. A Moroccan friend tells me that the French colonial type is pretty much like Blimp in this respect, a figure of fun at home and abroad. Unlike the Church, he is a Roman to the barbarians and a barbarian to the Romans. (The English version is the victim of a peculiarly cruel hoax, because organs like *The Times* and *London Illustrated News* may have given him the impression that he was keeping in touch right along with a changing Britain. But *The Times* is a Blimp among newspapers; it too has been billeted in a country—in this case England—in whose life it has no real share; it too exists in a state of arrested development.)

The tragedy of Blimp is that by now he would be no more at home in Edwardian England than he is in Rhodesia or Spain. Development is never really arrested: a man who tries to remain Edwardian will wind up being a caricature of Edwardian, with all the characteristics insanely exaggerated. He expands in a vacuum without reference to the facts, without reference to any living culture, a monstrous, pathetic distortion (Favorite author: Rider Haggard. Favorite composer: chap who wrote tararaboomdyay, what the deuce was his name?).

It is not stretching a point to say that the expatriate-artist is faced with a similar blockage, leading to similar sterility and malformation. Owing to the difference in sensibility, his response will be diametrically different. Blimp blames England for having changed, blames the world and the wogs and the decline in discipline. The artist turns ultimately on himself and tears at his own insides. He senses that he has somehow cut himself off from the main thing. He has lost sight of his audience and of his competition (he may even, like Hemingway, have lost his grip on the language). He can, of course, pick up the latest trends from three-months-old magazines—but a trend in art is not just a constellation of tricks: it is the result of pressures and influences, and these he no longer feels. The expatriate can imitate woodenly, remaining avant-garde by the skin of his teeth; but he will not fool the people whose work has burst genuinely out of a real social, historical setting; if they come to Spain, he will not know how to talk to them. They will find him "arty." (Just as Englishmen find Blimp too English to be true, English from memory.)

In other words, living abroad is an art that few people master. If you live "off the people," like a colonizer—and many quite liberal Americans and British do just that—you will find yourself cut off gradually from all sources of life, becoming an exotic, a freak, a sterile eccentric. (The floppy hat, the clothes that belong to no time or place, are a chilling symbol of this.) The sensitive man will feel it happening quite early on and will want immediately to wrestle all those fat fools at the bar, to start a fire in the washroom—anything to show he is still alive.

The alternatives would seem to be either (a) to make a willful renunciation, followed by a conversion to the new place, learning the language, sneering at nothing (except possibly the other tourists), drawing life and ultimately ideas from the same sources as the natives feed from: becoming, like El Greco, a naturalized artist. Or (b), like Joyce, to hammer out "in silence, exile and cunning" your own tradition: not trying to keep up with anybody, so sure of what you want to do that nothing can confuse or derail you. Merely to describe the task is to indicate its difficulty and to point out the fantastic psychic constitution needed to bring it off.

A third choice would be just to go home after the first scene in the restaurant, the first accident with the kerosene can, which might come any time from three weeks to two years after arrival: by then you will have either given up your painting or become hopelessly grafted to it, and you will not yet be a synthetic creation, a more sensitive Blimp, when you get home.

None of this has changed much. Morley Callaghan seems to have got back in time. Scott Fitzgerald got back more or less in time. Ernest Hemingway kept on wandering and wound up, in the persona of Colonel Cantwell, the greatest Blimp in American letters: an aesthete-colonial to end all aesthete-colonials, half poet, half club-bore, inevitably and tragically a figure of fun.

1963

II / *Racing the Clock with*

GREENE & PRITCHETT

AS WRITERS GET OLDER, THEIR SUBJECTS DIE
and leave them. Mr. Greene's whiskey priest, Mr. Pritchett's
sailor—all dead, quite dead. You can't bring them up to date. A
topical reference, a television set in the corner, and they're done
for. Like Bertie Wooster or Little Orphan Annie, they can't
survive under socialism, or Vatican II, or some one deathblow.

These two admirable writers have adopted radically different strategies by which to outlive their generations. In *Travels
with My Aunt*, Greene takes an old lady who has outlived *hers*
and shoots her into an adventure involving Istanbul and the Iron
Curtain, where time stands still, and Latin America, where it
runs backward. If modernity obtrudes, it can be seen through
jazzed-up old eyes. The Beatles are mentioned in passing, like the
dog that used to bark in the distance, for atmosphere; Greene's
obsession, Coca-Cola, is everywhere, amusing and American and
rather silly; people smoke pot.

Pritchett has gone the other way. Like our own John
Cheever, he simply removes the dates. His world, as laid out in
Blind Love & Other Stories, is as close as can be to timeless. If
he mentions the late war, it doesn't jar—it could be any one of
several wars. He manages, again like Cheever, dealing with a
Nike installation, to make it seem trivial.

Both strategies work only so far. There is no timeless world. Pritchett's England, dateless and newsless, stretches, by the sound of it, from about 1910 to 1940. The characters are cramped, hobbled by private concerns; they travel by slow trains and stay in residential hotels. The author won't necessarily bother you with these details, but you know that they are there. The performers are usually introduced formally in the first paragraph: Mr. Armitage, Mrs. Thwaite, Mrs. Hunstable—the names of English middle-class fiction between the wars, by now as classically abstract as the names of Greek legend. Pritchett neither hides his age nor stresses it: find the Universal in these stories if you can.

Greene has set himself a trickier task, if only because he has tried to beat the clock with comedy, and humor is of all arts the most "period." (Hence perhaps the short span of most humorists.) The notion expressed in the title—that aunts, as such, are funny—is period. And Greene must know it: he even calls the aunt Augusta, a name borrowed straight from Wodehouse—fair warning, I take it, that a parody is on its way.

He takes a characteristic risk that readers may mistake his purpose. If they do, they will find the book a wistful anachronism, next to Charlie Chaplin's *Countess from Hong Kong*. But Greene hews to the comic conventions so strictly that it has to be a plan. The aunt is a heller, her nephew is a prim housebody who raises dahlias. (Dahlias as such are also funny: Wodehouse names another aunt after them.) There is even someone off-stage who does tatting, for God's sake: a pre-Noel Coward way of indicating a stock spinster. The aunt, we know from page one, will shock the nephew to life and cure him of his dahlias. The only question is: how will the author manage to swing his pen in such a narrow area?

Inviting comparison with the great Wodehouse is certainly a mistake, and it should be said right away that the passages of straight slapstick are pretty awful. Greene has never been comfortable with humor; it seems too laborious an escape from his

*6*7

real concerns. He came to comedy rather late in writing life ("one must try every drink once," as he said in another connection), and has not been able to establish a technique. A man killed by a falling pig, a baby in a suitcase (both from his last collection of stories), might possibly be funny ideas, though I don't see how. But Greene hasn't worked out a tone for them, or developed the timing of the professionals. Besides, Wodehouse took Edwardian schoolboy humor to a pinnacle, like Joyce with the novel, and returning to the lower slopes hardly seems worthwhile.

But Greene is too serious to settle for parody even if he wants to. The book is also a study of old age and its stratagems. The aunt's capers are designed, quite self-consciously, to ward off death. She talks of a relative of her own who slept in a different room every night to make his last years seem longer. And when she runs gold bricks into Istanbul, or whatever the hell, she is doing the same thing. Further to that: an old person's chances of surviving accidental death are almost as good as a young one's; and to be on a par, even briefly, with youth is to be immortal.

Once upon a time, this vulgar love of life would have repelled Greene: witness his disgust with Rosie the Barmaid in *Brighton Rock*. But the breaking down of his own priggishness is another minor theme of the later Greene, and the square nephew, Henry, represents this process in stark caricature. Sin, so long as it is amusing, is not so bad as one had thought.

Unfortunately, the needs of comedy have provided us with the wrong prig. Greene has concocted one so totally outside his own range of sympathies—a sexless bank manager who has never trod the lawless roads of Pago Pago—that he can't be bothered to animate him, even comically. Although the story is told by the nephew, we never know what he sees in dahlias or banks or anything else. When his aunt dresses him down for a loveless zombie, we are told that he is "confused," but not what form this takes. He doesn't even have coherent prejudices for his mind to congeal around, or the pride of an assistant teller, but is kept utterly soft and unformed, the better for Auntie to kick around. Greene says that you should be hard on your characters, but surely not so hard that they can't breathe.

Had Greene devised a prig a little more like his old self, despising the aunt as a yellowing hag full of fake life and self-delusion, we would have lost our comedy but gained a story. The choice of comedy, therefore, can only strike one as a slight evasion or at least postponement. How would Aunt Augusta justify herself at the bar of Scobie and Pinky? Both of these earlier Greene men rejected life-at-all-costs. Is there something different about her that makes it all right? Or is that just in comedies?

Greene's fictional position may have changed on all this, but if so, he is not prepared yet to make a full statement. *Travels* comes off as a half statement, as lacking in resonance as a movie script. Aunt Augusta does present a serious point of view, but in a farcical context, in which erratic behavior is acceptable. An old lady can smuggle and lie and carry on with young men in a farce, and it means no more than if she murdered them, like the biddies in *Arsenic and Old Lace*. But there are moments when Auntie sneakily sobers up and presents this as a noble way of life. Silly Putty nephew simply bows and accepts. On second thought, it might have made a better *comedy* with Pinky the boy gunman to heckle her.

But Pinky is dead, and Aunt Augusta, half stage and half real, must do duty for the old Greene and the putative new one. She meets some of the canons: she has lost innocence all right and knows it, she is (from out of left field) a Catholic, she listens not to the commands of this world. So far, she is what he has been saying all along. But there is a sense here of sleazy compromise. In terms of consequences, innocence *is* her excuse—innocence, and being funny about it. No wonder Greene can't afford to put her in a fair fight. Innocence and being funny are the great English vices, gussy them up how you will: surely he would have hated this woman once upon a time.

Of course, none of this would be material if he were doing a detached character sketch, in the manner of Pritchett. But it is Greene's particular burden to appear to be pushing a position even when perhaps he isn't. Whether or not Auntie is meant for propaganda, she reads that way. And Square Henry, the nephew, sounds like more than a conventional straight man. To be sure, he represents the respectable world (which Greene detests, but which will love his book). But Henry's main characteristic, his refusal of life, relates him also to Pinky and to the boy in *This Gun for Hire*—young Englishmen with undeveloped hearts, terrified to nausea by the Flesh. Except that the prig is now a joke and not a theological problem.

The sensuality which used to give Greene's younger characters the shakes is now embodied attractively in a jolly old lady. The English often come to their naughtiness late. It is suggested that poor Henry had some early trauma concerning his parents and sex. Pinky, it will be recalled, never got over the Saturday night grunt and groan. But in Henry's case, it can be relieved, like a nasty head cold, by a wise older woman. There is no need to carry on about it, or drag God into it.

It is a funny place to find Greene. Tolerance and sensuality, à la Française: a note sounded more often by writers like Maugham and Coward, the languid English cosmopolitans. Aunt Augusta has all kinds of French and Italian connections. She will teach young Britannia how to live, she will take him on the Grand Tour. Travel may also have mellowed Mr. Greene. The old puritan hardness seems in retrospect more physical than spiritual, a revulsion from the smells and soot and tackiness of home. Under a tropic sun, with roaches in the basin, it got worse. But in a first-class Paris hotel, it really isn't so bad.

But Greene is unlikely to leave it at this. Auntie is also a flagrant sentimentalization, a schoolboy's dream of the "super" relative who talks bawdy and gives you a sip of her drink. It is bad fantasy to suppose she can wave away guilt and anguish for long. Worse yet, she is not even allowed to look old but must, like a crone being flattered, have the skin of a girl. Think young, as we say in Miami, and you will stay young forever. Americanism triumphant. It *has* to be a joke.

Pritchett has also lived much abroad, but it is a curiosity that almost all his stories are set in England. English expatriates carry worse wounds than most, old class wounds that throb at the sight of another Englishman. Pritchett hated his country because he was not a "Gloucestershire Pritchett," and never would be; yet a Gloucestershire Pritchett might have hated it even more. Snug in the lower middle class, V.S. had a juicier boyhood (as described in *A Cab at the Door*) than the public-school novelists; and much juicier than Greene's, with the headmaster father and the dingy reticences. The worst beatings of the upper-middles are reserved for their own.

At any rate, he has not escaped into Norman Douglas exotica, the Englishman in the floppy-white-hat syndrome, but returns again and again to that cranky world of commercial travelers and failed eccentrics in which he was, well, happy enough. Fragments of the autobiography bob up in the stories: a victim having sausage stuffed down his neck, a roué who kisses women's necks. Unlike the exotic authors, his characters are mired in circumstance. They cannot afford to travel for fun or wrestle with chintzy problems of the spirit. Pritchett sounds like the kind of writer who has to work for a living himself, a good sound to keep, whether justified or not.

Yet his people often have to ward off unspeakable pain, and they, too, are apt to resort to mental tricks. A lady takes pride in her husband's stinginess, another exults in his unfaithfulness. Make believe that the fire is your friend, and all will be well. There is nothing artificial about these tricks, they are not "attitudes," or secrets for better living; they are more like grotesque evolutionary adjustments which lurk down among the reflexes.

In his teens, V. S. Pritchett had a brief fling with Christian Science, and his interest in Salvation Through Self-deception may trace to that. It seems he accepted Mary Baker Eddy's belief that pain is unreal, mainly to please his father, a Micawberish salesman who raised his children in a web of dreams. Pritchett even had the same shock of waking as Dickens, when he was kicked out of the web at fifteen and put to work in the leather business. A Micawber guarantees you a rich childhood and a nasty day of reckoning.

The result is feelings so exquisitely mixed that Pritchett can seemingly get stories out of them forever. He is now sixty-eight, and this latest collection is as good as anything he has done. Dreams kill, dreams cure. The matter is never resolved, so the stories can go on.

In one of them, "The Liars," a bartender spends his afternoons swapping fibs with an old lady. This is lying as straight therapy, perhaps the best one can do. They both know they are lying, and enjoy the glow of the sport. In another called "The Speech," a dumpy woman politician has a voice that lies for her: it speaks of confidence and indestructibility, while its owner is shrunken and sodden with failure. The lie, the Voice, has trapped her into a false position vis-à-vis the world. Still, it is almost worth it. The audience loves her. (A classic example of how to write about the writing situation without mentioning it.)

The irony and balance are ideal for short stories. At the same time, they can make for a cumulative slightness of effect. Irony cuts off the emotional flow and tapers off too drastically itself (see O. Henry). Pritchett was long considered an incurably minor writer because of this tendency to avoid the kill. His Micawbers are neither condemned nor forgiven; they are simply rendered. "[My father's] main criticism of me was that I 'limited' myself and did not 'think big.' " The personal force, sometimes the hamminess, that makes a writer like Greene noticeable is strictly against Pritchett's rules. ("One must not write about oneself," he said in *A Cab at the Door;* and by this he means you must leave no trace of yourself at all, barely a signature.)

But without compromising his scrupulous tact, he can occasionally raise the temperature to scalding, using nothing but the situation and his own light impersonal commentary. In the best story, "The Skeleton," he follows his favorite pattern—one round character, all the others flat, and one saving lie—to show a real death grapple with old age, as opposed to Aunt Augusta's tank job. The hero has shaped and cooled a guilty episode from his past into a suitable meditation. This version is challenged by the truth, in the form of blackmail. But a self-deceiver who knows what he is doing has resources for this kind of thing. The old man routs the Arch Enemy, truth, without admitting a thing. The last note is triumphant: "By God, George thought, the Arch Enemy is a fool."

That is one solution. Since old age is incurable, what's the good of facing the facts about it? If life is too hard to face, by all means resort to myth. But be warned that this can be a hard road too, harder than Aunt Augusta would admit. "Awful things happen every day: they come without warning and—this is the trouble, for who knows?—the next one may be the Great Awful Thing. Whatever that is." When ordinary lying fails, one may have to descend to the bomb shelter of madness. Unless one is tough and agile, in which case eccentricity may do instead. In this story, and in so many others (particularly the classic "Sense of Humor" from another volume), the secret is to know what you're up to, to understand in the back of your mind why you need that particular myth, and to be prepared to go on believing, like a good Christian Scientist, in the teeth of the evidence.

These stories tend to be circular, ending as they began, with the challenge surmounted and the character exactly where he started. Of the exceptions, the title story, "Blind Love," is the most interesting. This one involves *two* round characters, and the lying which is good enough for solitaries is almost ruinous for combinations of people. Truth is a necessary arrangement among groups. A man can deny pain in himself, but not, say, in his children.

This is the only story about mutual love: in all the others, love is a lie told by a solitary to himself. In "Blind Love," a girl with a repulsive birthmark has an affair with a blind man, comforted by the knowledge that he can't see it. By a laborious ruse, he gets her to tell him about it anyway: at which point, they can begin to love each other properly. Any deception, however tangential, is a withholding of self, for the sake of safety. So, if you want more than accommodation in life—and don't knock that, you're lucky to get it—truth must be attempted.

This is the only kind of message you're likely to get from Pritchett, and its very modesty has led people to consider it a minor point of view. Immunized from faith early in life, he cannot pretend to believe more than he does. He has nothing like Greene's harsh Catholicism to offer his characters, no personal ideology to swell their importance. All he has is a cock-sparrow Cockney realism, and an exuberance about life as such, disciplined into a fine comic style.

From this equipment, two things follow. One is, as he says, that he must start afresh with each story, as if he had never written one before. And the other is that he must at all times write better than the "major" writers. Metaphysicians can be windy and sloppy, and be redeemed by big themes. Pritchett has to get everything just right—dialogue, motive, the actuality of things—because it's all he has.

Other writers must sometimes seem to him like the solitaries he writes about, with the one sustaining myth. The nearest he comes to a myth of his own, so he suggests in the introduction to *Sailor and Sense of Humor*, is an awestruck fascination with character, and its ultimate secrecy. Belief in character is an English superstition, yet Pritchett shares it only in the most limited sense. His people's secrets are bizarre, yet often pathetically small and cranky, and once you are on to them, the story is over. They do not, like a religious writer's secrets, testify to some transcendent inner self, but only to some bizarre situation being coped with. I would say of Pritchett that Situation is King, and Character its comic servant. (You don't have to judge Situation.) His real fascination, as with Dickens, Wells, and other spiritual Londoners, is with the simple variety and unexpectedness of life, the strangers in the street, the new people next door, bringing fresh short stories to town. And that may be myth enough.

1970

12 / JAMES BALDWIN:

Tell Me How Long the

Train's Been Gone

Nᴇᴡ ʏᴏʀᴋ, ɪsᴛᴀɴʙᴜʟ, sᴀɴ ꜰʀᴀɴᴄɪsᴄᴏ" ɪs ᴛʜᴇ
dateline; and you know how it is by the time a novelist gets to
Istanbul. Shall I tell them of the long journey I've come, of the
price I've paid? Would the folks like to hear about the loneliness
at the top? Told from an Istanbul point of view? It isn't all
roses, this fame and money.

You get, in James Baldwin's new novel, this sense of a man
rummaging in his trunk for a theme. It has been six years since
Another Country, and the crowd back home is beginning to
shuffle its feet and remember appointments. In other words, it's
novel time again. How about giving them the one about the
young writer who grows up in Harlem and leads a bisexual life
in the Village, etc.? You say they've heard it already? All right,
suppose we make him an actor instead of a writer?

Although Leo Proudhammer is an actor, you should have
no trouble recognizing him. He is small, not so much good-look-
ing as striking-looking, and he has large round eyes. (Sammy
Davis, Jr., I guess, only tragic.) Leo might really just as well
have been a writer—he shows no talent for mimicry or role-
playing, but quite a turn for rhetoric—except that, as I say, we
have heard that story.

The first section covers the early years in Harlem; and although Baldwin has been there before, and many writers have

been there since, this is still his turf and we get some good pages. No one evokes the Harlem of the thirties and forties more convincingly than Baldwin—never mind the occasion. The Proud-hammers out shopping on Saturday, with Mama angling for credit and Daddy seeing a thumb on every scale; Leo and his brother Caleb pretending to go to the movies together, so their parents would think they were all right; the faces at the window on a Sunday afternoon, waiting and watching—no wonder Leo Proudhammer got those big round eyes, from seeing so much.

But something seems to go wrong when he moves downtown. Baldwin's tone changes, he becomes shrill. Leo Proud-hammer goes to a party, and confronts the head of a famous acting school and wife. And it sounds just like the party scene from *Making of a Star*, or *A Star Is Made*, or *Star-Struck*. "Young man (lady), I see you have spirit—but have you got discipline?" His (her) lips tightened. "Try me."

Next scene: the kids doing summer stock. Shifting scenery, working their tails off, in fact. Not much money, but such laughs. J. B. Priestley's *Good Companions* is the prototype here, plus *A Star Is Born, Not Made*, etc. Show-biz sentimentality is notoriously as hard for outsiders to take as an Old Boys' dinner, especially when it includes a dirge for lost innocence. And one wonders, not for the first time, why Baldwin is bothering with this stuff.

These sequences also take much too long for their relative importance to the plot. We dawdle over minor dinners or drinks at the author's whim. Then, when we come to the part that seems more interesting, Proudhammer's slow rise through Negro bit parts, butlers, comic chauffeurs, etc., he inexplicably hurries us along. These years are synopsized, as they are in the movies: montage of cheap sets, part-time jobs, finally the Big Break. But the road to success has cut him off from his people. A breathless civil-rights coda is introduced. "You got to agree that we need us some guns. Right?" says a young admirer. "Yes, I see that," says Leo. We are not quite sure how we have arrived at this affirmation—unless we were somehow there all the time.

During this whole while, we are given many flashes forward and back of Leo's relationship with his family, and these differ in kind and quality from the rest of the book. In the chintzy scenes, Baldwin gropes like an amateur for nickel ribbons of observation to dress up his dialogue: people stare meaningfully; they pace moodily to the window, she looks at *her* so she can concentrate on *him*. It is all quite perfunctory: I counted no fewer than five hefty women and three red-faced men, mostly in walk-ons. In these matters, Baldwin leaves himself (to use his own favorite words) very, very vulnerable.

But when he gets back to the family, he dispenses with this nonsense and really writes. Leo's brother Caleb is the real star of the novel—a hell-raising kid whose spirit is broken in reform school and who finally escapes into bible-bashing. Leo's father, the proud drunk, and his mother, the domestic politician—these are Baldwin's real concern and you can tell, by the simple improvement in the writing, that he knows it.

Is it, then, that Baldwin, like so many writers, can only dial from the one booth? Is he disdainful of non-Harlem material, or does it make him nervous, or what? It is not simply that his white people look alike like Chinese waiters—good writing can be done from a fanatic's point of view. But he seems to lose his own identity, the authority leaves his voice, the mind-clearing arrogance fails him. He does not even write well about himself (I mean Proudhammer) in this setting.

One might call Baldwin a special victim of the race wars, a man trying to belong to both worlds, slipping in one and unsure in the other: but I think this is too drastic. I think he has paused in his travels and batted out a careless book, alive where it touches his own interests, borrowed and mechanical where it doesn't. He would not be the first writer to have done this.

1968

13 / ROBERT COOVER:

The Universal Baseball Association

THE ORIGINS OF BASEBALL ARE STRANGELY OB-
scure. Was there a single creator, or did the game slowly evolve?
If so, from what? Did that magical symmetry just happen? Or
is it necessary to invent Abner Doubleday?

Baseball and theology might seem to make strange bedfel-
lows. But, like a medieval schoolman who could make theology
out of just about anything, Robert Coover has spliced the two
together and produced a species of baseball scripture. His God
is a lonely middle-aged accountant who has devised a dice game
that approximates the probabilities of baseball. That is all. Upon
the void he projects the laws of chance, the percentages, what
managers call "the book."

Thus, the first day of creation. But as Henry Waugh
(JHWH) rolls his three dice, he ruminates. And his ruminations
conjure up a setting, sights, sounds, a paradisiacal ball park. For
dramatic interest, he assigns the players personalities proper to
their performances—as one might deduce a Babe Ruth or a Ty
Cobb simply from studying the record book. Waugh talks to
himself in different voices as he plays, and these voices become
independent people. God turns schizoid, giving up bits of himself that his creatures may live, and also that they may *interest*
Him.

As the players become conscious and separate, they become also contentious and political. History is now ready to roll. The Universal Baseball Association is soon a full-blown society, complete with ballads and a sex life, culture and continuity, even obituaries. Yet nothing moves it except the throw of the dice.

By the time the novel opens, we have already had a Golden Age, and the game is in the doldrums. Waugh hopes that the dice will turn up something exciting—otherwise he will destroy the league and take up something else. The players in his head are bored and restless. Where do you go after a Golden Age?

There is one hope: a rookie pitcher of greatness (i.e., divine luck) named Damon Rutherford, the son of a hero, a promising demigod, who might bring life back to the game. But fate turns ugly. Waugh gets his Adonis into a corner, where a roll of triple ones will fetch him a fatal beaning. Waugh could take Rutherford out and have a lesser man killed in his place—but this would be illogical, the players wouldn't like it. You can't remove a man who is working on a no-hitter. God must abide by his own rules. So the killing takes place. Evil triumphs, and to rub the pain in all the way, the dice go on a rampage and turn the game into a rout, favor of Evil.

The real-life Henry Waugh goes on a bender in the local tavern and impersonates all the players he has invented—the lechers, the drunks, the hard-nose aggression cases. A silly, fuddled man lunging around a bar is all the bar-flies see. But they don't understand, this man is holding a wake for his son, whose death he could not prevent.

The trouble with being a game-playing God is that, although one is all-powerful, one is still in the employ of the dice. Zeus stuck with his scales. If Waugh intervenes personally, the players will sense it and just give up, life will leave the game forever. But the dice keep favoring the Evil One (the pitcher who did the beaning), and the league is slowly dying of sorrow and bewilderment. Waugh is beside himself and stays up all night throwing, allowing his real life to go to hell in the process.

Ultimately, Waugh does intervene and fix the dice, and, in doing so, appears to descend into complete insanity. The players go their own way after that, found private religions and stage reformations, and proceed to talk like seventeenth-century parsons and death-of-God theologians. Is there really a Henry Waugh? Who knows? One continues to play for the sake of the game—whatever that is. It is impressive to realize that all this is going on in one man's skull.

All right, anyone can think of a cute parable. What makes this one work at book length is the complexity and congruity of Coover's whole *Summa Baseballica*. Take just one aspect, the relation of time to eternity. Waugh is on a different time plan from his creatures because he can roll out an entire season in a couple of weeks, a generation in one year. Thus, he sees further ahead and behind than they do. He is a futuristic God and a nostalgic God, all at once. And his present tense consists entirely of history and latency, "was" and "will be." As he enters the limited brains of his players, he shares his tenses with them, making them prophets (of the present and future) or poets (of the past), as the mood takes him; making them see the moment in its constituent parts, as he does.

The relationship is a relatively simple Old Testament one. Waugh is a very finite God. His creation is almost destroyed when a friend spills beer on it. And his world is a copy. The myths and personalities may be implicit in the rules of baseball (Lévi-Strauss would buy that), but the fact remains that real baseball got there first, and our accountant-God needs it to fertilize his imagination.

It would be a pity if the baseball buffs were put off by this mythology, or the mythology rooters dismayed by the baseball. Coover has in fact written a fine baseball novel, the best I can remember in an admittedly thin field, and based obviously on a study of the texts. The atmosphere is turn-of-the-century early

Lardner, when the game was in full swagger, but his averages are lively-ball 1930. The best of both worlds, in my opinion. The language is just right—colorful but not fancy. Take away the big metaphor in the middle, and the book still stands up. Conversely, not to read it because you don't like baseball is like not reading Balzac because you don't like boarding houses. Baseball provides as good a frame for dramatic encounter as any. The bat and ball are excuses. Baseball almost involves a real sub-culture, and tradition, a political history that were in some sense pre-ordained when the first diamond was laid out, that were implicit in the distance between bases, and that continue to make ball parks seem like unfrocked churches, places where even the boredom is of a finer quality. That the players and fans might be shadows in the mind of a Crazy Accountant up there is not only believable but curiously attractive.

Mr. Coover's admirable novel adds to our stock of benign legends. And how many books have you read lately that do that?

1968

14 / WILLIAM STYRON:

The Confessions of Nat Turner

Nat turner may have been the first of the great Negro preacher-reformers, a line that has fanned out since in such different directions as Martin Luther King, Adam Clayton Powell, and James Baldwin, the boy-preacher turned, or half turned, novelist. In an oppressive situation, ministers and men of the Book have a natural edge in literacy and self-confidence: and even a slave like Turner was able to accumulate enough white man's self-sufficiency, plus white man's cartography and logistics, to lead the only facsimile of a revolt the slaves were ever able to mount.

William Styron has undertaken to reconstruct Nat Turner, using the public record as skeleton and fleshing him out with motives and whatnot. The result, in view of current events, can hardly be read as an exercise in pure aesthetics. The author mumbles something in his introduction about "perhaps the reader will wish to draw a moral . . . but," etc., thus saving his book for art, but there is no "perhaps . . . but" about it. A novel on this subject has to be part politics, ours and his, at the moment.

Of course we are going to ransack it for parallels. And of course, under whatever light camouflage, the parallels are going to be there, for the author gets his ideas from the same place we do, from the air around us. And how better to learn about Turner's motives than from living man with the same (apparent) motives? Thus, Styron uses history quite properly to put his own experience into fancy dress and see how it looks. No historical novel has ever done more.

Turner's rebellion took place in the long hot summer of 1831, in the state of Virginia. (Farther south, in the unfoliated cotton fields, there was less privacy to conspire in.) When it was over, fifty-nine white people were dead; the insurgents were all rounded up and either hanged or shown a clemency worse than death; and the preacher himself, now safely in irons, was induced to write a confession which Mr. Styron has managed to merge quite smoothly into his novel.

The first of many such lessons for the white community; but they seem to have learned even less than usual from this one. The owners were baffled to find their Negroes acting together, which ran counter to the sub-scientific cant of the period. They were baffled twice over to find how much those tiny brains (read Dr. Pepper's monograph on the Negro skull) could hate. On the other hand, the slaves had acted with less than West Point precision. Some of them hit the cider presses, and some on the fat-cat plantations had even fired on their brothers. So, by the end, the clichés had rallied and were back in the saddle.

But, in truth, Turner had done an extraordinary job. He could not, in his rather cramped circumstances, have had personal contact with more than a handful of his troops. He picked them up one by one, zealots and slobs alike, as he burned his way from farm to farm, and tried to weld them instantaneously into an army. At that, he very nearly succeeded: he was within half a mile of the armory at Jerusalem, Va., his nicely titled goal, when his luck ran out.

At his sanctimonious trial another familiar argument introduced itself. The white folks began to talk backlash—we tried being nice to these baboons and look where it got us—and no doubt they were able to follow through on it and no doubt an era of repression was Turner's immediate legacy. At the same time, he gave the Negroes a legend which has not yet lost its potency. Turner was, for instance, a big influence on Marcus Garvey, the daddy of the Black Nationalist movement. Garvey's disciples included Malcolm X's father. And so on, through how many bloodlines, to today's Negro leaders.

The Turner revolt, as Styron tells it in this novel, was a revolution of rising expectations. His version of Nat grows up spoiled, comparatively, by a kind master who promises him eventual freedom. This mirage cuts Nat temporarily adrift from his own people and renders him something of a prig—not necessarily a handicap in a leader. Later, when the freedom bubble bursts messily and he is handed down through a homosexual parson to a medium-brutal redneck farmer, and finally up again, too late, to a decent master, his arrogance will endure, as both a comfort to himself and an inspiration to others.

Simultaneous with this quirky character training goes an even quirkier, self-inflicted theological training. The Good Book which the owners have fed to their darkies in selected spoonfuls turns out, in larger doses, to be equivalent to a keg of nitroglycerine. All the violence and underdog determination that the masters skip over blandly in their own Scripture readings nest deep in Nat Turner. For this is his whole education, his whole intellectual universe. Joshua, David, vengeance. If you can't get Mao Tse-tung on Revolution, the Old Testament is not bad for your one book.

To complete the package, Turner has natural spiritual gifts, sharpened to brilliance by fasting and strenuous chastity. His preaching, as Styron records it, is hard and urgent. The preacher was the natural leader for Negroes—not because of their ignorance and superstition (these were as likely to work against him), but because he could do the work of years in minutes. With one spellbinding performance he could weld his audience, give them some point of concentration and the energy to pursue it. Unfortunately, as the failure of Turner's rising shows, the hypnosis is likely to wear off at the wrong moment: preacher-intoxication is not enough for a whole campaign.

In fact, it even wears off Turner himself: before Armageddon commences, he decides he will have to break training and get himself a wife. Then, when battle is joined, the two sides of the Good Book split inside him, Vengeance against Love, and he cannot lift his sword. He believes in killing with all his heart, but as he tries to do it, God leaves him and does not return until, minutes before his own hanging, Turner has a vision of reconciliation.

The message seems to be that the Negro has every right to kill the white man but cannot escape pollution in the process. The ending is covertly sentimental, one of those chins-up sad endings, and part of its effectiveness will be determined, as I say, by your view of the race question and the other and smaller part by whether the novel has worked with you as a novel.

And here we run into difficulties. There is no doubt that Turner is still worth writing and speculating about; but whether he can be successfully written about fictionally is another question. The historical novel is traditionally so clumsy a method of investigation that the reader usually winds up doubting whether the characters ever existed at all, in any form. And Styron has only exaggerated the difficulties by telling his story in the first person.

First of all, there is the old diction problem—in this case, finding a language for an early-nineteenth-century slave and sticking to it. This involves writing a whole book in mimicry of a speech one has never actually heard. The best you can hope for is a language technically correct but thin and colorless as convent-school French: with all the idioms woodenly in place, but with none of the juice and flavor of a man at home in his own language. Since we are looking into the mind and motives of the narrator, it does not help to get our answers in Berlitz.

Styron has done as well as he could with this part of his problem. Nat's dialogue is not just a pedantic reconstruction but a plausible, timeless blend of Southern-biblical: a little stiff, but not by nineteenth-century standards (anything looser would rouse suspicions of another sort), and generally serviceable. One grows frustrated at times watching the author squeeze his own excellent prose into this whalebone of rhetoric: but he gets off some fine phrases, and the writing in fact carries one over a good deal of wasteland.

The diction problem turns up in a more acute form when it comes to Turner's own consciousness. We are in effect being asked to spend a short lifetime in the head of one skillfully animated museum piece. What does Turner think about all this time? Not the things we would think about, of course: the author has been careful to expunge the twentieth century. But equipping his hero with a complete 1831 sensibility is something else. Styron is on safe ground while he is sticking to a certain *type* of thought—just as a mimicker of movie stars is safe if he sticks to certain key phrases—but the result of this can only be monotony beyond the call of monomania. A long book told from one point of view is always a risk: here the risk is prohibitive.

To enrich the cramped psyche of his narrator, Styron has simply inserted endless chunks of his own nature writing—some of the best nature writing going, but largely irrelevant to the narrative and to Nat's focus at the particular moment. Important dramatic scenes are interrupted time and again for the sake of long weather and crop reports, almost as if the author's own attention had wandered. Worse, the weather is always just right for the scene: sultry for tension, cold for failure, etc. We even have clouds passing over the sun on cue.

These and other Victorian devices lend an artificiality to the whole enterprise. The tone is often closer to late-Victorian than early-Victorian. "For many years it had been my habit . . ."

"Thus my duties, compared to what I had been used to, were light and fairly free of strain." It reminds one of the novels that begin "When I was a boy at the turn of the century." And how about this for honest muttonchop indignation? "It was plain now that the sight of the dying child had caused even his adamantine heart to be smitten by guilt." Or for elegance of feeling, what about this tribute to a lady's hand? "That soothing many-fingered delicacy." One hears the voice of W. C. Fields fading away on that line; and then, as Turner refers (more than once) to "the days before my execution" we pick up Stephen Leacock. "I died, I buried myself. Would that all who write sea stories would do likewise."

I am not suggesting that the novel is full of false laughs: Styron's taste is much too good for that. But the question arises: can a pastiche of this kind, however skillful, serve as a vehicle for genuine feeling? The answer, in terms of fiction, of the "felt-life," surely has to be no. There are so many techniques for insuring immediacy and complicity that Styron is forced to deny himself. Instead, he must make do with that old pack-drill of declarative sentences, slowly marching past. *"I felt a blinding pain . . . for days I lay in a fever . . . I felt my cheeks burning,"* all the earnest devices of the Victorian novelist telling you what to feel and how strongly to feel it.

The only scenes that break loose from this rhetorical strait jacket for long are scenes of straight dialogue. (The monologues are characteristically tiresome.) Otherwise, a simple brief narration of Nat Turner's trials would be far more moving than this windy, florid elaboration of them. Unfortunately, the padding and the stentorian descriptions and the majestic theme make the novel look "important," instead of simply ingenious, and this kind of thing can cause trouble for authors. This is the novel Styron always wanted to write, and we should now be glad he's gotten it over with, and can get on with the ones he doesn't want to write. Four-hundred-page imitations can be left to less talented novelists.

But if the book fails by default, as a novel, it does succeed in many places as a kind of historical tone poem. Styron's version of the old South is not the usual derivative, Daddy's-plantation stuff but a place freshly imagined stone by stone. Some sense is conveyed of the many varieties of slave experience, and the many kinds of Negro it produced. The Amos 'n' Andy dialogue sounds note-perfect, and so does Nat Turner's contempt for it. The servant's need to play the buffoon (traditional to all cultures, but treated as unique in each one) required for corrective a dour, humorless scold like Turner. When he tells them to lay aside their banjos, he is striking the first blow against the Natural Rhythm Theory.

But, to return to our beginnings, did Turner strike the blow, or was it Styron himself? Is this book really, as Styron says, a meditation on history, or a meditation on the daily papers? The answer comes in two parts. Styron has nothing new to say about Negro motives—outside of a few period visions and voices, Turner's reasons for revolting are just what you would expect. But he does have something to say about the physical situation of slavery, the way that America looked and sounded and smelled from underneath: the only position the American Negro has known to this day. There may be something to be said for documenting this year by year, the 1820's and then the 1830's and after that the 1840's, until the size of the atrocity is recorded and dimly understood. If so, Styron has performed a signal, nonliterary service in writing this book.

1967

PART TWO

1 / *Confessions of a Sports Nut*

T HEY TOOK AWAY MY CRICKET BAT AT THE AGE
of nine and told me I wouldn't be needing it any more. Out of
kindness they didn't tell me I wouldn't need my soccer ball,
either. Otherwise, I don't think I would have come to America
at all. I would have lied about my age and joined the horse ma-
rines.

Exile is an ugly business at any age. Harold Pinter, the playwright, carted his bat with him all over England to remind him
of the past (he must have been eight when he started out). I was
forced to hand mine over at the frontier, and with it the long
summer evenings, the boys with the dangling suspenders, the
whole Fanny-by-gaslight world of cricket; my life for the next
few years would be a hunt for fresh symbols, a bat and ball I
could believe in.

Baseball dismayed me at first blush almost as much as the
big cars and the big faces in the street. In the dictionary of the
senses *cricket* stood for twilight, silence, flutter. (See also
Swans.) *Baseball* equaled noonday, harsh, noise, clatter. (See
Geese.) That was how it looked at first—boys milling around
dusty lots jabbering and hitching at their pants. But as I kept
craning from train windows and car windows in my first days
in America, I noticed something promising: that nothing ever

93

seemed to be happening at that particular moment—the same basic principle as cricket. The pitcher peering in to get the sign, the ritual chant of the infield, the whispered consultations and then, if you were very lucky, a foul tip, before you were whisked out of range. Baseball was not as busy as it seemed but lived, like the mother game, on pregnant pauses. This, plus the fact that it happened to be in season and you played it with a bat and ball, made it look like my best bet.

Unfortunately, the place where we first lived was an almost deserted village, so there was no one to play with. There was one boy about a mile down the road. He straightened out my batting stance and filled me in on the First World War, too, but he was five years older than I, with his own life to live, so I couldn't bother him too often.

Instead, I became perhaps the outstanding solitary baseball player of my generation, whaling fungoes down the long, narrow garden and plodding after them, chattering to myself and whaling them back again. Anything pulled or sliced got lost, so my first encounter with American botany was staring sightless through it, hunting the tawny baseball. When that palled, I would chalk a strike zone on the garage door and lob a tennis ball at it. Already I had the style, though God knows where it came from: the mock aggression and inscrutable loneliness. Gary Cooper high on a hill, twitching his cap, shaking off the sign: nodding, rearing, firing. Clunk, against the old garage door. The manner came with my first glove.

Another thing that stoked my love affair was the statistics. I like a game that has plenty of statistics, the more inconsequential the better, and I began soaking up baseball records like a sea sponge before I even knew what they meant. I liked the way you could read *around* baseball, without ever getting to the game at all. I devoured a long piece in the old *Satevepost* about Hank Greenberg, baseball's most eligible bachelor, and another about young Ted Williams, who only shaved twice a week. Official baseball sneaked up on me through its trivia. My learned friend up the road took me, at last, to an actual game at Shibe Park, and I was hooked for fair. It was the St. Louis Browns vs. the Philadelphia Athletics, hardly an offering to stir the blood, but more than enough to stir mine. The Brownies built up a big lead, but the A's, led by Wally Moses and Bob Johnson, staged one of their rare comebacks and pulled it out of the fire. The sand-lot games I had seen so far had not been beautiful to look at, only intellectually interesting (I used phrases like that occasionally, a real little snot in some ways); but here we had something as elegant as the Radio City Rockettes—explosively elegant and almost as fussily stylish as cricket.

Baseball became my constant, obsessive companion after that. Up and down the garden, faster and faster, first as Dick Siebert, the A's first baseman, then as Arky Vaughan, whose name and dour appearance I fancied, then right-handed as Jimmy Foxx. And at night I played out whole games in my head, in which I was always the quiet, unobtrusive professional (I detested showboating) who hit the penultimate single or made a key play in the *eighth* inning. It was as if I'd brought my cricket bat with me, after all.

The point about this was that it was all what D. H. Lawrence would have called "baseball in the head." When I came to play with other boys in the next few years, I continued my solipsistic ways, trotting out quietly to my position, chewing all the gum that my mouth would hold and gazing around with mild, shrewd eyes; or, for a time, grinning like Stan Hack, the Cub third baseman—a steady player on a steady club, the way I wanted to spend eternity.

A sociologist might (and I would probably agree with him, having just made him up) explain my choice of this particular type of athlete quite simply. Baseball was my social passport, and a slight averageness is good on a passport. It means that the officials look at you less closely. Who is that guy over there? Maybe he'd like to play. Say—he's quietly efficient, isn't he? I remember standing around picnic sites and county fairs, wistfully, with my glove half concealed under my arm as if I didn't mean anything by it. I was slightly ashamed of my accent and bitterly ashamed of my first name; but baseball did not judge you by those things. The Statue of Liberty, bat in hand, said, "Try this, kid."

Sometimes, magically, it happened. I was rather light for a ballplayer in spite of weighing myself a lot. I knew the names of all the light ballplayers (the Waner brothers were a special comfort), but still, 80 pounds was 80 pounds, and even with the most graceful swing in town I could rarely nudge the ball past second base. However, I waited out numerous walks, if there happened to be an umpire, fielded as well as the pebbles allowed and always looked a little better than the clumsy lout they had buried in right field. Afterwards they went their way, into houses I knew nothing about, to a life that contained other things besides baseball; and I went mine.

In the fall of '41 I left for boarding school. Although the baseball season was still raging, I found that it was all over as far as my new school was concerned. I felt as if I had lost a friend. My companion of the long, silent summer was replaced by a harsh, grunting affair, where people shouted like drill sergeants and made a big thing of getting in shape, being in shape, staying in shape. Suck in your gut, get those knees up.

I saw right away that football was the enemy. If 80 pounds was of dubious value in summer, it was downright ludicrous in fall. Beyond that, I distrusted the atmosphere of the game, all that crouching and barking. It was a side of America that might have appealed to a little German boy, but hardly to me. The essential solitude of baseball gave way to the false heartiness, the just-feel-that-stomach toughness. We only played touch football that year but, even so, managed to make a military thing of it.

God knows how, I came to love football anyway. The finished product, the game itself, transcended all the midweek drivel. I had seen the previous winter one game, in which Whizzer (now Sir Whizzer or Lord Byron) White scored two touchdowns against the woebegone Eagles of Philadelphia, and I guess I liked it all right. I drew some crayon pictures of it, anyway, showing little Davey O'Brien being smothered by Lions.

But there was an actuality to the game as played that was quite different from the game as watched or the game as planned. I became second-string quarterback in our rather peculiar school and got to run back a kickoff in a quasi-real game. Huddled in the lee of a gland case, a 250-pound eighth-grader, I made our only considerable gain of the day. I relished the swooping, shifting patterns that had to be diagnosed instantly, the hilarity of each yard gained, the pleasure of doing something you've practiced and getting it right.

It was quite different from my dreamy, poetic, half-mad relationship with baseball. This was crisp and outgoing, hep-two-three-four, and based on the realities of the game, not on some dream of it. Yet it filled the same social purpose. It became a shortcut, or substitute, for mastering the local culture. I still didn't know how to talk to these people but while I was playing I didn't have to. The soundless pat on the back, the "nice going, Sheed"—you could be any manner of clod, or even an English boy, and it didn't matter. I remember blocking a punt with my stomach and writhing in agony and feeling it was worth it for the brief respect I commanded.

This was canceled on another occasion, which is still almost too painful to describe, and which I write here only that it may be of help to others: that is, to any 80-pound English refugees who happen to be reading this. The setting was a pickup game played in semi-darkness. The agreed-on goal line was a fuzzy patch of trees off in the middle distance, I'm still not sure where. My team was losing 12–0, and it was understood that the next play would be the last one: hence meaningless, a lame-duck exercise. Their man threw a long pass. I intercepted it and stepped backward, some place in the area of the goal line.

Triumphant hands were clapped on me, and I was told that I had just handed two points to the enemy. Would (and I have woulded this would often since) that Zeus had smitten my tongue at that moment. The game would have been forgotten— 12–0, 14–0, who cared—and I would have been spared three lousy years. As it was, I said in fruitiest Cockney, "How was I supposed to know where the goal line was?"

Wrong thing to say. I heard no more about it that day. The saying went underground for a while, and when it emerged the context had been garbled slightly. I was now alleged to have run the wrong way, like Riegel in the Rose Bowl, and to have capped it, in what was now a horrible whine: " 'Ow was Aye suppowsed to know which why the gowl was!" Well, O.K., I was used to that by now, in an Irish school. But this legend so grabbed the popular imagination that I was still hearing it three years later from boys who had just entered the school.

The moral of this tragedy is that sport as a Julien Sorel passport has its treacherous side. It can bestow curses as carelessly as blessings, and the curses stick. However, those first two years would have been grim without sports, which played an unnaturally large part in my life, and still do in my mind, because they were, at times, all I had.

As to my life as a fan, that, too, was a social passport, and therefore doctored slightly. "Hey, how come you know so much about baseball?" could be a friendly question or it could be weighted with menace. Like a professional dumb blonde, I found there were circles where it paid to keep my knowledge to myself, even though it burned in the mouth and even though some fat fool was deluding the crowd with wrong statistics.

It was, though, an acceptable subject, and there weren't too many of those. I did not understand cars, had not been camping last summer, had a non-cooking mother: subject after subject broke in my hands. Only sports could be trusted. Fate had presented me with three frowsy teams to talk about: the Phillies, A's, and Eagles, all usually cemented into their respective last places. (I was foolishly pleased when a friend said, "Don't the A's usually finish around sixth?" The A's never finished anywhere near sixth.) Pennsylvania University was some small consolation—I saw it beat Army, Harvard, Cornell on various weekends—but hardly enough. My own social position was too sensitive to burden with three risible teams, so I decided to diversify. I took on board the Brooklyn Dodgers and the Washington Redskins. Sammy Baugh was a man I could identify with. Lean and steel-eyed, my winter self.

On balance, I would say that playing games didn't do much for my character. It gives one a highly specialized confidence and a highly qualified cooperativeness, but in return it makes one incurably childish. Intellectually, it teaches you that you can't argue with a fact, a mixed blessing. However, being a Brooklyn fan was useful. It taught me to suffer. The Dodgers immediately and definitively broke my heart. I had barely become a fan when Mickey Owen dropped the third strike and gave a World Series game away. Then the next season, 1942, Peter Reiser banged his head on the wall and the Bums blew a ten-game lead over the Cardinals. The Dodgers came to Philadelphia on July 4 strutting like gods and pasted the local scarecrows 14–0 and 5–4. Reiser hit the neatest, mellowest little home run you ever saw. Medwick, Camilli—players twice as big, twice as regal as any since.

On the Sunday after Labor Day the Cardinals came in. They had beaten the Dodgers the day previous, on Whitey Kurowski's home run, to reach first place for the first time. The Dodgers were playing two with Cincinnati. There was strangling doom in the air. I knew, everyone knew, what was going to happen. All afternoon I watched the scoreboard. The Phillies were managing to split with the Cards, an unlikely reprieve, but the Dodgers went down slowly, inexorably to total defeat.

I was insane with grief. It was worse than the fall of France, and the feelings were not dissimilar: the same sense of irreversible momentum and crushed dreams. It seemed strange even then that a misfortune suffered by a random collection of strangers could hurt so much. Yet for days I was sick with sorrow and actually tried to forget about baseball: a trick I wasn't to master for another twenty years. I recovered in time to root lustily for the Cardinals in the World Series. A defeat for the Yankees was already sweeter than a victory for anyone else. Hence, there was an element of vindictive nihilism in my baseball thinking, which was to run riot when Walter O'Malley took his team from Brooklyn to L.A. some sixteen years later, and which has dominated since that time.

In the fall of '43 we moved to New York. The Philadelphia hermitage was over. No more mowing lawns and hoeing vegetable beds in our victory garden to pay my way to Shibe Park, no more early-morning trolley rides to Frankford and long subway rides from there in order to get the whole of batting practice and two games for my buck and a quarter. I had not realized what a grueling regimen this was until I took a friend with a medium interest in baseball along for company. Even though we saw Ted Williams strike out three times on the knuckle ball and then hit a home run in the tenth, my friend never once mentioned baseball again.

But now I was in New York, the capital of baseball, and my appetite raged wantonly, like some Thomas Wolfe character in Europe, prowling the streets and roaring. In those days every barbershop had a radio, every butcher shop—the whole block was a symphony of baseball.

To be young in Paris, to be coming up for thirteen in New York! Unfortunately, the game itself was not in such hot shape right then. The stars were wafting, or drafting, away and being replaced by squinting, shambling defectives like the ones I had left behind in Philadelphia. The Dodgers tried out a sixteen-year-old shortstop. The lordly Yankees were reduced to the likes of

Joe Buzas and Ossie Grimes. The St. Louis Browns actually had a one-armed center-fielder. The hottest player in town was an aging retread called Phil Weintraub. You had to love baseball to survive those years.

But I liked going to the parks anyway. They offered the cultural continuity of churches. You could slip into one in a strange city and pick up the ceremony right away. College football stadiums made me nervous with their brutal cliquishness, and professional football stadiums always gave me rotten seats—the same one, it seemed like, high up and to the left, in back of the goal line. But ball parks were home and still are, a place where I understand what my neighbors are up to, even after a year abroad.

The football scene was a slight improvement over God-forsaken Philadelphia. The wartime Giants must have been one of the dullest teams in history, with their off-tackle smashes and their defensive genius. But they were usually able to make a game of it. I saw Don Hutson *throw* a touchdown pass off an end-around reverse, and my hero, Sammy Baugh, quick-kick 66 yards to the Giants' four. You didn't seem to see things like that in Philadelphia.

My own playing career mooned along all this while, striking me, at least, as promising. I had become a spottily effective left end, running solemn little down-and-outs and tackling with bravura (I found I wasn't afraid of head-on tackles, which put one in the elite automatically). I discovered that basketball yielded to humorless determination better than most games and I once succeeded in sinking seventeen foul shots in a row. But the game had no great emotional interest; it was more like a bar game of skill that whiles away the evenings. I liked the hot gymnasiums and the feel of the floor underfoot, and it was fun fretting about the score, but the game left no resonance afterwards. Fast breaks and the swishing of the strings—a thin collection of memories.

Baseball continued to intoxicate, worse than ever; tossing

the ball among snowdrifts at the beginning of spring, the sweet feeling in the hands when you connected and sent it scudding over the winter grass, the satisfaction of turning your back on a fly and turning round again in more or less the right place to catch it. I had grown off my 80-pound base and was now a gawky fanatic of 105 or so; willing to field for hours, taking my glove everywhere, pounding an endless pocket into it, scavenging for a game.

This sport, which I had needed so badly on arrival, was now making me pay for its favors. I was enslaved to it, like Emil Jannings to Marlene Dietrich. My life had become seriously lopsided. I refused to go swimming because it interfered with my career—tightened the skin on the chest and all that. I looked at the countryside with blank eyes. My father admonished me to throw away my baseball magazines after one reading, but I hid them like an addict. I don't recall reading anything else at all. Nothing, not even the war, interested me any more.

In my new neighborhood my passport was honored handsomely. I was the best shortstop, in an admittedly skimpy field, and I was always sure of a game. I didn't bother to make friends in any other context, seeing myself as an aloof professional who never mixed business with pleasure. I took an ascetic view of people who goofed off and had a mortal horror of games degenerating into horseplay. "Come on, let's play ball," I would say austerely, like some Dominican friar behind on his autos-da-fé. My father, who spent half the war in each country, took me to see a cricket match in Van Cortlandt Park, and it struck me as a vague, ramshackle game. We got into a discussion over the concept "not cricket." It seemed to me ridiculous not to take every advantage you could in a game. The slyness and bluff of baseball were as beautiful to me as the winging ball.

How long this would have lasted, I have no way of knowing. I might have snapped out of it in a year or two, under pressure of girls and such, or followed it glumly until some awaken-

ing in a Class A minor league. I contracted polio at the age of
fourteen, and my career was over just like that. I ran a fever and
for the first couple of nights I could see nothing in it but sports
images: football highlights, baseball highlights, boxing (I was
the only boy in school who had rooted for Louis over Conn, so
I had the films of the fight in my repertoire), all rushing through
my head like the Gadarene swine on their way to the sea. I was
allowed to switch sports, but not the main subject. My obsession
had to play itself out.

When calmness returned, I found my interest in sports had
fixated, frozen, at that particular point. I was to remain a four-
teen-year-old fan for the next twenty years. I continued thinking that the life of a professional ballplayer was attractive long
after a sensible man would have abandoned the notion. I returned to England for a while and became a cricket nut all over
again.

Yet it wasn't really the same. I knew now that my bat had
been taken for good and I had better find something else to do.
Sports still raged, but in one lobe only. The other was liberated,
free to grow up if it could. And my interest in sport was more
house-trained and philosophical: no more wrist-slashing over
defeat, no more hero worship, an occasional thin smile while losing at pool—all in all, about as much maturity as you can expect
from a hardened sports addict.

But when I see some Negro or Puerto Rican kid making
basket catches or running like an arrow, breaking the language
barrier and waving his passport, I feel like saying O.K., but don't
take it too seriously, don't let this be all. Sports are socially useful, up to a strictly limited point. I stopped being a foreigner the
moment I blocked that kick, and a moment is sometimes all it
takes. But blocking kicks or whacking baseballs only gets you so
far. (Don't bring those muddy boots in the living room.) The
mockery starts up again the minute you leave the park.

I thought sports had made me an American but in some ways

they actually retarded the process. I played them like an English colonial officer, exhausting himself with some amusing native game and missing too many other things. Having said that, let me double back on it: if you had to limit yourself to one aspect of American life, the showdowns between pitcher and hitter, quarterback and defense, hustler and fish, would tell you more about politics, manners, style in this country than any one other thing. Sports constitute a code, a language of the emotions, and a tourist who skips the stadiums will not recoup his losses at Lincoln Center and Grant's Tomb.

1969

2 / *The Good Old Days*

in California

THE FUN WENT OUT OF THE CAMPAIGN SO quickly it was hard to remember it had ever been there. Our show-biz names versus their show-biz names, our writers versus their writers, and which side was Barbra Streisand really on; the hysterical fun that followed the Kennedys everywhere they went, the sense of precariousness and racing the clock, and the counterfun of the McCarthy movement, with its kids and its cabarets—the buoyancy of an anti-royalist rising with a fantastic run of victories from Cork to Wexford, from New Hampshire to Wisconsin to Oregon. All gone now, like Jackie Kennedy's water skis. And all one could think was: If I had such a good time last night, why do I feel so rotten this morning?

Senator McCarthy came out in the corridor of the Beverly Hilton early on Wednesday and said a few spare words of regret. His face was white and ravaged, like a private man's, not just heavy and solemn like a politician's. He looked as if he had possibly spent the worst night in the history of Christendom; but since McCarthy keeps his feelings to himself, we could only guess at his thoughts. One thing that might have occurred to him, though, in passing, was that he had himself left a similar ballroom, by a similar exit, not an hour before Robert Kennedy had.

At least, one figured afterward that it must have been the kitchen he went through on the way back to his suite. Behind him, the ballroom was the usual swinging snake pit; next day the Los Angeles *Times* would describe the mood there as gloomy, but if so, saints preserve us from ecstasy. We had just sustained one of our most arresting defeats: Kennedy would now stay in the race, which was essential to our plans, deadlock the convention, and leave it to McCarthy to break the tie—an ambiguous situation to be whooping it up over, but we were used to that by now.

Upstairs, everything was a snarl of cables and cameras. There was nothing to photograph right now, but the roiling apparatus would sit there solemnly all night for people to trip over, just in case. McCarthy workers, great and humble, had piled into the bedrooms with the best TV sets, of which mine seemed to be one. So I edged in anonymously and watched, from a hard-won beachhead on my own bed, the scene over at Kennedy's place.

He looked, you may recall, unusually relaxed and content. Tales had been spreading of his total exhaustion, of his having to be helped into his car, and so on, but victory is politicians' medicine. His speech was humorous, in that limited but pleasant kidding style he had fallen into, and magnanimous. It had been a clean fight, as these things go, which meant that our loathing for each other was not quite irreparable; and Kennedy was mending fences as he went.

In retrospect, Sheed felt that this last speech had charmed him for the first time. But this, I fear, was an optical illusion. After a dogfight like that, you are in no shape to be charmed, not just yet. He left the platform, and we returned to our endless conjecturing, our audacious raids on delegates, and our happy Hubert-baiting. Even minor functionaries and hangers-on can fill a room with smoke and talk like power brokers. McCarthy's coup had been to offer this old man's dream to the under-thirties.

It was to wits woolly with role-playing and booze and the thought of no-work-tomorrow that the news arrived in grotesque bits and pieces. "Shooting . . . shot . . . somebody shot . . . clear the hall, *clear the hall* . . . Jesse Unruh, Bobby, don't know . . . in the hip, in the head." The TV was as confused as we were. The screen was a splurge of ungodly colors, baby blue and midnight orange. The young McCarthy workers sobbed and stared and said oh, no, and what's happening and I don't believe it. Bobby was reported to have gripped his rosary beads, a good sign. Somebody asked if receiving the Last Sacraments meant that the Church had given up on you. No, it was explained, just a routine precaution.

Time now to work on one's sermon. What's wrong with America, wrong with California, Los Angeles, guns, war, violence. Already the great popular preachers were wheeling like buzzards, coaching us in the right phrases and attitudes. "The fabric of our society torn . . . America sick, violence, guns, frontier . . ." By the next evening we would have heard it all; and we would be saying, we whores after novelty, that America wasn't so bad, that the question wasn't so simple, but prepared to abandon that position too if it became too crowded. Meanwhile, the President's meatball commission would set to work and slowly regurgitate Eric Sevareid's *aperçus*. Every journal able to lisp would start on its violence piece, and by fall the nation's bookshelves would be stocked to bursting with this new toy.

Knowing all this added a last thimble of gloom to that long evening, which ended when I introduced myself to my guests circa 3:30 A.M. and asked them to clear out. Whether or not America is sick or violent, it surely is preachy and predictable; and one shares in this quality oneself, as if it were a public utility.

Since I had been doing a little speaking for McCarthy in the Los Angeles area, I suppose my thoughts had been in synch with those of my numerous roommates. There I had been, bad-mouthing Kennedy all week, in a spirit of play; and now found myself staring at the top of his head, knowing for sure that he was dead, grip or no grip. "This wasn't what it was about, there's been a mistake," one wanted to tell someone. A lady journalist, unflaggingly keen for Gene, looked in at the last minute and said, "After this, I don't give a damn what happens to anybody," and tottered off to her room. The special quality of the moment was a moral squalor beyond tragedy. It was a messy and embarrassing thing, like someone throwing up on the rug; one felt reluctant to face the daylight, ashamed to have been there. Not, it was my gun, I pulled the trigger—ah, guilty me—but simply an embarrassed silence seemed best.

The next day (short-story gray and misty), we all crept quietly out of Los Angeles. The TWA hostesses hitched at their togas and tried to make like Italians. What year was it that the three emperors were gunned, or poisoned, down? Rome, a very violent society. The pilot had a comic routine, which he interrupted with bulletins about Kennedy. "Very critical, extremely critical as to life." The inflight movie was *A Dandy in Aspic*. When we landed in New York, we found everyone was a day behind in their grief and their theories, and we had to begin all over again.

An Easterner arrives in Los Angeles armored with notions. You feel your brain beginning to rot as you hit the runway. And the people in the airport look tanned out of their minds, offensively bland, and desperately superficial. The main impression, if you can shed the one you came in with, is no impression at all. If someone had said to me, ha-ha, this is really Detroit, I would scarcely have known what to answer, except to wave weakly at some palm tree.

However, the mind never stops working. A city that leaves no impression is sinister too, right? This would not seem quite so silly later. Meanwhile, there was nothing for it but to stare with frozen horror at the spastic taximeter and at the nameless pastels sliding past the window. The Beverly Hilton itself is a fine figure of a hotel, with a front some place in the middle and a string of off-mustard terraces to refresh your spirit on; but what you see from there is more of the same, pale greens and sickly beiges, and signs saying "Esther Feather's Reducing Salon," and Somebody's custom-made hats, operating out of dirty chartreuse warehouses; and beyond that—well, more of that. My one contribution to assassination-theory would be based on that first, blank look: namely, that all our assassins have been geographically dislocated; that our violence has something to do with feeling lost.

After a bath and supper (which I shall go into at corruscating length in the book version), I moseyed over to the Westwood CDA headquarters to see what work there was for a diffident, low-road speaker. This was the Wednesday night, a week from the primary. I got the impression that the smart writers had mostly headed for San Francisco already for the balmy cultural weather. Anyhow, they weren't here, in this vague, cheerful barn of a headquarters.

The girl in the spea ᷉er's bureau seemed confused and willing, the hallmark of a McCarthy student worker. The kids who had made the trek from New Hampshire had developed a style by now, flip, tired, gallant. Items: boy spread-eagled center floor in the Crenshaw headquarters taking the most ostentatious midday nap you ever saw—whacked out, poor devil; a girl staggering off from a party at 2 A.M. "to work the mimeograph for a few hours" (but, Dame Mitty, you *can't!*). And all the other Weary Warriors with their eighteen-hour days and tired grins.

The speaker's bureau girl was not of the theatrical persuasion, but she did have one thing in common with most of the others: she knew practically nothing about Los Angeles. This most labyrinthine of urban sprawls was being blitzkrieged by kids who couldn't tell a boulevard from a freeway. My first assignment was to a gentle middle-aged Jewish household, hardly my schtik, where I believe I was introduced as Wilbur Snead, or one of its variants, and then (quick glance at card) as literary

editor of *Life* magazine and *The New York Times*. The first
question I got concerned McCarthy's attitude toward Israel.

That night, as on others, I found the speaker's kit from
headquarters more or less useless. I had dutifully memorized all
the stock answers about oil depletion, poll tax, and so on, but
found that my little audiences didn't even know the questions.
The famous distorted version of McCarthy's voting record
(concocted by a New York group of Kennedy backers) was
still circulating briskly in Negro neighborhoods; but the white
folks didn't know or didn't care. How was McCarthy going to
end the war in Vietnam? Did he have executive ability? Or
(fringe stuff), what was wrong with the CIA anyway? were
the questions they asked.

I found myself sinking quickly into the deepest fens of
demagoguery. How far to the left or right was this particular
group was all I needed to know. Did they dig adventure, or was
responsibility in government their thing? As proxy brood sow,
I was there to serve. As to the enemy, Bobby became more two-
faced and Hubert more ludicrous every night. Until one sobered
up on Tuesday and looked at the mess. Unfortunately, I had
not followed the sound advice of Leonard Lewin (putative
author of *The Iron Mountain Report*), who had grown gray
stumping the country for Gene: to wit, ignore the other fellows,
be positive out here.

They do, I believe, like you to be positive in the L.A. area;
might stomp you if you were not. It is interesting, as you leave
some smiling hostess or other, to compare this resolute sunniness
with the vicious, in-turned quality of the Los Angeles driving
that waits for you outside. There seems to be no continuity
between life in the car and life in the house. The closest thing in
schizophrenia would be a Mafia gunman at a Holy Name rally.

A chronological rundown of the next few days would be misleading, because the mind has long since jumbled them, and

that's the form they now take. Speaking, driving, more speaking, more driving; Sunday now comes before Thursday, because that's the logical order. Prejudice gave ground slowly to glib observation. You notice right away the cool proto-movie-star routines of garage attendants, busboys, of the fellow who rents you the inevitable car, so stylized after New York, where manners are formed by abrasion and erosion, and where the doormen are old rock formations. You notice the fact that people not only have no accents but use no slang to speak of (this may not go for special groups, beach-and-bike enclaves, but it does for the middle-class students and such that I met). There is no common speech because there is no city. With so many people, it seems dangerous not to have a city.

These are thoughts to drive by. To Anaheim for a small give-'em-hell rally in an improvised Eugene's. To Santa Paula for a Mexican-American picnic, where you wish you could stay but can't—the stern demands of the stump whisking you from good scenes and bad alike. And through the airless Simi Valley in Ventura County, where the physical facts of campaigning become a little clearer.

A formidable motorcade had rolled up outside the local bowling alley, twenty to thirty cars covered in gorgeous bunting, and Michael McCarthy, the senator's sixteen-year-old son, perched on a back seat for display. With horns blasting and loudspeaker braying (bring our boys back, vote for Senator McCarthy), we set off through the desolate streets. Occasionally a stray dog would follow us. A small child would wave. Otherwise, silence, shuttered windows. It couldn't be every day that they had a motorcade out this way, yet they responded like people jaded, sick, with excitement.

One soon wearied of waving V-signs at stony-faced men who rubbed their cars in response, at stray gardeners who would not look up or around, even in anger. Occasionally on that long ride I thought I saw people actually lurking in their garages, peering from the shadows. All right, paranoia, but paranoia is modest good sense in the Simi Valley on a Sunday.

Meanwhile, a fellow in our car was trying to make a pitch to young Michael McCarthy. It seemed he wanted a civil-service job, had written to Michael's dad about six months ago, maybe the letter had been mislaid. I know your dad's been awful busy (laugh), but maybe he could find just a moment, used to be friends back in Minnesota, sixteen years ago. Roots still in Minnesota, you know, Dad's a wonderful man. "Mother would go back tomorrow if we could sell the house."

Michael is a boy of great poise, and he dealt with the matter gracefully. But this bleak cry for help combined badly with the dry sun and the cheerless wind and the endless bungalows— which, two days before the primary, showed no signs of pref- erence, no bumper stickers, no anything. The man told us he had been a salesman for twenty-seven years, had learned from selling that you had to believe in your product, that's why he believed in McCarthy; it was like religion or anything else, you had to sell it. Yet this Willy Loman of the Far West was one of the valley's live ones.

For a Presidential candidate, this would have been an off day. But for an out-of-shape dilettante, it brought the illumina- tions of fatigue. The first secret of campaigning must be to regulate your thermostat, to avoid excitement and depression equally, to save yourself for the next meeting and the next and the next. You cannot afford to feel like God, that would take too much out of you. Every excess must be paid for. Watch those naps, snacks, toilet habits. Remember the name of this man, and his wife, listen to his prattle and be prepared to prattle back in kind. I had always wondered at the steady, humming vitality of politicians, from breakfast rally to midnight caucus, but now I saw how it worked: the kind, empty eyes, the firm, indifferent handshake, everything economized on except ap- pearances.

That evening, I returned to L.A., passing on the way something described as the world's largest shopping center, set in a great vacuum, to talk to a group of, I think, Italian Catholics, more communal and New Yorky than anything I had struck so far. But all resilience was gone. I read the basic speech woodenly and hacked through the questions somehow. A professional politician would never have let this happen. He would not have wasted energy brooding about the denizens of the Simi Valley or about huge shopping centers where small ones would do, or about all the failures and solitaries who cluster about Los Angeles looking on the bright side and driving like werewolves.

All the while, this microscopic private campaign was trotting alongside the real one, and following its contours. Senator McCarthy had come to Los Angeles and gone, making his usual mild but favorable impression. Private observation informed me that he looked wretched before breakfast, an excellent thing in a candidate (how else could he represent the interests of my group?). More significantly, in some ways, Clarence Jones, Martin Luther King's legal adviser and co-chairman of McCarthy's New York campaign, had come to town, snapped his fingers at the easygoing Westwood staff, and had set to work making an eleventh-hour pitch to the racial minorities, which the McCarthy workers had prematurely conceded to Kennedy.

Jones's scheme included talking to as many Negro ministers as possible before they hit their pulpits on the Sunday before Tuesday's primary, and circulating reprints of an editorial endorsement of McCarthy by the influential Negro newspaper the *Sun Reporter* outside the churches. McCarthy workers were reluctant to enter Watts at all, where pro-Kennedy fervor could, if inclined, wreak much damage to cars and sound trucks. But, as it turned out, the editorial was circulated safely enough, and so was Louis Lomax's endorsement of McCarthy after the Saturday night debate. And who knows, perhaps a percentage point was affected by this frenetic activity.

Meanwhile, one had had at least one glimpse of the incurable triviality of history. I went to a party on Thursday thrown by the Negro head of the CDA headquarters in Crenshaw, hoping to meet whatever other black supporters were around, only to find some sort of boycott in progress. A wistful spread was laid on, but only a few white workers and Myrna Loy showed up for it. Later a couple of Negro friends dropped in. With a lifetime to feud in, the matter had chosen primary week to erupt.

But the important thing now was the Saturday night debate. We had high hopes for this. McCarthy was reported to be indignant over the ground rules, and if his face shows a weakness, it is for petulance. But he was resting well and looked strong as a lumberjack. He would cream their boy.

Thank God (I suppose), he did not. For their own different reasons, the two men dealt gently with each other. The group I was with laughed when Senator Kennedy brought Israel into a question where it didn't strictly belong: a routine political stunt, no hard feelings. His reference to the ten thousand Negroes who might descend on white-Republican Orange County if McCarthy had his way was not so well received. We took that to be a backlash pitch, and hoped that Negroes picked it up. Otherwise, the mildness of the occasion was unbroken. Kennedy might have lost, by looking less Presidential and all that, but McCarthy had hardly won.

It was obvious that the big question the next day would be: what is the difference between them anyway? I thought the debate had revealed some significant ones, notably on the question of negotiating with the NLF, but it was hard to tell whether Californians cared about this, or anything else in particular. The task suddenly seemed to be to interest them in their own primary. There were on the margins random signs of Bobby-love and Bobby-hatred, both echoing through the squeal that followed him everywhere; but of serious political feeling, there seemed to be surprisingly little. Eighteen percent Undecided in a Saturday night poll. Eighteen percent, after all this.

On Monday, I talked to a bunch of Catholic colleges, plus the normal allotment of housewives. It took an act of faith to believe that this was still making a difference. I was told of one student who had changed his mind as a consequence of my harangue, but he was probably under voting age. Otherwise, the important question now was whether to ring doorbells, or to phone up the neighbors and bother them that way. The activists in the audience threshed this out while the rest of us listened. I had no thoughts on the subject. Los Angelenos seemed infinitely inaccessible by any means at all.

That evening, the Senator ambled around the seventh (McCarthy) floor chatting with his cohorts, and I had a chance to gauge him up close. He is physically imposing, and I could understand why his admirers had wished him to be photographed standing next to Kennedy. Americans would always like an extra few inches of President, all else being equal. He has a politician's memory—I had met him briefly some seven years before, and he remembered this without faking. He listens fairly well, for a politician, looking beyond you, but picking up the drift. He seemed sharper and more concentrated than I remembered, as if the campaign had summoned his wits together.

Beyond that, he is the kind of wry Irishman that I have known more than my share of, feel comfortable with, would trust crossing a bog. The famous cynicism is *de rigueur* with this Irish-uncle type—emotions being for special occasions and cynicism for everyday wear; at any rate, a matter of style, not of moral conviction, and nothing to worry about. I felt no doubt that he would make a good President, if he wanted to; there remained some small doubt about that, however. We talked briefly about the debate, and he said that he thought Kennedy had made one or two mistakes. "Put him on bread and water for forty days and he'll blurt out the truth," he said, smiling. When I reminded the Senator that he had been on that same diet himself, he said, still smiling, "Yes, but I'm tougher than he is." Not hostile, but decidedly scrappy.

Robert Lowell (without whom no account of this sort would be complete) also turned up that evening, but our conversation was not noteworthy. The Boston Brahmin and the Roxy dropout sparred briefly, using the light gloves, is probably the simplest way to put it. There was nothing to do now but wait. At the Westwood headquarters next morning, a parking-lot attendant tried first to stop me, then, failing that, to extort an unprecedented fee. I pointed out that the lot was half empty, and he said, "It's as full as I want it to be." When I rejoined rather pompously that people like him were hurting McCarthy's cause, he said, "I don't give a shit about McCarthy. I'm for Kennedy." And a smirking crony drove this home: "We just want to get you people out of here."

Upstairs, one of the sillier girls was going on about last night's sniping mission—a couple of delirious hours spent tearing down Bobby posters and slapping up Gene ones. So the eighteenth-century spirit, bullyboys, street goons, and vandalism, was alive in both sides, the more grotesque because there were no special interests involved to speak of, only personalities—and in a sense, only one personality, Kennedy's, followed by that weird squeal. The speaker's bureau was closed. There was some action downstairs—dubious small boys from Port Said and the Levant collecting stickers and hats, and so on—but upstairs it was like the last day of school, feet on the desk, detective story out, last-minute gossip.

This prompted a few last thoughts about the scholar-gypsies who had followed the McCarthy caravan from coast to coast.

Some of the McCarthy youth corps had run through a life cycle, from zealous to slightly smug, in a few months. The best of them, including their leader, Curt Gans, kept their heads down all the way; the worst would chat while a phone went unanswered, or would pick it up and sound ineffably bored into it. "She isn't in. I don't know. Yes, why don't you do that." Office work was clearly not their thing, and it was probably time for the more languid of these to be phased out and replaced by semi-pros, yet how could you fire them? They had gone to God knows what sacrifices in order to be able to lounge around here; they came at bargain prices—always a factor in the McCarthy campaign; they represented McCarthy's appeal to youth, which Kennedy was alleged to envy; and their departure, however tactfully managed, would be interpreted as an erosion of this.

That evening I invited Lowell to my room for a drink. The usual election-day liquor crisis was raging, and I had to advertise up and down the corridor for a tooth-mug of bourbon. After a bit, the Senator himself appeared, along with Blair Clark, both looking noncommittally morose. Although the polls were still open, the word was in from the kill-joys at the networks that McCarthy had already lost by nine percentage points; a miracle could shave this to six.

McCarthy accepted a cigar and a small Scotch and went out on the terrace with Lowell. Being as snoopy and star-struck as the next man, I wanted badly to follow them, but it was one of those scenes—the two tall men motionless, leaning on the rail looking out at Esther Feather's Reducing Salon—that you don't intrude on. I stayed inside and talked instead to Blair Clark (a man destined from birth to smoke a pipe). I had not quite gathered until now how precarious our man's position actually was. If Kennedy lost and dropped from the race, enough of his delegates would split to Humphrey to scuttle McCarthy for good. If Kennedy won, our puny funds would dry up still further, and some of our workers would defect. The closest thing to a success would be what we finally got, a close defeat. But, of course, when we got it, it wasn't worth having.

I finally did go out, on some ruse, and did a little light eavesdropping. They were talking about how the Indians lived in Arizona (McCarthy had spent the day there) and the virtues of living out of a canoe. The Senator looked wistful. "Everyone should try living out of a canoe," he said. "Do them good." The talk turned to poetry, and he brightened. Lowell had been a good poet once upon a time, he conceded, before taking up obscurity; now, who could tell?

It was not a typical conversation, I gathered, but a sensible attempt to ward off stress, the banter of athletes or soldiers. Mc-Carthy knows how to handle his nerves—he couldn't have come so far otherwise—and talking with Robert Lowell is part of his strategy. They talked about which of his own poems he should read tonight if the mood was on him; Lowell had helped him with one or two of them and made his recommendation meticulously, liking the rhythm of this one, the imagery of that one.

For something to say, I asked McCarthy about his sports metaphors. He didn't seem to understand the question at first; his eyes were tired and withdrawn, and it occurred to me that he had probably been thinking politics all along, deciding when and how to concede, while humoring Lowell and me with small talk. Lowell asked if he would join us for dinner, and he said, sadly, "You know I can't do that. I'm a public figure now." Charlie Callinan, his tiny bodyguard, came up to tell him he was wanted some place or other, and he said, "Charlie has graduated from a presence to a force," and left us. I noticed that he had smoked his cigar twice as quickly as I had mine.

That brings us almost back to the beginning. I had dinner with Lowell after that, and he talked about the Catholic politeness of the TV debate, and the Catholic nastiness. Every culture has it own forms of the virtues and vices. Then he talked about whether McCarthy would make a good President. Well, there were only two great ones in our whole history (I forget which). McCarthy would be a lot better than most. He also spoke fondly of Kennedy, and was sorry to have to choose between them. Earlier in the evening, a Washington correspondent had been asked to compare the Kennedy boys. "Next to Jack, Bobby is all heart," he said. These scraps came back to mind later in the evening.

I saw the Senator twice more that night. The first time was in Mary McGrory's room, where he was watching television. He seemed severe now, bordering on the vexed—possibly over the incredible CBS projection of the final vote, which had him losing 52 percent to 39 percent or thereabouts. A mistake like that must play hob with a candidate's blood pressure. But I fancy he was simply saving his strength and doing a little light planning. Because the next time I saw him, down in the ballroom, he was as serene as ever. They were having voting-machine trouble in Los Angeles County (some were stolen), so we were still leading by a thin margin at midnight. To hell with the projections. We would stage a miracle during the night. "I want to be in that number," we sang, and waved our fingers aloft. On to Chicago.

The next time I inquired after the Senator, I was invited courteously to return to my room. Security guards had sprouted from every crevice, and the seventh floor had been quarantined for the night; not quite George Wallace's dream of a bayonet every thirty yards, but we were on our way.

Back in the good old days, back on the Monday night, I had a friendly argument with a man about whether Southern California was the wave of the future. I thought about the separateness and the car cleaning and the people who learn their accents from TV; the next night I would think also of people who find the faces on TV realer than friends, closer than family, and for whom, *a fortiori*, young glamorous politicians can be brain-shaking torments, things to be loved and killed; but tonight I just thought about the car cleaning.

And I thought about the hippies and New Lefters who crowd together so as not to get like that, and who, for all their foolishness, do wish to form real cities and inner cities and bring the old ones back to life. And I stacked them against the losers, and disengaged winners and solitaries ranged along the Coast, who still think that they are the future, but who are too scattered and weak to affect even the present, even the neighborhood, and whose collective response to the future is Max Rafferty. And I thought (after all, the campaign was resting, no speech tomorrow. Indulge): we'll just see about that. You had your day in the forties and fifties, Southern California, when people still thought there was magic in that stuff, split-level ranch houses and bloated shopping centers and drive-in banks, but just now, for a little while, I think humanity is going to win.

That, of course, was Monday night.

1968

3 / EUGENE McCARTHY:

The Politician as Professor

WHEN SENATOR MCCARTHY LOOKED OUT THE window and saw the troops lined up below, he said that it reminded him of the Battle of Lake Trasimeno. (Later he amended this to the Battle of Cannae, I don't know why.) It was amusing at first. He talked about sending down Hannibal's escape plans to the hippies. No blood had been shed yet and from the twenty-third floor the men on the bridge looked like toys.

All the same, an average citizen looking in would have said: There you are, that's an intellectual for you—making Punic War jokes while Chicago prepares to incinerate. But it struck me, as the Senator pushed on with his joke, citing Scipio Africanus in the wrong battle, that there was nothing especially intellectual about this. The people who indulge in it most heavily are generally lightweight schoolmasters and clergymen, intellectual kibitzers and con men. McCarthy might or might not be an intellectual, but you couldn't prove it by Scipio Africanus.

It didn't seem too important at the time—just something to think about in the intervals of being shoved and growled at by the world's ugliest cops. McCarthy had now lost for sure and was taking refuge in his hobby. A witty man has to be careful, on a campaign, against the one joke too many that can make him seem fatuous. But now, among friends, it came out in rivers, cascades, and he was at first very funny with his mock-erudition and later wearily facetious as fatigue wound him down.

The next morning, when he crossed to Grant Park to address his "government in exile," one saw the other side of this hobby of his. His first words were strong, and he had gone back to watching his jokes. The anarchists dotted around the crowd murmured their "shits" and "motherfuckers," but they were mismatched. He answered the main question without breaking stride. "Not necessarily in the Democratic Party," he said. He looked the part of the Irish rebel, gigantic in defeat, dwarfing his enemies.

And then he blew it, or, as usual, half blew it. He said that he wanted to quote from two of his favorite authors, Péguy and Robert Lowell. The microphone was not that strong, not strong enough to pick up a quote from Péguy. People at the edges slumped back. The shit-sayers started up again, a little more confidently. "You're a loser," "I'm not going to die for a motherfucker like you." The neurotic self-loathers were back in business, on his time.

After that, Robert Lowell read his own poems: and what had seemed wrong for McCarthy seemed quite all right for him. Poet versus schoolmaster. And one wandered off thinking: What is this business with quotations? What's with Lake Trasimeno? It has nothing to do with intellectual force, or even with great oratory. The Kennedys had their reasons for using quotationship, partly to endorse culture as such after Eisenhower, and partly to show that they had other friends besides Mayor Daley, Charles Buckley, et al. For most other politicians, it is just a silly, parvenu form of showing off. For McCarthy, it seemed to serve no purpose at all, except to make a man of rather direct and earthy intellect seem vague and woolly.

Since much of the public expects this of intellectuals anyway, and despises them accordingly, it seemed a pity that McCarthy had played into their hands so consistently. Did he suppose that woolly professors were coming back? Or was it his true nature, the only style he had? The publicity certainly ran that way. One heard again and again about his days as a teacher and his days in the seminary, until his years in Washington seemed like an interlude; secular reporters, who had never seen the like, had him sounding like a thirteenth-century eccentric, a man of crazed frivolity.

Thus the man who had done so much to put intellect back in politics seemed to be working with the other hand to confirm the prejudice against it. Public opinion makes no fine distinctions about this: you've seen one egghead, you've seen them all; and in recent years we'd seen two, Stevenson and McCarthy, both witty and ineffectual, and that was quite enough. But for those who know that no two intellectuals are exactly alike, it raised questions about types and modes of intellect—whether what the public took to be intellect in these men was that at all, or some misleading spore or musk.

The subject can hardly be discussed in the abstract, so we shall have to take some liberties with Senator McCarthy, currently our most important piece of evidence—but with the understanding that a public figure, or campaign creature, is always a fictional character with no resemblance to a living person.

To clear a little obvious ground: non-Catholics might be surprised to know how many bright Catholics give the seminary a whirl and how little significance this may have for their later lives. Curiosity, youthful imitation, idealism, escapism, whatever causes people of a certain age to enlist in things—one would have to know which of these impulses was strongest in a given instance and which survived the experience; also, whether the seminarian became fixated at that point or grew a new skin.

The obvious thing about this, as about his teaching, is that McCarthy turned his back on both a long time ago. He has been a politician for the last twenty years, of his own free choice. It

is romantic to assume that he really pined to be a priest or a professor all along; nobody, so far as we know, was stopping him,
at least from the latter, and he would not be an easy man to
stop. He may have fancied those styles, as Everett Dirksen likes
the style of a country preacher, or as an American might like to
sound like an Englishman. But McCarthy is wise enough to
know that this is just a game, that a politician is not *really* a professor. As an heir to existential Thomism, he knows that ultimately it is his real work that defines him, not his dreams or his
memory of Latin. At the same time, part of being a good politician is to seem like a little more than a politician, and here a
memory of Latin might come in handy. Government is a branch
of theatrics, and it pays to have a recognizable persona which
distinguishes you from your fellow tradesmen.

Thus we arrive at Eugene McCarthy, the professor: not
fooling himself, for sure, or faking his interests, but still, a
politician-professor rather than a plain professor—just as a banjo-
playing senator is a politician first. It is impossible for so
essentially serious a man to have been in this business for twenty
years without both learning it and believing in it. And, in fact,
Mary McGrory, the Washington columnist, described him once,
in conversation, as the most intuitive politician she had ever met.

How did this become obscured in the campaign, behind
the mask of learned ineffectuality? Was this, in itself, intuitive
politics—a sense that after Johnson people wanted an amateur,
à l'anglaise? Before the primaries, this could almost have been so.
There is a connection in American myth between ineffectuality
and integrity, but this stops at the clubhouse door. McCarthy's
first interest was to wave his public popularity at the pros; but
his second was to impress the pros himself, and all summer long
we kept hearing about how he was failing to do this. It seems
now that it may all have been a charade anyway, that the delegates were all in place back in May and that impressing them
would have been an empty exercise in charm; and perhaps Mc-
Carthy knew this and concentrated entirely on making a public

record. But he made it easier for the pros and their apologists by seeming like a lofty bumbler, sacrificing precision for the sake of a cute reference.

One obvious explanation is that the pressure of campaigning brings out all manner of tics and twitches that are normally under control. We have seen that literally happen to certain candidates, making their faces an embarrassment to behold. And even secondary characteristics, like Bobby Kennedy's joking or Hubert Humphrey's babble, may inhere more deeply after this brain-blowing experience. Bobby, you may remember, was rather a solemn public figure until the last year or so, when he fell upon humor with the zeal of a convert and made a lifetime of jokes in a few weeks.

There was certainly something of this about McCarthy's scholarship. What might well have started out as a joke, a playful signature, was hammered deep into his style and character by repetition and nervous exhaustion. And where he had probably written the occasional poem for fun, he now began to publish in earnest: rather as if Harry Truman had decided to give a concert tour (although McCarthy's poetry is better than that, of course).

It seemed that now, as he approached the peak of political success, he began to yearn for something else, anything else. This must happen sometimes to politicians who wholeheartedly want power; to one in two minds about it, it must be a real aggravation. One wants to say to the public: Look, I could have been that, if I'd tried; my real gift was always for such and such. And some small hobby that was long ago relegated to the attic is brought down and dusted off and perhaps really taken seriously.

And like the Emperor Nero traveling with his violin instructor and his track coach as living symbols of his other side, so McCarthy traveled with Robert Lowell. (According to revisionists, Nero was a pretty good emperor—but those avocations have hurt.) It wasn't, of course, a mere friendship of convenience. But it did have this functional aspect, of giving Mc-Carthy a way out. On the day he was due to debate Robert Kennedy, easily the most important day of his campaign, he spent the afternoon walking around Alcatraz with Lowell, talking everything but politics.* And so it went: the hotter things became, the more literary became McCarthy, and the more one saw of Lowell.

Nothing to do with intellect, but quite understandable. If a man is going to have to campaign for nine months, he should be allowed to take his violin along. Or even to learn the violin for the first time. And, up to a point, it was good tactics too: much better than Hubert Humphrey calling his sheep. (He should have stuck in his thumb and pulled out a plum while he was about it.) But there was something askew about McCarthy's attitude to his literary self, some element of put-on that struck many people as perverse: sinister, foolish, or both together. To be an antiquarian was bad enough, but a self-mocking antiquarian—?

There were several explanations which were kicked around rather randomly by his admirers, each with its little grain of truth. But I think the most important one concerns the intellectual tradition to which Eugene McCarthy does genuinely belong: namely, that branch of Catholic thought loosely described as "*Commonweal* Catholic," here used to connote a generation of Americans from thirty-five to sixty, shaped politically by the great labor encyclicals, by the rise of unionism and the Catholic Worker phenomenon, etc.—a mix of old-fashioned religious training and successive trends of progressivism. In this context, McCarthy is not so unusual, but almost, in many respects, to be expected.

To begin with, there is the matter of personal style. Although most *Commonweal* Catholics would rather conscientiously reject

* I got this from a very good source, but Lowell says he was never in Alcatraz in his life. At any rate, the Senator was not in his office that day. See Jeremy Larner's fine book, *Nobody Knows*.

any allegiance to G. K. Chesterton, I believe that most of them would, by temperament, accept his assertion that Martin Luther set a bad precedent when he used his personality as a weapon in argument. (There are, by policy, virtually no personality pieces in the *Commonweal* magazine itself.) From which it follows that whatever use a *Commonweal* Catholic makes of his own personality is likely to be peripheral, playful. When McCarthy was serious, he was very, very serious. His discussion of the issues was lugubriously impersonal. But his flights of personality were such as to say: This isn't important, this is not what we're here for; his jokes were more skittish even than Stevenson's, and less biting.

One could almost say that whether he knew his Roman history or not, his references to it had to be frivolous—because that was his persona, not his real self. Why in that case make the references at all? One guess is that he did it to amuse his friend Lowell (a sometime *Commonweal* Catholic himself, although that's another story). At least, in my own brief observation, he tended to drop this line when Lowell was out of the room and pick it up when he returned. My first notion, that he was simply showing off for Lowell, seemed unfair, because as he did it, he looked at Lowell with a slightly baiting expression: this is your game, not mine. But let's see how I do at it. Some parody, much respect, much, always, self-mockery.

The *Commonweal* Catholic in essence tends to combine a belief in the secular world, social progress, etc., with an abstract, quasi-scholastic style, left over from school, and the remains of a self-scourging conscience. McCarthy's first response to the Czechoslovakian crisis, worthy of St. Anselm, was an extreme example of both. It was based on the theorem that personal feelings do not constitute an argument. His contempt for "weeping politicians" may seem like new politics, but it is much more analogous to the old-fashioned spiritual director who says: Don't come in here crying; don't show off about your damned sins.

And above all, don't show off about your damned virtues. McCarthy could not, if life depended on it, act out his compassion for the poor. Politically, this subject demands a certain amount of Mammy-singing. You can denounce the war calmly, and the emotion will take care of itself. But when you come to poverty, you must perform. It was a little-noted fact that McCarthy spoke precisely as strongly about both subjects—no more, no less; yet he was felt to be passionate about Vietnam, indifferent about race.

His distaste for the Kennedys must have had something to do with their ability to find in themselves great wells of compassion, and their willingness to share this discovery with the public. The Kennedys are not *Commonweal* Catholics, for better or worse. Even their self-mockery is tactical. McCarthy's is compulsive.

The *Commonweal* Catholic is also congenitally mistrustful of ambition. On average, he is likely to settle for a place lower than he might have—to wind up just outside of *Who's Who*, as sociologists were noting a few years back, and to be scornful of those who push themselves beyond their merits. Laziness is his characteristic defense against getting uppity. It neatly resolves the problem of ambition. (So, incidentally, does an obsession with sports—that staple of American Catholic education.) When the *Commonweal* Catholic finds himself going further than nature intended, and feels himself succumbing to ambition, he scourges himself all the harder. He reminds himself over and over that he isn't that hot; and to keep his own bearings, he keeps a cynical eye on his ambitious competitors. If you don't watch out, you'll get to be like Mr. Nixon.

What confused people about McCarthy was that his self-disparagement apparently coexisted with arrogance toward the rest of the world. But again, in a climate of spiritual sophistication this is not unusual. People of rigorous introspection commonly work their tension off with lofty but basically harmless wisecracks about others. Anyone who has ever sat around a rectory, or even an Irish living room, will have heard many duplicates of McCarthy's wit. The instruction to be charitable makes malice all the more seductive; at the same time it enforces a basic gentleness, which is also part of McCarthy. When I met him seven years ago, I had the impression (which others have confirmed) that his wife Abigail was both brighter and waspier than he, that she was making the gags he would like to make if he could. Under the lash of the campaign, McCarthy became a master of insult, but still with that deprecation, that slight silliness if you will, that pays the tithe to charity.

So far, I have made his temperament sound like a series of handicaps (which is perhaps not a bad definition of most people's temperaments). But it gave McCarthy certain strengths too. Besides the obvious ones—courage, nice nerves, a relative selflessness—it gave him novelty value. It was a great irony to some of us that this type which has been knocking around this country in various forms since the last century should suddenly be unveiled as the latest thing. Not that McCarthy didn't provide his own quirks and innovations; but so many of the things that people puzzled over—the wit, the laziness, the detachment—go back beyond Richard Brinsley Sheridan.

Humility is hammered perhaps a little too roughly into young Catholic skulls. I have known more promise gone to waste for want of a doting Jewish mother than history will ever hear about. After this boot training in self-abnegation, you may find that no matter how hard you come to believe in the secular world and what needs doing there, you will retain this reflex about yourself: I must not use it for my own glory—even if what it needs is my own glory.

The political benefit of this is a kind of freedom quite unknown to the ambitious office-seeker. McCarthy's freedom from deals, from routine sycophancy and duplicity, may finally have sunk him. But in the meantime it enabled him to make a sustained statement about American political reality unlike anything in recent history (yes, I know about Stevenson). The need for a minimum wage, for negotiation with the NLF—even the tweaking of J. Edgar Hoover's nose: no one, not even Bobby operating from the Kennedy bastion, could have discussed these matters so lucidly. If this effort in political education goes for nothing, it will be only partly the fault of McCarthy's flippancy. Our own will have something to do with it too.

Intellectually, McCarthy's strength was his weakness—a gift for abstraction that has gone out of fashion even in Catholic circles. Taken too far (as in the question of how many angels to let into your bomb shelter), it is foolish enough. But when done in moderation, and in combination with a good head for concrete example—and here McCarthy's poetry is relevant, as was Thomas Aquinas's—it still has its uses. The best scholastic thought always proceeded by analogy, so that one's sense of specific reality was also the test of one's metaphysics.

This might seem in itself a metapolitical talent in most modern countries, but the United States is not most modern countries. Our political discourse is still larded with eighteenth-century abstractions—freedom, law and order, what have you—and so our discussion can never go straight to: Where do we build the sewer? but must always run back over the great questions like, Whose freedom to do what? Whose law, whose order? In the circumstance, it is only reasonable to take this discourse away from the mountebanks at specified intervals and hand it to someone at home in that conceptual world, who abides by its discipline and does not use his words like Humpty Dumpty. This rinsing of rhetoric makes it usable for the next generation of slatterns.

If a thirteenth-century philosopher washed upon our shores, we might expect the following questions of him. What is your CIA *for?* Define the phrase "free world." *Cui bono* in Vietnam?

What's so great about gold? McCarthy did not ask all the questions, only the ones in Group A. He did, after all, have some interests to protect: he was not a saint, else he would not have reached the point where the Presidency arises. But he introduced a method, a mode of discussing public questions, which would bring some minimal rationality to them. Had he remained a priest or a Catholic college teacher, it is unlikely he would have done so; out on the periphery, this tradition of thought has tended to stagnate. Anyhow, it is in this special area that his claim to intellect lies; and with the jokes scraped off, it is no bad claim.

Whether better discussion leads to better politics, or is simply an end in itself, is another question. The significance of intellectuals in politics, in the conventional sense of a Stevenson or a McCarthy, hinges on it. Both these men believed first and last in an educational Presidency. Their critics have felt this was a little schoolmarmy, that Stevenson could do his teaching much better without having to worry about the Bomb and the Mexican ambassador every day. So, too, the Pope might be a better spiritual leader if he didn't have all those diplomatic relations.

But whatever one decides about that, whether one feels that McCarthy has already performed his best possible function or whether he could have gone on performing under the ton of rubble known as the Presidency, it is worth remembering that both he and Stevenson were special kinds of intellectuals and that judgment about them should not be extended to the other kinds. Whimsy is not necessarily part of the package—nor the pressures that create whimsy. Teacher-politicians use it. But Mind has other functions in politics besides teaching.

I believe that McCarthy would have made a good President simply because he would have felt it his duty to be. Those catechism reflexes have their value. (I am leaving aside his manifest superiority over the other candidates.) But I am not sure of it. The habit of frivolity is tyrannical, wants to make a joke of everything. With McCarthy, it appeared to perform so many necessary functions that when it lapsed, a very deep melancholy seemed to take over. For a supposedly cool man, he was probably the most mercurial of the candidates; his mood could change sharply three times in five minutes. But because he is so clearly a grownup, these things go unremarked. He does not exploit his emotions.

It is hard to estimate his Presidential capacity because, in *Commonweal* Catholic style, he underestimated himself sinfully. He was, I believe, after the first shock, delighted to be free of his role, to escape from his Secret Service man and return to that niche a little below the top. The campaign must have expanded his consciousness—the rush of poetry; the friendship with Lowell (the star athlete and his coach); the friendship with Peter, Paul, and Mary. Now he could make the most of all that. As President, the difficulty of being himself would have been excruciating. Make us a joke, Mr. President. Make one of those apt comparisons to country life. Everything laughed at (even the bad ones), everything published. The melancholy would have deepened.

Just one man, not precisely like any other: his friends, the *Commonweal* Catholics, children or thereabouts of immigrants who wanted a toehold in this country and expected no more; grandchildren of four centuries of defeat and frustration made bearable by mockery and songs and by thumbing their noses at the reigning LBJ's. Some Irishmen wanted to try their own hand at power when they got to the New World and make like overlords themselves. Others did not. It has been nice to hear from one of those for a change.

1968

PART THREE

I / *The Kitchen*

EVERY WRITER HAS HIS FAVORITE STAGE SET: some hotel lobby or colliery or back room which forms the perfect setting to his act: sometimes, sometimes not, a replica of the place where he saw his first vision.

For Arnold Wesker, this shrine will always be a restaurant-kitchen. Even when, for variety's sake, Wesker writes about something else, it usually manages to sound a lot like a kitchen. His plays have titles like *Roots* and *Chips with Everything*—foodsome, kitcheny titles. He is a master at conveying steamy desperation, the cramp and twitch of work in hot places. The rooms have a way of being a little too warm and crowded in a Wesker play. His characters flare up and subside like gas jets. The orders come pouring in from the faceless carnivores outside. All the world's a kitchen, where the poor work in squalor and ugliness to feed the faces of the rich.

All of which has given Wesker a powerful if sometimes unwieldy metaphor to work with. Mr. Wesker is of Russian-Hungarian descent, and he was employed for four years in an English restaurant: and to have approached English society from this particular angle is to be privy to a peculiarly gruesome secret. For English restaurants teach the banality of evil as nothing else does, and the drabness of class warfare. The line "chips with everything" recurs obsessively in Wesker's work:

and one imagines that after gazing for four years into a pan of french fries, the dullness hurt worse than the cruelty. To work in a sweatshop is bad enough: but to work in a sweatshop filling a thousand orders of boiled cod—that is obscene.

Wesker's early play *The Kitchen* is his most frontal assault on this theme: and, as might be anticipated, it profits from being frontal, from not having to transvest the Wesker metaphor. If one of the characters boils over, we understand what has happened. The smell of cabbage has gotten to him. The author does not have to trump up plot devices to explain it. In fact, he does not need to trump up a plot at all, for in this case the medium is the message, and the kitchen is the plot.

The dramatic action consists entirely in the serving of two meals in a nightmarish English restaurant (the director Jack Gelber has turned it into an American restaurant, but it remains English under the skin). Wesker's attitude to this setup is, as usual, slightly ambiguous. The kitchen is awful, but the restaurant out front is worse: a cold dark place into which the waitresses plummet and where the world's competitiveness is thrust upon them. They come back screaming for meat and fish, bearing greed and rapacity with them, turning the chefs into savages, into a scale model of the people outside.

Yet to be engaged in a common enterprise, even a debased one, is a step toward fraternity: and between meals the kitchen people grope toward the Wesker ideal: "friendship." It is central to Wesker's thesis that the working class has some memory of purity that is kept in severe check by the demands of middle-class culture; but whereas in *Chips* he sentimentalized this thesis outrageously, here he understates it almost out of existence. One of the chefs asks the others to tell him their dreams; the dreams are of representative banality—sex and money (the kitchen is too close to the restaurant for anything better). But there is a hint of responsiveness, of rigidly limited poetry, in their answers. Humanity burns low in the kitchen: yet things being as they are, it is still the best place to be right now.

By his steadfast underplotting, Wesker manages to avoid a good many mistakes. The diner-exploiters never appear onstage, so that Wesker's class venom does not betray him into caricature as it did in *Chips*. (The owner shows up a couple of times, but Wesker is on his best behavior, and the owner is quite believable.) The absence of a central story saves him from the last-minute melodramatics that also hurt *Chips*. The last scene, where one of the chefs runs amuck and the owner wrings his hands and wonders where he has gone wrong, is ever so slightly stagy. But, otherwise, Wesker has simply rendered us one hell of a kitchen. If avoidance of pitfalls is your criterion, this could be Wesker's masterpiece: but only a very unambitious writer would be content to stop at this, and Wesker has in fact taken several bigger chances since.

Gelber's direction is a model of something or other. He has choreographed the pig-swill rush hour with the greatest attention to detail. The chefs are always either over- or under-occupied so that they can strike no rhythm, but are kept in a maximum stage of futile jumpiness.

Mr. Gelber has also defted the accent problem, simply by not bothering about it much. Ostensibly, the waiters are polyglots, whose points of view are reinforced by their accents. But it is hard to find actors who can sustain these imitations for long, and Gelber seems not to have worried his cast about it. They all sound vaguely foreign: Rip Torn is meant to be a German, but he could pass for Welsh or Scandinavian at any given moment. The point is that by not trying self-consciously for authenticity, Gelber has kept the problem from grating.

Of the actors, Mr. Torn is sprightly and intelligent, and Conrad Bain does his usual solid job. The rest range, as usual, from adequate to forget-it.

1966

2 / *An Evening's* FROST

A*n Evening's Frost* IS EASILY THE HIGH POINT
of the new season—a modest enough compliment, but a heart-
felt one.

Most of it was written by Frost himself, so it contains some
real language: not spastic wisecracks or eclectic chitchat, but the
real stuff, coarse, personal, sly; shaped and hardened like an old
man's face by geologic layers of experience and cunning. Since
Frost had only one good voice, you could hardly make a decent
verse play out of it; but you can turn its narrow, incantatory
power onto Frost himself, and this is what Donald Hall has done,
with considerable success.

Frost's writings, when assembled in this way, are not only
pretty to listen to, but dramatically intriguing; for Frost is in a
way a genuine dramatic creation. Although his poems are seldom
directly about himself, they justify T. S. Eliot's accusation "self-
centered." Each of them does a job for Frost: each of them projects the persona. He is never off-guard for a moment.

The first part of the evening deals with his long apprenticeship, in the self-imposed exile on his Vermont farm. He wrote
whimsically about his farming period, because the older Frost
tended to look back in whimsy. But as Mr. Hall juggles the
writings something else comes through—the shadowy quality

that Lionel Trilling noted in Frost and that Frost so characteristically denied.

Unless the production overemphasizes the split in his life, Frost's exile lasted twenty years, a long time for an exile. For all this time—and it covers most of his young manhood—Frost says he heartily disliked the human race. He could say this lightly, because he had already made sure everyone knew that his misanthropy had had a happy ending. But such conversions make one suspicious and you find yourself wondering more than once about that happy ending. When a man emerges from a long misanthropic exile with a gruff tenderness for humanity, you look for tricks. (And all the more so when you later find him spewing folksy venom over most of his poetic rivals. For a warm man, his record of behind-the-back insult is striking.)

You have to wonder whether what he was working out during that endless hermitage was not how to love people but how to handle them: how to look through them and dominate them with his own performance. One thing he seems to have acquired from his contact with nature was a certain cold, hard quality which was to aid him considerably in his own survival (always a big problem for a Grand Old Man). His elation and depression were as cyclic and impersonal as the seasons and he weathered them like a farmer. In the splendid early poem "Home Burial" his wife accuses Frost of a lack of real feeling, and we sense that she is right. Like many poets, he was an opportunist of feeling; no emotion was ever so imperious that he hadn't got one eye cocked on whether he could use it in a poem. Part of Frost's equipment was a surgical coolness—so highly developed that he could even write a poem about it.

The end of the first act coincides with the end of his private ministry. He says at this point that his life was a risk that he had to take, and took, which suggests (though I daresay he didn't mean it to be read that way—like Hemingway, he only admitted to attractive weaknesses) that he had been kept in exile by real fears. At any rate, he was better equipped at the end of it for the risks of literary life than most writers. He had an ego like a rock, an ever-normal reserve of smug wisdom to fall back on, a personal language already fully developed, and a sense of his own limits almost unique in modern American writing. He was altogether his own creation, based, like Jay Gatsby, on his platonic idea of himself.

His performance in the second part of his life, and the second act of the play, is easier to understand if we think of him as a self-taught celebrity. He knew that it was wrong to be as corny as Carl Sandburg, and he made heavy fun of Sandburg, but he often came closer to this routine than he knew. His literary taste was exquisite, and he was usually saved from the ultimate foolishness by felicitous phrasing; but his public style was out-rageous—a crazy quilt of early-American, middle-high Harvard, and all-round Huck Finnery stitched together in solitude, one supposes, for purposes of disguise.

If the public picture is to be trusted, he exploited this gim-crack personality fairly shamelessly. Frost is reputed to have been two different things in the faculty lounge and the public platform. If he was cautious, like a New England farmer, at the beginning of his career, he was blatantly, insolently overcon-fident in manipulating the scene as a celebrity. Of all the great literary men's acts (songs, dances, imitations), his is surely one of the broadest. If he was at all a shy man, he must have been amazed and delighted to find how much he could get away with.

All this may make him sound more than a little buffoonish; but the tricks *did* protect him and enable him to write the poems. And what distinguished Frost from so many literary stuntmen is that his act never got into his work. His public performance was so unreal to him—possibly the world of campuses and women's clubs was sometimes so unreal to him—that it never corrupted what he called the secret places of his mind. He con-tinued, with exceptions, to work the small but rich mine he had staked off as a hermit, and to caper on his own time.

It is to the credit of Mr. Hall's production that even if one had nothing else to go on, a good deal of this character would come through. The mélange of verses, scraps of letters, etc., winds up forming a credible mosaic. In fact, if it could be established that the real Frost was not like that at all, the production would still stand up as a dramatic sketch.

Of the performers, Will Geer does well by the elderly Frost, once you get over the notion that he is really Jonathan Winters doing his old-lady bit. Donald Davis makes an unlikely enough younger Frost, but my chief quarrel with Mr. Davis concerns his brief interpretations of Pound and Eliot. I know that this is the night we root for Frost, but that is no excuse for caricaturing his contemporaries so childishly. Davis plays Eliot, in particular, as a malignant sissy, and this is gross. Marcella Cisney, whose direction is otherwise fine, should do something about this right away—it's a real, bush-league embarrassment. John Randolph as interlocutor does a good straight job, but he ought to watch that simper—the point about Frost's jokes was that they were not very good. But perhaps, at that, Mr. Randolph is parodying the kind of brainless approval that encouraged him to go on with them.

1965

3 / *Marat / Sade*

FOR FLAT CRITICISM THAT COMPLETELY MISSES the point, there is nothing to compare with an author's explanation of his own work. With rare exceptions, "what I really meant" pieces are tantalizingly vague and misleading—almost as if some friendly spirit had stupefied the writer to keep him from giving too much away.

What brings this to mind is an interview that Peter Weiss gave a while back concerning his play *Marat/Sade*. Although one interview should never be held against an interview-prone author (Mr. Weiss has presumably planted contradictory theories in other places), I can only say that if this is all he got out of the play, he was wasting his time writing it up for the stage.

It seems that Weiss's main concern in the play was with the revolutionary ideas debated by the Messrs. Marat and Sade. These ideas are certainly interesting, and a good cut above the ideas most people have in their bathtubs, but nothing you would be surprised to find in a good German quarterly. Weiss's belief that they form the heart of the play has lent some small ammunition to his detractors, who claim that he hasn't written a play at all and that Peter Brook's direction is a trick to make it seem that he has.

But the really interesting thing about the ideas is that they are undercut all the way through by matching ironies, which then proceed to undercut each other. To begin with, both sides of the debate are presented as originating in the same brain—and the brain of the Marquis de Sade, at that. (In case you don't know the play's premise—the Marquis has written a play for his fellow inmates in the asylum of Charenton: significantly, a play intended for the patients' therapy. Mr. Weiss gives us both the play and a play enclosing the play. Thus the refraction is infinite.) Marat, the revolutionary, is a character in the mind of the Marquis and thus partakes of Sade's particular pathology; but to densify matters, the part has been given to one of the asylum's paranoid patients—therapeutic casting, indeed. Marat's radicalism and the actor's paranoia periodically intertwine so that you can't always be sure which is talking. Is Mr. Weiss suggesting that they are at bottom the same thing? Or is this simply Sade's idea? Or is it—and this isn't as absurd as it sounds—a defense of paranoia in a stinking world? (As a response to the Weiss/Sade world, paranoia hardly goes far enough.)

The audience gradually becomes implicated in this confusion. The night I was there, and presumably on other nights as well, people began to applaud their favorite ideas, only to waver when they realized that the avowed lunatics on the stage were clapping even louder. Does this concurrence make the lunatics sane or us mad? The uncertainty reached a screaming crescendo at the end when the lunatics marched forward and solemnly applauded the audience.

As you sit there clapping the lunatics and watching them clap back, you are part of a regulation-absurd tableau—Sade and Weiss have obliterated all distinctions or reversed them: the monkeys are outside the bars, the visitors inside. My own reaction, for what it's worth, was that if they want to clap me I certainly don't want to clap them: which, of course, completed the reversal.

In discussing the play, Weiss has explicitly rejected absurdity, as if he found the concept (or un-concept) repugnant. But this is one of the most misleading things about his analysis. For the whole point of having historic events acted out by lunatics is to demonstrate a corresponding berserk element in the world of fact. In between Sade's discussions with Marat, which are rational enough, various segments of the French Revolution are acted out, and these are steeped in dementia and prove entirely suitable to insane actors. The Paris mob, mighty right arm of revolution, is reduced to a stamping and gibbering of lunatics; and you would hardly know the difference. Marat, the quintessential reformer, lurks in his tub working off childhood spites; his murderess, Charlotte Corday, is a victim of melancholia and sleeping sickness, who has to be woken up before she can do anything at all; and her companion, Duperret, turns out to be a raving satyr, who makes high-minded speeches while fumbling grotesquely for Charlotte at the same time.

It is not so much that the world is insane—which would be a stale one-dimensional observation—as that in the world of consequences it hardly matters one way or the other. Supposing the French Revolution had been performed in a lunatic asylum, would the results have been any different? Could not madmen with totally different goals and motives have achieved the same effects? Or, arguing backwards, is there anything in the effects of the actual revolution—the carnage, the distortion of language and of ideals—to prove that it wasn't the work of madmen?

At the end, the lunatics sing a song about the glorious fifteen years that have passed since the Revolution, and it is at once a perfectly good patriotic song and perfectly insane. And if we return a moment to the debate between Sade and Marat we find in a roundabout way the same conclusion: that revolutionary action is noble and necessary, but that its consequences are as absurd as those of any other kind of action, or of no action at all. Rationality is a quality of thought, not of events.

Mr. Weiss is reported to have Marxist sympathies himself,

but if so this is a classic case of the artist's powerful subterranean drive to subvert his own ideology—or, in this case, all ideology. He has used tricks whose implications he has not been willing to understand: even down to the trick of shamming insanity. It is not surprising that he has talked stupidly about his own play. The ideas as such are presented in all seriousness, and Weiss ingenuously says, There—that's your play, the ideas. But by handing them over to lunatics, and by having them illustrated in drooling pantomime, he has shown what he really thinks of them. This is what becomes of ideas in the real order, he says—demonstrating a conviction much stronger than anything he may think he thinks.

(Lest anyone suggest that this is a routine case of a capitalist critic jeering at a Marxist lapse, it should be said parenthetically that what Graham Greene calls "the artist's duty to disloyalty" applies in all situations: a sense that something is missing in the going formulation, and an urge to reintroduce it. An artist's obligations toward the fullness of creation always override his sectarian opinions.)

Much of the credit for *Marat/Sade*'s effectiveness has, as noted, been attributed to Peter Brook's direction—sometimes with a slight surliness, as if Brook had done something slightly dishonorable in staging the play so well. But although the direction is all that it is said to be, it is no better than the play deserves. In fact, a reading of the play is almost as impressive as a viewing. The language is vivid without ever lapsing into the boozy woolgathering that threatens most verse plays at one time or another; and Adrian Mitchell's translation is a model of its kind. The absence of conventional plot movement is more than made up for by the dance of ironies, itself a kind of complicated ballet with a definite formal structure. This play gives itself to a director and says, in effect, Do everything you know, shoot the works—enlist every gesture and sound effect you know; it won't be too much.

Richard Peaslee's music, played by a bathhouse five that makes Spike Jones's band look like the Budapest String Quartet, adds considerable atmospheric assistance. The tunes are a kind of Brechtian-baroque, suitable to whichever century your thoughts happen to have strayed to. The cast has already been praised to a crisp elsewhere, but one more Zen handclap might go to Glenda Jackson, Clifford Rose, and John Steiner. As with most English companies, the Royal Shakespeare has enough good actors to go round, so that there isn't that dismal gap between the leads and the bit parts which bedevils so many American casts, notoriously the one currently laboring with *The Country Wife* at Lincoln Center.

A good deal more could be said about the play—its religious and sexual motifs, which get whirled up in the general ambiguity; the role of the asylum governor, who is surrogate for the sane world, and for us the audience—but enough. A play of this kind has a different face for everyone who sees it. So maybe one should recommend it with caution. It is at the very least a theatrical event which uses every inch of the theater and bombards senses you didn't know you had. Mr. Weiss claims that he has tried to combine Brecht and Artaud—a logical impossibility, but so much the worse for logic. The result is combustible, and whatever way you react to it, you have never seen anything like it before.

1966

4 / *The Glass Menagerie*

THE FIRST TIME AROUND, THERE WAS NO DOUBT about it: Arthur Miller was the playwright of social awareness; Tennessee Williams's *Glass Menagerie* was the play of private sensibility. The second time around, none of this seems quite so clear. As Miller's plays are revived, we may find that they are more private and socially thinner than everyone had supposed. Conversely, *The Glass Menagerie*, which has just been revived, proves to be a much solider piece of work than memory had painted it.

It contains, to begin with, a density of social atmosphere, and even detail, beyond anything that Miller has yet offered us. Williams may have thrown everyone off the scent by calling his play a dream: because, in point of fact, we know the exact year, the neighborhood, the family's income—Mr. Williams is dreamy like a fox: I wish I knew half as much about Willy Loman as I know about both the past and present of Mr. Williams's specters.

The main characters in *The Glass Menagerie* have escaped from social pressures, much as Willy Loman has. And the pressures they escape from are actually rather more substantial, and less subjective, than Willy's were. They are a rural Southern family withering away in the border city of St. Louis, and their social style is totally inadequate to an urban setting. The mother is a Southern belle, whose natural methods of survival are coyness and passivity, interspersed with a series of cobra-like lunges. In the first scene she tenderly recounts how every one of her old friends married money, and the aroma of magnolias and greenbacks is suffocatingly poignant. Unfortunately, she has raised her daughter in the same school, not realizing that in a big city passivity gets you nowhere. You must first learn to go out and nail your victim. And the past offers no clues as to how you do this in a big modern city in the heart of a depression.

So it is that the daughter stays at home waiting for the famous gentleman callers who never arrive; and of course, since she gets no practice, she doesn't even know how to be coy properly when the time comes. She is passive all right, but not with the watchful, predatory passivity of the Southern belle: only with the paralytic diffidence of the lonely city girl. When the caller shows up in the last scenes, she faints, in horrible mime of a real belle; she flutters and shrinks to order, and all she arouses in the caller is dimwitted pity and mail-order encouragement.

To complete the debacle (which is surely one of the most shattering ever staged), the mother has also grown rusty in the ways of seduction. She flutters rather too aggressively, and one gets more than a notion that she wasn't too good at this kind of thing even in the old days. Many people have pulled this suggestion out further and have assumed that her own amorous reminiscences were straight make-believe: that she is a dreamer pure and simple who has destroyed her daughter by forcing her into the dreams.

But I believe that this multiplication of ironies weakens the play unnecessarily. The horrifying thing about the mother is that she is not a "natural" dreamer at all but a woman of action. She is always willing to take steps, to call up someone, to put her daughter through business school or whatever seems necessary.

148

She shows traces of what might even be called competence, in a different kind of setting. She simply is unwilling, or unable, to adjust this competence to the actual situation: to admit (for this is what it would involve) the total irrelevance of her own past.

This aspect of the play is forcefully—too forcefully perhaps—brought out in the new production by Maureen Stapleton's interpretation of the mother and Piper Laurie's of the daughter. These two constitute as robust a pair of girls as ever fled from reality. Miss Laurie's voice is much too strong for the wistful lines it has to deliver; and Miss Stapleton's style is such that her house would always be full of terrified gentleman callers and anything else she wanted.

But this is a mistake in the right direction. The play is full of acute social observations that could easily be obscured in a misty production. The world has of recent times been flooded with shabby aristocrats of this kind, and it would be easy to guess from their current helplessness that they were never of much use. But Williams seems to suggest that dreaminess has been thrust upon them by circumstance: their actions may now be grotesquely unreal, because their decline is too painful to face; but it was not always so.

To emphasize the social import of his play, Williams has actually interpolated several rather clumsy bits of commentary, bringing in the Spanish Civil War and the labor unrest of the period. One is reminded by this that Williams was still very much a playwright of the thirties: the diction is portentously March of Timey, those war clouds were gathering, etc.—the helplessness of these people is forced into a larger context. The playwright wishes to point out that they were not the only Americans to lose their way in the Depression, or to resort to dreams.

None of this is to say that *The Glass Menagerie* contains nothing but social message: my aim is merely to emphasize an aspect of the play that has received too little attention. Williams has probably never used such broad social symbols since. The gentleman caller ("who has learned poise through public speaking") represents another kind of city waif. The mother and, by proxy, the daughter, live at least in a sort of past; the caller lives only in a shallow, impossible future, where his poise and his confidence lessons will magically "pay off." Pat Hingle plays the part with gross effectiveness, making it easily the most tragic thing in the play.

And surviving the wreck, like Ishmael, floating aimlessly—but floating—is the son, admirably played by George Grizzard. The son is cursed by memories which make no sense, by experience which teaches nothing and points nowhere; but he is free of the wreck. Or so Mr. Williams hopes.

1965

5 / The Seven Descents of Myrtle

T ENNESSEE WILLIAMS'S PLACE IN THE AMERI-can theater is secure, no matter how hard he tries to dislodge himself. *The Glass Menagerie* and *Streetcar, et al.*, founded a school and then proceeded to dominate it; and Posterity seldom asks better than that. However, a writer never knows. He wants Posterity to put his immortality in writing; failing that, he gets out one more play, to be on the safe side.

Unfortunately, it seems there are no more masterpieces to be coaxed out of Mr. Williams's corner of the South, for love or money. Outside of anything else, the whole scene has been parodied to death: all those whacked-out belles wandering around in their slips, the lusty men with the fatal flaw, and the lustless men with the feet of clay, all the tattered hopes and the flaking undershirts—a play would have to be great indeed to get by with that stuff today.

Williams probably knows this better than anybody (he sometimes seems almost too intelligent to be a primitive), and not too long ago he undertook to do a straight parody of him-self called *Slapstick Tragedy*. But this was too much: gilding the magnolia, putting silicone in the hog fat. So this year he has done a modified parody, a play that some audiences can take straight and others with salt.

Unfortunately, even with salt, the taste is bad. *The Seven Descents of Myrtle* chronicles, in the tradition of neo-homosexual theater, the steady, fly wing-pulling humiliation of a woman, whipsawed and put upon by a fag and a stud. Myrtle (Estelle Parsons) comes on as a braying chucklehead, so we don't mind too much watching her get her lumps; still, just for the sake of interest, it would be nice to see her win at least one trick before the night is out.

Brother Lot (Brian Bedford) has married Myrtle on a TV show and brought her home to his decaying mansion, which is also on the point of being flooded (Old South going, going). Lot is a bit of a fop and none too good in the sack, a non-starter in fact, but Myrtle has more than her share of the mother in her and hopes to work things out—if she can get to him before he dies of T.B. (You see what I mean about parody.)

Meanwhile, down in the kitchen, there lurks half brother Chicken, adrinkin' and abroodin'. And we know—ah mean, we jest *know*—that he's going to wind up playing much-needed footsie with Myrtle. His ace card is that when the waters rise he can hoist her up on the roof and they can drink chicken's blood until things blow over. Brother Lot is beyond such exercises. True, Chicken has a little colored blood, but no one is perfect.

At the height of the revels, Brother Lot comes tottering down the stairs in his dead mother's nightie, croaks a few pleasantries in her voice, and passes out on the floor. Myrtle would seem to be well rid of so, what is the word, *moody* a husband, but we are led to suppose she is now in the seventh circle of hell, as she gallumphs up to the roof with Chicken to commence her vigil.

There is no way of taking this play seriously. As a comedy, Sid Caesar would have done it better and quicker in a television skit years ago. By now, even the parody is exhausted. And, unfortunately, Williams has thrown in a few unmistakably serious lines that undercut the vestigial humor—some trumpetings about life being for the strong, some pathos about old Chicken and his pesky past, some feeble attempts to elevate Myrtle above the level of punching bag.

You don't direct a play like this. You simply give it a whump on the tail and tell it to keep moving. José Quintero has, alas, failed to do this but has allowed Estelle Parsons in particular to snuffle and whinny interminably, generating feeling where there is no feeling. Harry Guardino as the inevitable overendowed male in the boys' department jeans is good enough to show how bad his part really is. Brian Bedford as Lot keeps busy struggling gamely with his Southern accent and his consumptive cough, which gives him a curious effect of laughing at certain key moments.

But I don't think he is laughing. It isn't that funny. A good writer making a joke of himself is a sorry sight, whether he is doing it on purpose or not. I can't believe that Tennessee Williams takes this material seriously any more. Even from Rome, or wherever he is at the moment, he must have heard that the flood finally rose up and that Myrtle and Chicken and the whole crazy lot were drowned, and that kind of play, straight or funny, went out of business a long time ago.

1968

6 / Inadmissible Evidence

O NE SONG, I HAVE BUT ONE SONG," SAID THAT
bloody little squit Snow White, and John Osborne would probably grunt a surly "amen, ducks" to that. For Osborne also has
but one song, and but one way of singing it. The Osborneman,
who is both the singer and the song, the actor and the play, has
billowed forth in a number of different disguises, his grievances
modulated, and his responsibility for them reshuffled (that is
how you tell one play from another); but Osborne has never
bothered to devise a new rhetoric for him, or a new angle of
vision.

However, what Osborne lacks in variety he can more than
make up in intensity. Within the confines of his gunny sack he
agitates like a religious sensitive. And he always plays it with
feeling; an honest tradesman in a dirty stinking world.

What gives some slight movement to the surface doldrums
of Osborne's work is the way his interpretation of the Osborneman fluctuates. Is he dirty and stinking too? Sometimes yes,
sometimes no. In *Look Back in Anger*, Jimmy Porter seemed
to stand outside society, a wounded saint looking down in judgment. Although Porter ran his own ménage like a concentration
camp, he rattled off humanist verdicts on the outside world like
a Gatling gun. In *The Entertainer*, the Osborneman is still vic-

tim and part-time judge, but he is closer to the world's rottenness and has contributed to it. The ambiguity is primitively handled, particularly in *The Entertainer*, in the bursts of littlefellow decency which seems to place him temporarily outside and above society (of course, they really are images of society's own sentimentality, but it isn't clear whether Osborne means this).

Now in *Inadmissible Evidence* we have a hero who is so totally merged with society's evils that you can no longer tell who has done what to which. Society is to blame for him, but he is equally to blame for it. The Osborneman is victim and executioner, debaser and debased—and either way he loses. In bullying his subordinates, he is imitating one of society's unpleasanter aspects; in crawling to them, he is imitating another. Society is ourselves, and the man who would flay the one must flay the other.

With such an advance in psychological realism, it would be too much to expect a comparable advance in narrative technique. In fact, *Inadmissible Evidence* is as dramatically and intellectually static as anything he has done. Since it concerns a man in hell, one could argue that staticness is part of the point; but things do not even get worse, although they try hard to, and even a fiendishly versatile performance by Nicol Williamson cannot keep a certain Osborne-fatigue at bay. The playwright's logorrhea rolls over everything in the end, neutralizing events and characters like a lava that turns living matter to stone. Everything that occurs is broken down into the same type of statement, the same pattern of words, so that the only hell left is the fact that the Osborneman will not stop talking. Hell enough, but we have been there before.

But again there is a psychological advance here, because Osborne seems to have realized for the first time that the factual situation is usually secondary to the verbal situation in his world, so he has turned the whole play into a verbal situation, a talk-nightmare as opposed to an image-nightmare. He has converted all his actual happenings into mental events, and has reduced his characters to one, making the others into backdrops, metaphors, dream figures. This leaves him free to wrestle with the central psychological data without cluttering the place with weak secondary characters and significant plot twists.

He has, in brief, locked himself up in one skull and found there all the rottenness and stagnation and aimlessness of a whole society. A few years ago, he wrote his famous "I hate you, England" letter, a croak of anguish which made him something of a butt for a while. Here he is saying through the Osborneman, "I hate me, I am England"—a more interesting and less vulnerable statement.

Bill Maitland, his latest incarnation, is a divorce lawyer, who absorbs into himself all the pain and cruelty of his clients' lives, because they are also his life. In the hallucinating insomnia of drink and pills, he can barely tell which life is which, it is all a great sea of pain. In his mind (the whole thing takes place somewhere between his sub- and his semi-conscious) he acts out the lust, cruelty, and self-pity that are the mainstays of his profession. By the end, the stage is empty: even his phantom companions have fled in disgust.

A scoundrel, without a doubt—yet the condemnation comes from his own mouth and no one else's (this presumably is what is meant by *Inadmissible Evidence*, this and the fact that you can't use a man's dreams against him). And even at that he is a better man than Jimmy Porter, further along in the life of the spirit, and he graces, on the whole, a better play.

1965

7 / *Hughie*

Aɴʏᴏɴᴇ ᴡʜᴏ ᴡɪꜱʜᴇꜱ ᴛᴏ ᴇxᴛʀᴀᴄᴛ ᴛʜᴇ ꜰᴜʟʟ juice from Eugene O'Neill's *Hughie* should first hie himself to Robert Brustein's chapter on O'Neill in *The Theatre of Revolt* (Atlantic, Little-Brown). This is by all means the best analysis of the pipe-dream plays, to which *Hughie* forms an intriguing footnote. Mr. Brustein contends that O'Neill had his own pipe-dream—that of being a "literary" playwright, full of arty tricks and classical razzle-dazzle—and that only when he had confronted this, played Hickey as it were to his own illusions, was he able to achieve real stature.

Hughie is an aggressively non-literary play, a glossary of 1920's slang recited in a mangy hotel lobby. It deals with a single aspect of the pipe-dream syndrome—the I-thou relationship of dreamer and listener. The dreamer cannot quite believe his own story until someone else has heard it, nodded, said, "Is that so." After that the dream enters the world of fact: it has gained, so to speak, a witness.

The action of *Hughie* consists of a drunken horse player floundering round and round the elevator cage, looking for a witness to his dreams. He had a listener once and they were happy together, giving birth to a host of little pseudo-events, but that listener has recently died; and now the dreamer must woo himself a new one.

Like a man who always marries the same girl, Erie Smith, the dreaming horse player, always falls for the same kind of listener; he is a pushover for night clerks. Hughie, his dream dream-listener, was night clerk at this same hotel; and now Erie is trying to court his replacement.

This in itself tells us a good deal about Erie's conversational prowess. A night clerk in this kind of hotel is the listening equivalent of a prostitute. He is paid to sit there and take it; in fact, he is literally a captive audience, because he works in a cage. Erie Smith cannot find a listener on the open market. He probably could not even keep a bartender at his end of the bar. His partner must virtually be strapped down.

In courting an audience, Erie Smith's "line" consists in reminiscing about his former one, Hughie. There was a *real* listener, boy; and as Erie describes the dreams he told to Hughie, and Hughie's superb reactions to them, we realize that the witness has actually been absorbed into the dream. Erie Smith is boasting, lying, about having been listened to; he dreams about the act of being heard.

As to his new prospect, Hughie's replacement: this fellow may be consigned to a cage, but his favors are not so easily won. As a professional solitary, he is accustomed to being his own listener. He talks to himself in a bemused kind of way of the possibility of making more noise than the garbagemen make in the morning, or of burning down the *whole* city, cement and all. This is narcissistic, closed-circuit listening, a heck of a thing to come across at three in the morning.

But Smith does not give up, and finally he succeeds in making a freak connection. His soliloquy happens to mesh at one point with the night clerk's interior monologue. The name of Arnold Rothstein the gambler comes up. Rothstein was a celebrity of his time—and even then (the play takes place in 1928) celebrities were the stuff that dreams were made on. On the understanding that they are talking about Rothstein, and nothing but Rothstein, the new night clerk consents to listen.

What follows is as tragic, on a small scale, as anything in O'Neill. Erie Smith is perfectly satisfied to have a listener on these terms; he acts as if he had made a conquest. And we suddenly see how little he asks of his listeners—the merest appearance of acquiescence will do; Smith will supply the rest. The night clerk remains fast in his narcissistic slumbers, but Smith's fantasies of gambling and wenching have inserted themselves into these, by virtue of the Rothstein connection.

And from Erie Smith's zest in this new affair, we gather not only that there is a new Hughie in the making, but the converse, that the old Hughie was probably no better than the new one. Although death has transformed him into the perfect listener, he probably listened in his day just as perfunctorily as his successor does now. Smith has already observed several similarities between them, particularly their unmistakable "night clerkness"—a quality, it appears, of patience and passivity, of simply being there.

In other words, the I-thou of pipe-dream listening is among the most corrupt of relationships. The listener is allowed to think his own thoughts. Like the witness to a legal deed, he is required to provide only superficial assent. It may be wondered why he is needed at all: but Erie Smith is a gambler, not a night clerk; he needs the appearance of action, of something happening. He has not yet sunk into the torpor of his victims, the self-absorbed listeners of this world.

Unfortunately, Jason Robards doesn't get anything like full mileage out of or into Erie Smith. He doesn't seem observant enough to be a really first-rate actor. His frenzied pirouettings around the lobby are no substitute for drunken dither. He looks as if he is about to plunge up the stairs or out into the street; even when he drops his key, he is much too decisive about it.

It may be that José Quintero the director was trying to

inject some spurious action into this splendidly static situation; if so, he has been unfair to drunks. The drunk who wants to make just one more point before going to bed should *teeter* more than Mr. Robards does.

Mr. Robards is not a very accomplished physical actor (his finest scene, in *A Long Day's Journey into Night*, was played seated) at the best of times, but he makes a few amends in the important final scenes where voice and baleful glee—his specialties—are the order of the day. Jack Dodson is properly glassy-eyed as the night clerk.

Several critics have questioned whether *Hughie* is a play at all. But O'Neill, by the end of his career, was so total a dramatist that he could mount a complete drama in a ten-minute speech. The one-hour length of *Hughie* is more than enough to make it the most interesting play of the season.

1965

8 / Baker Street

AFTER THRASHING ABOUT WILDLY FOR HALF the night (well, not a second less than fifteen minutes anyway) trying to think of something to say about *Baker Street* that would be worth bothering a printer with, I fell into a fitful doze. I must have been brooding about Hemingway's famous boast that he had outboxed the Messrs. Stendhal and Turgenev but would hesitate to enter a ring with Tolstoy, and had fused this with my normal discontents, because when I awoke I found I had typed—or rather, goose-quilled—the following paragraph:

Although I once fought a draw with Saint-Beuve, and later took a truly popular split decision from Matthew Arnold, I have been getting that obsolete feeling more and more lately. For some time now, I have been in training to challenge Edmund "Bunny" Wilson for the championship—normally nothing would get me into a ring with Bunny unless I get a lot better, but I am a strange old man and maybe I am better than I think— but just recently I've begun to wonder whether it is worth all the effort: the roadwork and the sparring partners who try to take you out in one . . .

The sources for this piece of automatic writing were not hard to trace. The style had obviously been borrowed from Lillian Ross, whose famous interview with Hemingway I had recently been rereading with the old slack-jawed amazement; but the thought was recognizably my own. For a number of reasons which I won't go into here, a conviction has been growing that criticism as we know it today may be on the way out. It is certainly redundant and obsolete—who needs a hundred oracles belching dark contradictions from separate caves when you could have one oracle belching dark contradictions, etc.—and now it seems that the British have actually perfected a new critical machine . . .

Well, perhaps "perfected" is putting it too strongly. The muggeridge II has certainly superseded the American macdonald, and it produces more words per month than the old sontag, but it still has a few bugs. For one thing, it is not very good at fiction; it tries gamely, with gears clanking and little iron jaws masticating like fury; but its aesthetic sense is still in the rudimentary stage. It registers stupidity and cant accurately enough, but is all at sea with nuance.

Perhaps the outstanding feature of the new muggeridge is its formidable second-strike capacity. Woe to anyone who controverts it—the muggeridge strikes back with the speed of a cobra, with a suave giggle and lick of the steel tongue. The macdonald was good in this respect, but hopelessly wasteful: it used to try to answer its enemies point by point. The muggeridge simply giggles and licks, and its enemies become instantly paralyzed.

The muggeridge's extraordinary output also enables it to review the same book in several places at once, which clears up a lot of silly confusion. The old machines used to disagree sometimes and then they fought like old tin battleships, circling slowly and pelting the landscape with shot. It was a mess. One hardly knew what to think.

Nowadays, none of this is necessary. Simply install a muggeridge in your office (the only thing a muggeridge will not fight with is another muggeridge). Several magazines have already purchased one—and these magazines among our best. An imported criticism machine adds a cachet that anyone can feel proud of.

And perhaps future models will prove even more efficient. The new muggeridge is already much smoother than the old one—the old one which wrote that Churchill was senile at a time when the information could be of use to no one and could only cause pain, and which sneered at Queen Elizabeth with a peculiar, chop-licking relish that even anti-monarchists found it hard to warm up to. The new muggeridge doesn't do things like that. Or if it does, it prefaces the assassination with words like, "Dearly as I love you Americans" . . . The new muggeridge has had what Cyril Connolly calls a "gland of charm" built into it.

The muggeridge II has not so far as I know been fed any movies or plays yet. But I see no reason why it should not process them with the same success, since there is nothing specifically literary about its methods (its prototype was, I would imagine, a political gossip writer, which was later found to work just as well on books). If a muggeridge II was faced, as I am right now —and have been right along, daughter—with the task of reviewing the musical *Baker Street*, I don't see why it shouldn't click out something like the following:

"I never cease to be amazed at the patience of Americans. I never cease . . . ," whir whir. (Tell him it's a *play*. About Sherlock Holmes.) "When I was a boy, I remember" . . . (better just let him talk—he'll get round to it in a moment) "but I never thought I'd live to see the day" (hasn't he got a lovely accent, though?). "Now, as to this so-called play. Poor Fritz Weaver has been cajoled into doing the impossible: playing this degenerate, not particularly interesting monument of Victorian sexlessness—a countryman of mine, I fear, but I don't boast about it—and poor Inga Swenson, forced to make love to this sexless charlatan—I myself am quite sexy, thank you very much. In my day we didn't talk about it, that's all—and poor Martin Gabel as the sexless Dr. Moriarty. Poor everybody. Not excepting poor me."

This kind of thing is tough to compete with; if *Common-weal* ever decides to install a muggeridge II, my days are probably numbered. Meanwhile, let me just add to the above that *Baker Street* is an uncommonly weak musical with one of the poorest scores I have ever heard on Broadway. Fritz Weaver talks his songs, which helps—except that the words aren't particularly good either.

Sherlock Holmes is not really a good subject for a musical. The satirical possibilities have been mined to a faretheewell by Leacock and others; and the detective side was done very well in the old Basil Rathbone movies, with all the advantages of screen magic, and none of the encumbrances of music. Presumably, this was not discovered until too late. Anyhow, the fog is excellent.

(And now tell me the news, daughter—is it true that Bunny Wilson has a glass jaw? I am a strange old man, to put it mildly, and if I remember to keep my guard up, I may win the championship yet.)

1965

9 / *A Delicate Balance*

Edward Albee breaks out the bottles early in his new play *A Delicate Balance*. Which means that for the first two acts, it's strictly drink and pour, pour and drink, to the point where reviewing it becomes thirsty work indeed. The third act is set at 7:30 in the morning, which promises a rest to the company elbow; but lo, dawn's early light finds them at it again, lacing their orange juice with vodka and carrying on about the wonder of it as if they had discovered Atlantis.

This is not meant to be the beginning of a temperance lecture—although watching other people drink has never been my particular brand of voyeurism. The boozing in *Virginia Woolf* I found absolutely B-12 (morally acceptable in part with exceptions for unusually mature monsignors) because it was a character in the story. But the drinking in *A Delicate Balance* is not really about anything at all—or at least the small dramatic points it makes are out of proportion to the liquid volume. Filling the glasses has become all too evidently a nervous tic, like the fiction writer's "he shot her a glance": something to do for your characters when your characters have nothing to do.

And this is the story with *A Delicate Balance*, which is no more than half a play, about a year's work from completion. The author, scurrying to keep up with his white rabbit schedule, did not have time to finish it, but simply stuffed the cracks with cotton and was on his way. Before the situation has even been established, the characters are philosophizing about it over their brandy—which reminds one of Ogden Nash's definitive dictum about ice-breaking. Dramatically, too, liquor is quicker. Albee is like a jumpy hostess who can't wait to get her guests' tongues loosened, but brings them their drinks out on the driveway.

This tactic may be taken as a likely sign of creative fatigue. One of the great problems connected with writing too much is that it becomes such a bore setting things up every time, making those first weary moves with the pawns. (One novelist I know vows to start his next book at chapter 6.) So the hostess analogy is not bad: your play or party does get going quicker with the aid of liquor. Emotional situations can be ripened artificially and you get to your shout scene sooner. But the neighbors are not fooled and neither is the audience: unless you can arrange to keep the onlookers loaded too, they will see just how little the shouting amounts to.

Anyhow, within minutes we find the cast chaffering over a half-formed situation and a half-empty jug. The husband and wife have failed each other, by the looks of things. Their daughter is about to come home after failing her fourth husband (she hates her parents, but keeps coming home anyway). Upstairs lurks the wife's sister, an honest-to-goodness lush who has failed everybody within the three-mile limit.

Onto this stimulating scene burst a couple of neighbors who are frightened by their own house. This has interesting Thurberish possibilities, and might very well have made the play: but instead of allowing it to grow, Albee first force-feeds it and then impatiently stuns it with talk. The neighbors are escaping from a plague, they have brought their plague with them, do you like their plague? Albee can no longer wait to tell us what's on his mind: his plays are coming perilously close to his interviews, in fact.

The point he wants to make about the neighbors is that they have discovered lovelessness in their own house and have brought a cup of it over—only to discover that their hosts already have plenty. This puts the neighbors in the same bag as the daughter, which calls for another round of drinks. The smart-alecky sister enjoys rubbing their collective noses in these home truths and is told, for her pains, that she is the strongest of all of them. "The walking-wounded are often the strongest . . ."

This latter is a common superstition or wish-think of writing folk, who would be king of the hill if it were so. In this case, being strong consists mostly of making wisecracks while someone else's ship sinks—someone she has been parasiting off, by the by. Since the sister has taken no responsibility for anything that happens, she demonstrates about as much strength as one of the ushers. It is glib and sentimental to equate her with those few walking-wounded in real life who have managed to make themselves strong.

Probably the only way to save the play would be to dump all the harangues, and explanations, and most of the ideas, and to replace them with scenes. But scenes take longer to write. Those two people who are afraid of their own house are worth a play, and for the few minutes that they are treated comically (à la his own *American Dream*) Albee shows us what he might have done with them.

1966

10 / *A View from the Bridge*

THE TALE OF THE GOOD WRITER GONE RANCID IS such a commonplace in America that a new example hardly raises a flutter. Arthur Miller has joined an all-too familiar procession—the league of uprooted, transplanted writers; the Southern novelist who lives in Antibes, the California novelist holed up at Sag Harbor, the Midwesterner ending his days in Havana, all the migrant workers of American letters, Van Wyck Brooks's army of displaced talents.

Arthur Miller has written pretty good plays about Brooklyn, so naturally he goes to Hollywood and writes about Europe or goes to Europe and writes about Hollywood—who knows where these people are writing from anyway? His new mailing address is the Everywhere-Hilton and his new subject is Life. He doesn't write the Brooklyn vulgate any more, but that nice neutral stuff you can't quite place, the stuff they taught Clifford Odets (and Cary Grant) in Hollywood. Since he looks like an intellectual with his pipe and all, this least intellectual of playwrights has added that to his routine, making thoughtful noises about key subjects of the day. Albee the mystic, Miller the intellectual: the American Dream.

Miller's recent writing has been so uncompromisingly bad that one is tempted to say that he never was any good. Laid out in a critic's morgue, his Brooklyn plays don't look as impressive as they did: social moralities from the thirties (we are all guilty) crossbred with psychiatry-mongering from the forty-fifties (relax, nobody's guilty) to the disadvantage of both. To be stranded between Clifford Odets and William Inge is to be stranded indeed.

But the plays do not belong in a morgue yet, they belong on a stage. And there, to judge from the current revival of *A View from the Bridge*, they still work. This is the last of the early Miller: with this one he has already begun moving away from the old neighborhood, the voice is getting thinner. His people are heavily mythologized and dreamlike. The poverty of language, which is to embarrass him sorely when he tries writing about less primitive people, is already weakening his big effects. Twice, we are told that the hero's eyes look like tunnels; a passion possesses him "like a stranger in his body"; old man cliché is taking an ever more obtrusive hand in the speeches.

But the play works: you can sit in the stalls ticking off its defects all evening, but in the end something has happened. And the thought occurs that perhaps Miller was always trying to write bad plays, and that this was a sizable step in that direction, but that he still was some way from mastering the art. The cheap-jack universalizing, the sociological gospel-singing, the terrible flatness of characterization are there in force, have been there all along, in fact, but there is something else working vigorously against them.

To put it briefly, Miller's characters up to and through this play were always more specific than he meant them to be. He left out details, in the hope that we would see his people as Giant Myths: but luckily for him, we didn't need details. The basic Miller family had an unmistakable flavor: we knew the neighborhood, the school, what year the characters had dropped out, how many payments were due on the car.

Miller has always tried to keep these things dark. He wants

Willy Loman to be all salesmen everywhere; he wants us to think big—and of course on a superficial, 100-great-books level, we do. We think about salesmanship, American values, Is It All Worth It, etc., all the things that Miller thinks about (and probably taught poor Miss Monroe to think about, too). But the real experience of the evening has always consisted of meeting a particular man in a particular setting: meeting Willy Loman of 221 Atlantic Avenue, or wherever it was.

A writer like Miller is like nothing so much as a medieval monk solemnly inscribing what he thinks ought to be inscribed while Hieronymus Bosch devils fly around his cell and dance on his pen. *A View from the Bridge* is a classic tale of jealousy and revenge, etc., etc., but the dramatic tension does not come from the story; it comes from the setting: it comes from the haunted Miller house which we have visited several times before. The narrowness of lower middle-class life (the house is cramped, the neighborhood is cramped) has, long before the play opens, brought his people into rasping alignment, generating the steam that will make the play move. The child in the Miller house has to go through the parents' bedroom to get to the bathroom; the people upstairs can hear every word, which means that private quarrels double as public statements; all the actions and passions that richer people can work out in a large, varied setting must be confined to these few small rooms. (What goes on outside the rooms tends to be sketchy, even in the good plays.)

In *A View from the Bridge*, the uncle falls in love with his niece, as a man might fall in love with a girl on the subway, just because she has been standing on his foot all the way from Pelham. Rich people have a choice of relationships; Miller's people must take what is at hand. The intensity of Miller's plays comes from the fact that a family must find among its own members the whole range of human encounter. A rich man has friends in Quogue and a girl in the East eighties; a Miller man can only fall in love with his niece.

Whatever the Brooklyn plays are ostensibly about (and I use the word "Brooklyn" generically), this background must be kept in place by the viewer. Future audiences may find this harder to do. The Depression still lingers in the Miller house. In real life, the old neighborhood has already changed. Miller's Brooklyners sound slightly out of date, which gives the plays an undeserved air of spuriousness. (Danny Kaye's Brooklyn imitation also sounds slightly out of date; Brooklyn jokes in general sound out of date.) It may be partly this speed of change that makes writers like Miller leave home in the first place. The neighborhood leaves them before they leave it. Houses go down, highways go in, people move out. What's to stay for? And if Miller wanted to get out of the Miller house, who can blame this man? Talent in America is a ticket to somewhere else, and even if you have to leave the ticket at home, it may still be worth it.

In the new production, Robert Duvall as the tormented uncle and Ramond Bieri as his vengeful Sicilian cousin-in-law are particularly fine. The shout scene in the last act might seem a bit too much for sensitive ears, but if you like a good shout in the theater, well, here you have one.

1965

11 / *Theater Revisited*

LAST NIGHT I DREAMED I WENT BACK TO BROAD-way (picture Joan Fontaine loping up the driveway smothered in shawls, if you must picture something). The ushers were smaller than I remembered and the seats had shrunk to the size of baby's high chairs. The customers were exactly where I had left them, and when I brushed one of them by mistake, powder started to run helplessly down his trouser leg. Quite dead, poor devil.

The curtain that I had watched with trembling excitement as a child (picture Freddie Bartholomew in nankeen breeches if you can't see it any other way) was covered in thin green mold. It hung as listless as a fat man's dressing gown, and from the ceiling descended a fine, warm dust, coating my tonsils and driving me half mad with thirst.

The play, now this was strange, was called *The Goosing Game:* fresh, I read in the flickering gaslight, from a triumphant run off-Broadway, where it played to twelve people over five years. The ghost of Theater Past clutched at my bony wrist. After the mutton and cheese, I was to be spared nothing tonight.

The curtain sagged up at last, and we all applauded the set, which consisted of plain brown paper and chalk graffiti. The vast stage, where choruses of fifty used to gambol, contained a single mattress and a skinny young man in his underpants. He was, let's speed things up here, on the lam from his brutal father who wanted his heir to join him in the napalm business, and from his understanding—too understanding—mother.

At some point he is joined by a chum similarly clad. They embrace awkwardly. Our hero says nervously, "You understand, this doesn't mean I don't like girls." "Yes, yes. I understand," his new roommate breathes hotly. Our hero flings loose, as the necking threatens to get furious. "Christ, I don't know what I'm doing. You've got me going crazy." Friend rises up, fetches beer can. "Make up your mind, kid." Or, alternatively, "You bit my lip, you bastard." My notes are hopelessly unclear at this point.

There followed, in feverish sequence, a visit from blustering Dad, whom the hero tries defiantly to goose, and flip mother ("I think your young man is cute"). Having driven them both out with flailing wit and ruthless honesty, he strips off his shorts in the half dark, for the scene they said couldn't be made and lunges blindly in the direction of his buddy's hips.

The second act introduces the sex element. An old girl friend heaves up the invisible stairs and knocks on the invisible door. Hero clings to friend for protection (they are back safely in their jockey shorts by now) and shouts a defiant "Come in." "For Christsake what are you two doing," says the girl carelessly, taking out her pillow and lying down.

Well, much to-ing and fro-ing here, but what it comes to is that Miss Daisy, his old high-school sweetheart, wants to move in with the two of them along with her favorite librarian, the first grownup who ever made any sense to her. (These two will later proceed to peel off their sweaters and read Emily Dickinson.) An old man falls across my lap at this point, streaming powder and moaning soundlessly. He knows, and *I* know, that at the bottom of the invisible stairs lurk her dithering, lackluster father, who hasn't had a job in thirty years and who raises bees in the attic, and her brutal henna-haired mother, who wants her to finish Harvard law school. She will flail them both insensible with her wit and her honesty.

I groped down the glamorous aisle at last and out to the glamorous White Way: but I hadn't yet paid my full debt to Society, it seemed. The ghost of Theater Present took me by the scruff and dragged me downtown, through a series of forced marches, to a basement on Avenue B and lower Canal Street. Here conditions were Stygian, and I could barely make out the $10 price on my stub. The man in front was so tall, I couldn't even *see* the mattress this time. And his curious swaying motion blotted out most of the actors as well. Thus, since I could only see the tops of their heads, it booted little how far down they stripped. I think the boy's mother hauled off her brassière at one point, causing the lad to laugh bitterly. And the father from Murder Chemicals, Inc., may have done some light disrobing too. But short of flinging myself into the aisles, there was no way of proving any of this.

The ghost of Theater Future looked a lot like a redesigned bowling alley. There are at least two other basic plays on at the moment, besides the above. But there does seem to be an ominous shrinkage of subject matter, particularly off-Broadway, where the new ideas are supposed to come from: the family play, the play of homosexual discovery, or else some kind of symbolism, preferably about man's life cycle. Plays like *Geese* (both ends of it), *War Games*, or even the much superior *Spiro Who?* all tell the same story about where the adults went wrong—largely because, for drab economic reasons, playwriting has become a young man's game and partly because derision about the aging process is as American as our sentimentality about the old.

Theater is drastically short on the sort of lumpen middle-aged writer who still turns up in the Novel, who has discovered that life is a bitch at all ages and that, as James Joyce said, anyone who succeeds in raising a family at all is worthy of some respect. Elaine May's one-acter *Adaptation* is a partial exception, dealing its lumps out evenly to all generations. But her satire on the American life cycle is mechanical and second-hand and not quite as funny as it used to be. In the old days, when she worked with Mike Nichols, her teenagers were real teenagers. Now they are copied out of newspapers and medical journals. As successful writers pass, what, twenty-five? they seem to drift further from primary material: after they leave that dreadful family, all is journalism.

Plays slither in and out of New York so fast that your only chance is to watch the playwrights. On the bill with *Adaptation* is a fine little play called *Next* by Terrence McNally. It deals with a hopelessly inappropriate man (James Coco) trying to reason with his draftboard, only to find there is a lot of draftboard in all of us. McNally began life with a play called *Things That Go Bump in the Dark,* which managed to combine the worst features of the Big Symbol play; so it is good to see him working away from the prevailing categories.

He is one of several young playwrights (in this business you go on being young until you become famous) to make book on in the next few years. Israel Horowitz, whose *Honest to God Schnozzola* tries to parody too many things at once but squeaks by on theatrical virtuosity; Lanford Wilson, whose *Gingham Dog* I missed, but I'm an old Wilson fan; and John Ford Noonan, author of *The Year Boston Won the Pennant,* a play fairly groaning with symbols, alternately banal and mystifying; John Guare's *Cop Out* gets us aback to journalism, but Guare has talent too.

These and other names crop up punctually on lists of promising playwrights, but they never seem to crash the celebrity register, which remains frozen like the Peerage. We badly need more celebrities to be disappointed by. Williams and Miller shouldn't be asked to carry this load indefinitely.

The most written-up theatrical event (because everybody in the house turned out to be a writer of sorts) of the past season was the invasion of the Theater for Ideas by the Living Theater. The occasion was a debate between the Becks and the Others about the nature of Theater—the Becks maintaining that its primary purpose is to melt the wax in your navel, and the Others (mainly Robert Brustein) suggesting that even this takes talent and strategy. The Beck's principal argument was to wreck the joint. And since this did cause some excitement, I guess they proved their point: though a lynching or a Bund rally would have proved it just as well. It isn't that difficult to get people excited, and never was; a sharp bite on the knee will do it in most cases.

Unfortunately, before her wrecking crew got to work, Judith Malina made the mistake of saying something. Which was, in effect, why watch Hedda Gabler when you could be watching me? Why should an actress be chained to some dead Norwegian when she can be her own throbbing self? And this point was very far from proved by the events of the evening. Ibsen would have written a much better riot.

The question of self-expression needs a little clarifying. Some people have it in very high degree, and they are known as artists and writers. Even for them it is bloody work, their own voices sounding only occasionally in a lifetime of effort. The outcome of their cranking and winding is occasionally known as a play. Then there are people whose powers of mimicry are so abnormally developed that they cannot express themselves at all without borrowing. And these are known as actors and actresses. Ask the brightest performer ten questions, and be lucky to get off with only seven clichés. The dumbest ones actually believe they made up the clichés.

What Miss Malina is demanding is that these charming phonograph machines should move into the creating business—and this, not just on their good days, but every time out. Ibsen himself would shrink from inventing a new Hedda Gabler for each performance. But this is, in effect, what the Becks must expect from their goon squad. Because if the actors ever start repeating their improvisations, what is to keep these from becoming as stale as the stuffy old script was? By the second night, they are imitating their own imitations.

In fact, this seems to be what has happened. As the Becks' crew of chimps came screeching down the aisles, one sensed a flatness even in their hysteria. They had done this before, and it showed like the thousandth night of a run. Their lines, if you take out the blanks, were tired and out of date. To tell this particular audience that they should be home watching their televisions was the kind of mistake you make after too many years in France. I doubt there were three TV watchers in the house, and at least one of them belonged to the Becks. As to their other swifty, "Yah, yah, you paid ten dollars," this was not only mystifying as a wisecrack, but sailed harmlessly past the many freeby holders that Shirley Broughton (director of the Theater for Ideas) had generously let in. True improvisers would know at once the difference between culture-benefit folk and freeloading eggheads.

There may be an art to breaking up symposiums, and God knows, I wouldn't mind seeing it practiced more often. Free speech is all very well in its place, but if Groucho had been there to heckle Paul Goodman and Harpo to sit in Miss Malina's lap, I would have waived the right. But, however hard the talentless try to escape them, the demands of Art are everywhere: insult is an art, gesture is an art. Doing away with words is a promising start, for so backward a group. But, alas, physical movement can be as stereotyped as any verbal cliché, and clowning is the most exacting art of all. Loutishness is not enough.

It was an irony sufficiently hackneyed that they should pick on Robert Brustein for their jungle warfare. Brustein's admirable new book *The Third Season* shows a theater lover on the rack, looking wildly for escape from the sterilities of Broadway and the dead hand of the schoolroom classics. Such was his despair that he even gave the Becks houseroom at the Yale Drama School, where he is dean. Yet here they were, treating him like any old dean, doing everything but lock him in his room. Take that, you good liberal.

The effectiveness of the invasion depended entirely on how angry they made you. Your own liver was the stage and your spleen the plot. The Becks have to keep moving, because, like all emotions, rage runs down, and they haven't the wit to fuel it. All the funny lines that evening came from the audience, and there weren't enough of those. Even critics have trouble with spontaneity. The theater of improvisation depends on a rarer talent than the old theater ever did. And although we were all jumping from chair to chair and gibbering like gibbons, I don't suppose any of us would have shown up for a second night.

Hatred of art is, God knows, an old story. It is a natural human response, like stoning saints. But lately it has taken on a new chic, in the name of relevance. E.g., if playwright's Nazi father were to say of Shakespeare, "What's in it for me?" we would just say, There he goes again. But a member of the relevance generation can say such things and worse—and we think immediately it must be Shakespeare's fault. We do not, as better listeners would, hear Daddy's tired old voice, piping through fresh adenoids.

Philistinism and youth-worship have formed a sinister merger, and Theater is the first to hurt. A young writer in the *Village Voice* recently washed his hands of culture completely after Nicol Williamson's dismal *Hamlet*—lumping it all together, like an out-of-town buyer trapped at *Madame Butterfly*. Ironically, the production pandered to youth by making *Hamlet* into a generation-gap play and endowing the Prince with a sulky whine that might actually prompt youth to sue. But nothing brings out a play's irrelevance more embarrassingly than attempts to deny it.

If McLuhanism would just go away, as even the inventor

must wish by now, and take its weedy derivatives with it, classical theater might well flourish among young people for the first time in years. Older Americans have always been bored by it, whatever they may pretend, so they find it easy to accept a theory which explains why kids should be bored by it too. And certain youths, aping their elders, say yes, yes, I'm bored; it's irrelevant—not recognizing that irrelevant is a word from the businessman's culture (see *functional*), and that they, like aristocrats of the past, can now afford to be irrelevant without shame; and even to write plays which are not about their own families, or about the morning newspaper.

1969

12 / *Theater 1980:*

(*as seen by The New York Times*)

I HAD A LOT OF FUN AT THE PRODUCTION OF *Little Women* at the New York A.C., though I confess there were moments when I was curiously nauseated by it. As a sheer aesthetic statement, I preferred the New Delhi version, where we all just, so to speak, "did" it, on the steps of the temple. But the breakaway nuns' costumes of the Athletic Club retain all their wistful gaiety and I fell completely for the cheeky sincerity of the Black Mass sequence. As I say, I thoroughly enjoyed myself, except for those moments of racking nausea, and so did my friends, on the whole.

What was the play trying to say? I confess I am not familiar with the American classic on which it was based, but I assume it is not unlike our English game of rounders. Anyway, the adaptation is first and last great fun (and when did you last have an evening of *pure fun* in the theater?) except for those puzzling stretches of blind repulsion, which I suppose I ought to say something about.

The fornication was, let's face it, not up to snuff. American actors have many virtues—robust innocence, rugged naïveté, and so forth—but they just can't copulate. Rufus Snavely looked utterly wretched, as if a small dog was tugging at his trouser leg, and Mavis Yardley looked as if she might well have been that dog. She can, of course, tug at my trouser leg any time she wants to. Also, that of my friend Waldo Figley of *News* magazine, who was snoring cheerfully in the next seat, a victim of the excellent lobster thermidor at Voisin.

Figley and I left after the first act, Figley still dead to this world, and I not quite sure whether to laugh or throw up. I believe the copulation problem, to get back to that for a moment, may be linked to the Supreme Court ruling that the participants must wear gloves at all times. I don't know how you feel about this, but I never wear gloves myself, only an undershirt or light towel of some kind. Gloves strike me as tacky and cloying, but others may feel different about this of course.

To get back to the play. What *was* it saying? The marvelous thing is that it was saying different things to different people. To me it said that man's loneliness laps on the endless shore of his indifference. There is something of Ibsen in this and not a little bit of Chekhov too, although it is all really Arthur Pettibone the playwright who speaks in his own voice, God bless him.

You may find quite a different meaning. You are perfectly entitled to, because the play is larger than life, and yet infinitely smaller. It is a fascinating evening of theater, which fails essentially. Figley says that the title is homosexual.

1969

PART FOUR

1 / *Blow-Up*

Michaelangelo Antonioni, the big a., has come and gone, and to judge from a spattering of interviews, the old comedy of errorful manners took place: the aesthetes rolled up expecting to meet one of their own, and received for their pains answers worthy of Primo Carnera. To hear him tell it, Antonioni doesn't know what the hell he's doing when he makes a movie, and despises anyone else who thinks he does. At one point, if *The New York Times* is to be trusted, he even uttered the cry of the stage-Italian, "I am Antonioni!"—only failing to add, like Erik Rhodes in *Top Hat*—"I am reech and I am preetty."

None of this will discourage, or instruct, the hardier snobs, who will see it all as devastating commentary or as the wonderful simplicity of genius, or something. It reminds one slightly of English academics chaffering over, say, William Faulkner—except that the English are always on the alert for ironies and delicious put-downs, while we tend to take our celebrities straight. When Antonioni says, "I cannot make a comedy, because nothing amuses me except sex," this is no simple boor talking; this is *Antonioni*. Or how about: "They [women] are the most important invention in the world for me." (Mr. Rhodes: "For the woman, the keess; for the man—the sword!")

Whether the master was telling his interlocutors to blank off or was really trying his best may never be known. In any event, the movie he had come over here to celebrate, namely *Blow-Up*, impressed this observer as being gorgeous but a little bit dumb, like his repartee. Antonioni confides that his previous movies had been made with his stomach but this one was made with his brain (for this and the other sidesplitting quotes, full credit should be given to Rex Reed of the *Times*); but clearly he must get back to his stomach right away. For that is the seat of his talent.

Undeniably, *Blow-Up* is a handsome movie—the kind Granny might have called "almost too handsome." The shots of London are extraordinary, all the more so since A. was working without his usual cameraman. It seems that the Mediterranean eyeball can find beauty anywhere or, if it can't, puts it there anyway. A. says he actually painted the grass greener—which, considering how the English carry on about their grass, was a nice piece of bravado. As a result, his London sparkles like Siena.

Then, having spread this feast, he falls to examining his big toe. When your toes are as finely wrought as Antonioni's, this is perfectly in order; but some viewers have mistaken the size of the subject. They believe for instance that the movie is about the cult of photography (the central character is a photographer)—but Antonioni has nothing to say about photography; and nothing to say, this time around, about modern society.

In fact, as soon as he comes within sight of an idea, he begins to sound like the man in the interviews. Take the photography idea. Everybody knows by now that this apparently harmless little art has a brutal dehumanizing effect on all concerned, turning people into cameras or camera fodder, as the case may be. Has Antonioni got anything to add to this? Well, no. He simply presents us with a particularly gross photographer (David Hemmings) with no feelings whatsoever; shows him in lugubrious close-up, feeling nothing; carefully numbers his footsteps—tap,

tap, tap (pause) taptaptap, one of the master's more intriguing trademarks. Who he is, how he got that way, or whether he was human before he stumbled on his first Brownie, you will have to find out from some other director. Antonioni neither knows (and this I'll swear) nor cares.

Not that Antonioni has a duty to tell us these things, or anything else; but he wastes an awful lot of time appearing to tell us. The close-ups, the footsteps, all look so meaningful, but are all sheer style, like a Roman traffic cop. Even the pregnant pauses are mostly false pregnancies. I would be the last to hurry a director who likes to linger in the tub; but even a slow film has to be doing *something*, and some of the sequences in *Blow-Up* do nothing at all, except sit around and admire themselves. As a result, the film lacks not only pace but interior rhythm.

And what has Antonioni found out about England? Only that under the swingingness there lurks a great tedium. This discovery dates back at least to Piers Plowman and has since been confirmed by John Betjeman. And since Antonioni has noted the same phenomenon in Italy in previous outings, we have to wonder exactly what it is he has discovered. On close consideration, it occurred to me that he had hardly noticed England at all, any more than he noticed New York. Great directors are pretty well buffered from their surroundings; and if the only thing that amuses you is sex, you'll not get much fun out of England anyway.

The nightclub and pot-party scenes are not only not specifically English—they are movie-conventionalized to a point that we wouldn't tolerate from Hollywood. And the central character might as well be a Dutchman. All right—give Antonioni the benefit of the doubt and call the whole thing a parody (and invest him with a sense of humor which apparently he leaves behind on long journeys) and you still haven't got much. For the woods are full of parodists, and all this stuff has been done much better by local wise guys.

Yet time works on *Blow-Up*'s side. By the next day the narcissism has shrunk to size, and the gaudy images have swollen into near-masterpieces. Two sequences alone—the posing of the fashion models, and Vanessa Redgrave's gambol in the impossibly green park—would be enough to justify all the yawnsome footage and plottage. Close up in the obligatory seduction scene, Miss Redgrave looks like a hockey captain; but outdoors she makes a fine gawky nymph and the setting, now in focus, now out, compares with the best color-dream you ever had.

The film ends with a tennis game in mime which summarizes *Blow-Up*'s great weakness and its great strength—the galumphing non-organic symbolism, and the drenching beauty which makes you forgive it. If a beautiful babe wants to talk about the levels of meaning in Immanuel Kant, that's her privilege. And so it is when Signor Michaelangelo Antonioni wants to shoot us another film about meaninglessness and alienation.

As Truffaut demonstrated in *Fahrenheit 451*, great directors are not necessarily intellectual giants. A philosophical discussion between him and the Big A. would no doubt be something painful to hear—a riot of truisms and banal outspokenness, earnestly arrived at. Yet, like crazy prophets, they see intelligently, their eyes light on the right clues even when their mouths press them into clichés. Both their last films were shot in England, where they were temporarily at sea and were forced to rely unduly on their brains; but these slips are no cause for dismay. Prophets have never traveled well (except, presumably, to receive honors).

1967

2 / La Guerre est Finie

ALAIN RESNAIS'S *La Guerre est Finie* IS A great improvement on his last one, *Muriel*. With M. Resnais the parts are so nicely mixed that you never know when you are going to get the artist or when the mountebank will pop up. It seems to depend more on his material than on his mood. There are huge gaps in his literary sensibility, and when he applies one of his elaborate settings to some piece of costume junk he has picked up, the result can be excruciatingly pretentious.

In *La Guerre* he has got himself a script nicely suited to his means. It is an elegy to the revolution game. A group of aging troublemakers shuttle back and forth from Paris to Madrid, with forged passports and cryptic instructions: *we must warn Jean; we must get him out of/into town with/without delay*, etc. They have been doing this for twenty years now, and nobody really cares any more.

The plot is so complex as to be no plot at all—meaningless complexity is the very essence of their lives, as, at times, of Resnais's art. Every now and then, one of their number is absentmindedly captured, or killed, just often enough to fill their lives with endless terror and to heighten their sense of mission; but the mission has lost its point years ago. The war is over, and they are simply its leftover twitches.

The film is above all a study in pure process. The professional spy must do his job and so must the professional spy hunter, even when there is nothing special to do; and so they hatch their plans and stockpile aliases, effacing and reeffacing their identities, in a beautiful Resnais vacuum; switching trains to shake off nonexistent pursuit, and sweating over every traffic cop; overvaluing their game outrageously, as athletes are wont.

And yet, Resnais has not fallen into the European political novelist's bag of making his story *too* abstract. His spies are working for something tangible—a General Strike in Madrid, which will derange the tourist trade and unhorse General Franco. (The latter took their efforts seriously enough to ban the film in Spain—but possibly his sense of reality is as defective as theirs. A couple of years ago, *Life* magazine was also banned in Spain.) Resnais's special knack is to make concrete evidence seem as abstract as the old town of K in the province of X.

In the end, the efforts of his spies are going to be futile because they are living in that kind of dream; and from the very way they walk and the sound of their voices, you know that they know it. Yves Montand, the hero, is a very model of dogged futility. His every move is exhausted: a man lost in a strange city in a night that won't end.

Montand lends the kind of weight and sobriety that Resnais often needs; even so, someone should kneel on this director's chest and oblige him to cut when he has made his point twice. Economy is vital to this kind of movie. On the heavy credit side, Resnais's use of flashbacks and -fronts to suggest a rhythm between past and present is miles beyond anything he accomplished in *Hiroshima, Mon Amour*, and the love scenes between Montand and Ingrid Thulin must be among the most beautiful ever filmed.

1967

3 / *Persona*

Scatter your concentration for a minute and stop trying to follow the plot. In no time you find yourself in an underwater kingdom of custom and fetish. The Swedes—to start with an easy one—live on beaches all year round, where they romp glumly to-and-fro, in heavy sweaters and birthday suits, wondering what it's all about. The French are great eaters, led by the nonpareil Jean Gabin, who can chew his way through an entire movie, and formidable neck-kissers too, possibly in the same vein. (On the other hand, these French do not wear raincoats the way they used to.)

The English have taken to jumping in and out of their little cars and banging the doors with vigor. No more pouncing onto buses for them. The Italians do more walking than most, stopping to make their point, and then trudging on. You need an especially sturdy pair of shoes to make an Antonioni film—and where better to buy them than in Italy? Of course Americans are still wedded to the telephone, although those long dialing sequences seem to be on the wane. The numbers have gotten too long by now, and your finger goes to sleep just thinking about them.

These and countless other bits of business may or may not be of social significance. (I sometimes fancy their insignificance may be breathtaking.) But they have much to say about the overall quality of a film. Reviewers pay them small mind, lumping them under the general heading of photography. But in fact they have little to do with photography. When Jean Gabin is working over his pre-dinner roll, it boots it little whether he is being shot from overhead or under the plate. It is still old Jean eating.

The quality of a director's imagination can be cruelly tested by these water-treading sequences. If his mind keeps drifting back to the café or the phone booth, as in the recent *Galia*, we sense some kind of a visual starvation; if he keeps wanting to drop everything to go for a drive, à la *The Deadly Affair*, we can call him on motion sickness. A repetition of locales may be inevitable, but a repetition of certain *types* of scene, without due cause, suggests either a narcissistic trance or a galloping staleness.

The really good movie should have had all of its parts tested down to the winches. There should be no flat, here-you-keep-them-entertained-while-I-change sequences. No one can or should keep a movie at full intensity for two hours. But at those prices there is no excuse for cheap, throwaway shots or make-work dialogue. For all his fur-licking languor, Antonioni always honors his obligations frame by frame (a bone to Signor Paranoia); so, consummately, does the subject of this rather windy introduction, Ingmar Bergman.

Many things will have been said about Bergman's new movie, *Persona*, by this time. But I should like to stress here its aristocratic gold-plated quality, remarkable even for Bergman. It does not, like even the best movies, use superior filler material; it uses no filler material at all. Every sight and sound counts: and when Bergman comes to the end of these, he ends his picture.

The subject helps him. Whatever may be said about schizoid derangements, they are still a moviemaker's delight. From the lush old *Spellbound* days (calendar art insanity) through Polanski's *Repulsion*, we have had a gaudy slew of schizoid images; but none so exact, or strung together so tightly, as the ones in *Persona*. The movie opens with a series of actual hallucinations; hands being crucified, some kind of Krazy Kat cartoon, etc. These are to be our frame of reference. We will not need to see them again—although Bergman reinserts them in the middle as a memory freshener. He can proceed to tell his story on the literal level, within an aureole of dream: actuality will henceforth seem as fragmented as a nightmare; a mirror breaks, a drinking glass shatters—these are the outward signs, the sacraments, of schizophrenia.

Persona is the story of a catatonic actress who diabolically possesses the soul of her nurse. The nurse carries the demon of this silent, smiling woman within her, and writhes in fever with it, like a religious sensitive. The actress finds peace in this arrangement until her old self confronts her, like seven devils returning, in the form of the nurse. The weaker character proceeds to flail the stronger with the stronger one's own demon, but also to pander to her; for demonic possession has its coquettish side. Besides, these are two women living together with a relationship outside the spirit world, and Ingmar Bergman doesn't miss a beat of this either.

The actress is schizoid, but has projected the split half onto somebody else; the nurse is schizoid by accumulation. One lends a superfluity of personality to the other. Each remains true to her professional role. The giver and the receiver intermingle and devour each other, but then separate again, like some weird bivalve.

This is a very bald account of a very hairy movie. Bergman has brought all his interests together in an extraordinary film. The long Swedish twilight zone between religion and clinical psychology, the dark chapel and the bleached hospital corridor, the intuition of being and nothingness as manifest in the female soul; even the magic-lantern slides that are said to have fascinated him as a boy (the movie has some of the flashing herky-jerkiness of a sleight-of-hand performance). With so much going for him, there is no need for the pointless slamming of doors and lighting of cigarettes. When the girls romp on the mandatory Swedish beach, they mean business.

1967

4 / On Violence

Everybody gets to do at least one violence column before returning to work. The subject was worked over pretty thoroughly in *Esquire* a few numbers back, but it retains an inexhaustible chic. Besides, the craving to write about it on the part of scrawny, pigeon-chested critics is itself part of the violence phenomenon.

"I don't mind a risqué joke so long as it's *really funny*" was the way Auntie used to put it (no joke ever made it, so far as you can recall, but it took many years and some vicious welts before you discovered that), and I suppose you would have to find a similar formula for violent movies.

Granted that you need a passing strong stomach to go to any movie these days, with skulls splitting across the seams and eyeballs dropping like chestnuts in even the mildest of them, certain distinctions are still worth making. "Violence belongs, it's American," to paraphrase the old beer ads, so total prohibition is probably out; the choice lies between good violence and bad, my kind and yours. Non-violent gangster movies and Westerns may some day be concocted, like vegetarian lamb chops, but I can't see junior buying them—not with his record, not with his tastes.

So all we can do is make sure he gets a clean bomb. This

lets out *The Penthouse*, the latest scraping from England, right away. *The Penthouse* belongs to that seediest of genres, the lubricious sermon. See how decadent our young have become, watch them rape each other—yea, brethren, watch closely. This device sells a lot of newspapers in countries where people are embarrassed to take their vice straight, but remains an indifferent art form. Man who wants to make a decadent film will do a better job if he admits that that is what he wants to do, that decadence grabs him, the way Sadie Thompson grabbed the Reverend Davidson, and not pretend that he is making it under protest and in the public interest. An artist's opinions are his own business; what matters to us are his reflexes.

There are some non-violent things to be said about *Penthouse*, and we may get back to that some day, but meanwhile I would cite this as one of the illegitimate uses of violence. The director Peter Collinson has thrown in a sanctimonious program note (on the press sheet) about all the decadence going around —for all the world as if he were in some other line of business himself. Peter Watkins's intellectually lamentable movie *Privilege* (discussed in this space some centuries back) spouts its indignation higher and truer, because Watkins is a true Puritan and not a camped-up imitation, and he doesn't dally in Miss Thompson's cabin.

Second cousin, or idiot nephew, to Horrible Example violence is Righteous, or Good Guy, violence, the kind where the detective pistol-whips some enemy of society to a jelly. This is excessively obscene because it is sadism with the brakes off. Having been given some good reason to loathe the victim, we can sink our boot into his flesh along with Officer Duffy and, even while our man is squealing like a rabbit, we know we are doing the Lord's work.

To get angry at the violence in *Bonnie and Clyde* is, in contrast, to misdirect one's quota of spleen badly. In that admirable movie, pain is shown in two aspects: the unreal pain that a child deals out when he says, "Bang bang, you're dead," and the reality when he is hurt himself. When Bonnie and Clyde shoot people, it is all in fun, just like an old gangster movie; when they are hit themselves, reality floods in on them. Significantly, it is after this first strike that Clyde becomes sexually potent for the first time. It is not Bonnie's poetry that does this, but his initiation into the world of feeling via pain.

What distinguishes this violence from the usual Good Guy variety is, of course, our sympathy for the victims. This keeps our balance of powers in order, love against death. When virtue and brutality are on the same side, there is no court of appeal and the victim is literally in hell. When they clash, as in *Bonnie and Clyde*, our feelings are mixed. We still enjoy the victim's pain, but not too much. This harsh verdict on ourselves seems inescapable: we *do* enjoy the pain; otherwise there would be no violence problem at all. But our enjoyment is monitored by pity. This is the best most of us can hope for right now.

The alternative to closeness and identification is to distance yourself as far as possible from the action: to emulate the infantilism of Clyde Barrow, with all its implications of personal impotence and irresponsibility, and to deny outright the reality of other people's pain. No harm in this, necessarily. Art doesn't mind performing these messy functions for you, making representations of your more squalid wishes, fashioning voodoo dolls for you to stab or cry over and renting you fantasies of adultery, sloth, gluttony or whatever the local crowd needs. Only for a Puritan is miming a sin the same thing as the sin itself. But in the case of violence, it must be decided whether pity is the point or not; and if pity is not the point, it must further be arranged that no pity is felt. Which means, in a humane society, that the victim be kept as remote as possible.

This distancing of violence is something akin to what happens in pornography. The good bourgeois pornographer understands that his readers will peep at strangers making love, where they would hesitate to peep at friends. Hence, it is pornography's business to make sure that you never become friends with the performers. Human distinctions must be kept blurred, like the features in a stag film: even fictional functionaries have a right to privacy. Besides, if you do get to know them even a little bit, you are out of the tight little realm of pornography altogether. (If you *were* to watch friends making love, your response would be much more complicated than your response to strangers, even, if you like, more "literary.")

So too with pornographic violence. The essence is to keep the victims in silhouette. *The Dirty Dozen* is a fine example of this: the German officers killed at the end are cardboard dummies—too attractive, according to some critics, but certainly not too real. To watch total strangers being knocked off in carloads is the most harmless form of movie violence. (Hence the essential innocuousness of James Bond.) Preferably the killing should also be done briskly and in long shot. A human face mashed in and soaked in blood makes unfair demands. It breaks the childish contract and enlists real feelings, but in a vacuum: the situation is unreal, the person is unreal; therefore the pain has a duty to be unreal too. If the character in the stag movie pauses to tell us that she is doing it to raise the rent for her three retarded children, we don't want her to leave it at that and just go on with the movie. Real pain cannot be used for a walk-on.

So—these would seem to be the basic requirements: the audience must be lined up on the victim's side, if there is real suffering involved; otherwise, if the fun is all in the dishing out, the victim should be a pornographic dummy beyond sympathy. If you don't like to see human beings treated in that way, you are probably quite right—but then you must also argue with a good deal of comedy, all farce, all horror stories, and beyond that the whole idea of theatrical representation, which demands that some human beings be treated as objects and not subjects.

Provided these requirements are met, the question of who is

doing what to whom—whether Americans are killing Germans or Bulgars are roughing up Croats—seems relatively trivial. There are people who worry about things like this, the effect on world opinion of, say, films like *The Dirty Dozen,* but that can only be because they take world opinion for a bigger damn fool than it is. That most armies, ours and theirs, are wretched, unsporting affairs can hardly come as news to any alert citizen. And anyone who isn't onto it by now probably does not swing much weight in the chanceries.

The problem of kids sympathizing with gangsters is one for the criminologists. My guess is that it vexes aging property owners out of all proportion. All my acquaintances grew up sympathizing with gangsters, and you couldn't ask for a milder group. I would be much more nervous about a boy who grew up rooting for the cops, a boy with edifying fantasies. But in any event, we cannot brick up this line of imagery, any more than we can censor people's dreams. The outlaw, however unsympathetically presented, is a powerfully attractive figure; no one can prevent us from joining him in our dreams, or from looting and killing and carrying on in his service. If anything, movies domesticate these impulses, directing them and resolving them acceptably: but undoubtedly such movies are going to set some people off. Somebody is being set off by something every hour of the day. Girls are even ruined by books, Mayor Walker notwithstanding. One must estimate the risks. Violence can be made overpoweringly seductive. Which is why I would seriously consider banning, for minors at least, movies which encourage us to relish pain without sharing it.

Wouldn't we be better off without any representation of violence at all? The answer to that is the old one—we would be better people if we were better people. I would be sorry for a boy who had never seen violence until one day some bully beat him to a pulp; or until, in dreams, he took a knife to his old man. Movies must keep pace with events.

Which came first, the bad movie or the bad dream? People raised in the country will likely remember boys who had never seen a movie behaving with a most sophisticated brutality; and the bullying in English boarding schools certainly needed no encouragement from Hollywood. Violence is there all right, in the bones. Art enables us to look at it in detachment and semireality, to ponder its aesthetics, and to learn something about our own reactions to it (the shock of finding we enjoy it, the relief of finding we don't). A movie industry that did not provide this service in America would be even more remote and artificial than the one we have.

The question of squeamishness deserves special treatment. I used to wonder, while staring bravely at those full-color photos of intestines and tripes in *Life* magazine, whether I really had a duty to know about my intestines: there was no question, I was as guilty as anyone of maintaining one of these greasy complexes inside me, but it was a fact I preferred not to face. So too with the various disembowelings and mutilations that flash across our screens; one's distaste is at least partly a distaste for human flesh in any but its more conventional forms. Unlike the medical student who faints at his first operation, we can flatter ourselves by putting our dismay down to simple distaste for cruelty; but sometimes I think we don't mind the cruelty half so much as the exposed flesh.

Anyhow, grotesquerie of this type is most often found in a kind of movie that is seldom attacked any more by our moral guardians, if indeed it ever was: the traditional horror movie. Here the violence is so steadfastly fantastic that human psychology is not involved at all, and appearance is everything. This is a realm of super-pornography, in which human characteristics are all but abandoned and unimaginable horrors can be permitted. In the recent movie, *Games*, for instance, we have what looks like a nasty face injury, eye shot away and all that, but never fear; the eye may be real but its owner is not. Also, the wife is driven methodically crazy with fear, like Ingrid Bergman in *Gaslight*, but the insanity is superficial. (*Games*, by the by, is a poor horror movie on any terms, signaling its tiny secret miles in advance; but even a good one would be bound by the same laws.) There can be no pain in the horror world, only hideous grimaces. Only the sights and sounds of pain.

Finally, outright sexual violence, or sadism proper, probably requires separate discussion. It is widely maintained that all violence is sexual, even, presumably, the bombing of cities, but I refer here only to that kind which causes specific arousal by contemporary community standards etc., etc. (beasts and perverts are on their own). Complication here is that a mime of a sexual act is a sexual act in the sense that the mime of a murder is not a murder. A stab can be faked, but a lifted skirt is a lifted skirt. But we'd better not get on to that stuff or we'll be up half the night.

Why is violence booming at the moment? There are a few non-political explanations besides the old state-of-the-world stuff. We have, for instance, more leisure to enjoy it now—all our pleasures must grow to fill the space. It is also easier to distance ourselves from pain than it used to be, since it is now almost possible to live a whole lifetime without it ourselves; like savages, we are fascinated by this alien experience, this strange dance people do when they are hurt. My guess is that the great consumers of violence are not themselves dealers in it but full-time onlookers in the last of the great American spectator sports. And finally, the art itself has improved so much; screen violence is far prettier than it used to be, a regular ballet; and technology has opened a treasure trove of methods that has to be explored to the bottom.

1967

5 / *Les Carabiniers / How I Won*

the War / Cinéma Vérité

Nnot for me, the relentless pounding of
the Film Festivals; as soon read three novels a day for a week;
the raw celluloid burns your eyes and coats your tongue in no
time. However, a modest sampling, supplemented by pathological
eavesdropping, suggests that the New York Film Festival proved
this year what it proves every year: that we aren't missing much
the rest of the time, but that we are missing something, and that
anyway it is good clean fun to clank up and down the glass
corridors of Lincoln Center with the international set, Roberto,
Alain, and the gang from Poland.

There were several anti-war films on hand, confirming one's
impression that this is slowly replacing music as the international
language. ("Your people hate war, Ivan? My people hate war
too." "Fine, Joe.") As a film genre, it seems limited—although it
takes a master like Jean-Luc Godard to show exactly how
limited. His *Les Carabiniers* wears out the whole vein like a
blunt hypodermic.

The reasons are not far to seek. Film, by necessity, can deal
only with the phenomenology of war, not its substance. It is
next to impossible to dramatize the warm-water port or the
mining rights that brought the whole thing on, let alone any
niceties of ideology: so your standard anti-war film disguises its

limp, its limitations, by suggesting that motives don't matter anyhow, that they are always equally silly, and that war is so horrible no motive would be good enough for it: two arguments, one good and one so-so, jumbled and commingled in the undeveloped areas that most directors use for heads.

Godard's attack is quite traditional. He takes the killing and looting to *be* the motive, and to hell with the warm-water port. Two French hillbillies are recruited on the understanding that they will be allowed to set fire to women and drive Maseratis, which is what war always comes down to in the end. Then, as they go bounding off on a weird campaign that takes them through Egypt and Mexico (Godard's little joke), they send home postcards, rapturously describing the atrocities they are getting a chance to commit, their big break at last after all those dull years on the farm.

This is what movies do best: never mind what war is supposed to be about, this is what it is. Existentialism is the official philosophy of movies. What matters is what's happening on screen: this child being killed, that woman being raped; what doesn't matter, because it doesn't photograph so well, is why it's happening. For movies, all war is the same war. Or, to put it McLuhanly, it doesn't matter which program you turn to, France vs. Germany, Egypt vs. Israel—the slaughter is still the message.

Godard lumbers into this hoary nest of concepts as though no one had ever been there before. He discovers ironies that go back to Homer, and shakes them until they rattle—which raises the old Godard question. It is, I guess, possible for a movie director to get by on the literary sensibility of a fifth-rate Armenian novelist, provided he keeps away from literary turf altogether; but when he blunders like this into the world of words and ideas and fictional forms, he had better send for help. Truffaut, Godard, and Antonioni have all come to grief lately over defective literary ideas. In their best early work they had each appeared to bypass literature; but literature has been getting its own back.

The trouble is that they don't always recognize a literary problem when they see one. *Les Carabiniers* is the equivalent of a terribly banal novel, and Godard doesn't know it because presumably he doesn't know novels. Fortunately, his claque at Lincoln Center seems to be in similar case, and they stare open-mouthed as Godard rediscovers the wheel and the steam kettle.

Richard Lester (to leave the Festival for a breather) would not make such a horrible mistake. Lester has a precise sense of the medium and never strays an inch from it. *How I Won the War* is not about a real war at all, but about the phony wars that scamper alongside the real ones—that is, the entertainment war, the rhetoric war, the home-front-morale war. He has taken these and superimposed them helter-skelter on scenes of actual agony, producing a bloodcurdling collage, funny only because you can't have a war without fun, can you, love? Fun is a big war industry.

Lester's main target is the war movie itself. His thought, extrapolated from many earnest press conferences, seems to go like this: since movies can only deal with the surface of war, you would suppose that the form would be, by its nature, anti-war. He is outraged therefore to find that, by a multimillion-dollar distortion, the movies have gone against nature and glorified war beyond the wildest ravings of General Patton.

Lester is trying, in one movie, to reverse this whole process. His method, loosely described, is to concentrate on one of those small, synthetic groups that the movies employ to make war seem simple, warm, and human, and to alternate their totally unreal doings with newsreel shots, showing the same men isolated in vast groups being mowed down in the waters of Dieppe, having their brains shot out over Arnhem, or their legs mangled, or their privates blown off: always in bitter anonymity.

Lester has a problem here, because there was of course a real

World War II as well as a phony one, and he seems to be de-
bunking real pain as well as its ethereal movie counterpart, and
also (such are the inscrutable twists of commerce) to be exploiting it himself as black entertainment. These risks seem to me
inevitable, and Lester has done his best with them. To his credit,
he has chosen an attractive war to pick on, rather than a silly
mythic one like Godard's. World War II, he has said off-screen,
was a pretty good cause. Yet it grew, on its own juice and
energy, into something just as monstrous as a bad cause would
have. A war doesn't remember why it was born, it only knows
that it is having a good time.

Lester's own use of violence comes as a series of grotesque
shocks to the system, rather than as the well-prepared, quasi-
erotic climax that it is in most war movies. His troupe of strolling
soldiers do a snatch of *In Which We Serve*, and another from
Desert Victory, showing their wonderful Cockney humor and
British pluck until their real-life counterparts catch a bullet and
the dance ends abruptly. The use of a real bullet, artistically
speaking, instead of a stage one runs the blood cold.

The movie is admittedly propaganda, an anti-recruiting
poster which assumes you have already heard the other side.
Lester's point is that the charm of war must be discredited
somehow or other, by showing it drunk and sick and imbecile:
otherwise, the seduction will be renewed indefinitely. He shows
heroism to be pathetic on the scale of a modern war—argue with
him about that if you like. At least his version is less of a cheat
than the Hollywood one, in which Errol Flynn really matters:
the myth that you will die propped in the arms of an admiring
buddy, which keeps war in a nice way of business.

Where Lester does go wrong, to my taste, is in making his
movie too parochially English. He has said, in answer to this,
that you have to start with some army, and that's right: Godard's
Little People from the land of Y have told us all they know. But
in bearing down so hard on British Army particularities, Lester

has gotten his feet all tangled up in the old class-system business. The officer class, in the person of Michael Crawford, cannot see a body of water without falling into it; in fact, cannot stand up without falling down. This is a private joke, and a dull one. Officers may be murderously stupid, but to spend two hours emphasizing their physical clumsiness is a waste of at least one hour and fifty-eight minutes.

The other sense in which the film is too English is in its actual texture, that sense of madcap improvisation, of aren't-we-having-fun, that blights so many English comedies. Instead of the smooth, deadly attack of *Strangelove*, we get another joke-book thrown at us. The movie bogs down in the desert sand for, I would guess, about half an hour, while Lester rams through a whole variety show of army gags; then pulls itself together and returns to its melancholy attack. As his one-shot assault on war, Lester has overcrowded his movie outrageously, put in everything he knows, with the result that you have to like some of it, and couldn't possibly like all of it. (Incidentally, to answer the second question everyone asks: John Lennon is adequate.)

If *cinéma vérité* had existed at the turn of the century (as opposed to the good old *cinéma mendacité*), the archives would bulge by now with films of Caruso talking to his manager, Dame Melba twitting her friends, Paderewski jogging thoughtfully to work, etc., a trove of trivia. As it is, we have to make do with Bob Dylan, doing more or less the above, exhaustively as a *New Yorker* profile, in *Don't Look Back*.

This kind of celebrity fetishism probably makes more sense with Dylan than with most people, because his art is his life, or vice versa, a seamless gesture throughout. But if we didn't know this, and had nothing to go on but this movie, we might take him for a rather average wise guy, a Bobby Darin for highbrows, working full time at his role, with a nasty habit of bullying his intellectual inferiors and pulling his celebrity badge on them. Dylan's put-downs sound snappy for a while, until we recognize their mechanical nature, a mass-produced stream of quibble and negation ("I'm not a pop singer . . . why should I communicate with you?" etc.). Perfectly okay for around the house, but not perhaps worth immortalizing on film.

The trouble with this kind of movie, as with this kind of journalism, is its gelid, indeterminate quality: this is not the best of Dylan, nor is it precisely the worst. It's just this film that we happen to have. The viewer, who looks for some principle of selection, is sniffing up a cul-de-sac. For instance, why is Joan Baez, the ultimate camp-follower, depicted in her one scene as the butt of another camp-follower's nasty crack? Meant to tell us something? Probably not. If the film had a conscious purpose, it could only be to make Dylan look bad, and this I doubt.

Unless (you never really know with this kind of journalism) Pennebaker is playing a double game: inventing a spoiled punk out of a serious artist. Certainly he makes a bum out of Dylan's business manager, whom he portrays as a slimy, avaricious toad straight out of Ben Jonson, revealed here in pornographic-financial action, scratching and whinnying for more money for his boy, one of the most indecent sights ever filmed. There are, also, some fair samples of Dylan's ranting incantations, which musically have all the charm and variety of an Andy Warhol movie, but verbally are haunting, opening doors in back of the brain and letting the old cats out. The only music in the film is provided by Donovan, in an interesting eyeball-to-eyeball with Dylan.

Another specimen of *cinéma vérité* which makes one want to take the hand camera and hand-flush it to hell and gone is Peter Whitehead's *Tonight Let's All Make Love in London*, another Festival item. The thesis, presented with the inevitable protective irony (like a fat soldier advancing behind a thin sprig of camouflage), is that swinging England is at heart empty and muddled. Whitehead's means of conveying this truism, besides his own execrable photography which can hardly be blamed on

England, is a series of close-up interviews with such inarticulate spokesmen of the New Thing as Julie Christie, Michael Caine, and a chap who paints on live bosoms.

The result is like a prolonged Eisenhower press conference. "Happiness is, sort of, well, pleasure," I think I heard Miss Christie say, between squirms. What it all proves is hard to say. Even in the age of Pericles, most people probably had a sticky time justifying their lives philosophically, especially actors and chest painters. To badger them about it then or now is a low form of sport, worse than bear-baiting. Whether England swings with vitality, or like a corpse on the end of a rope, Julie Christie would be the last to be able to tell you. This kind of meaningless social commentary is catnip to *cinéma vérité* and I fear we're in for a heap of it. The desperately honest camera work compels trust the way the first printing presses must have, and we have yet to develop antibodies to the possible thesis-mongering that goes with it. Peace to André Bazin—nothing lies like the camera.

1968

6 / In Cold Blood

W̲HAT THEY'VE DONE IS TAKEN TRUMAN CA-
pote's whatchamacallit and made a non-fiction movie (or something) out of it. Which means, if Truman has a run-of-the-play
contract, that Perry Smith and Dick Hickock, the Kansas killers,
may soon find themselves financing yet another glittering bash
for The Beautiful People. It would probably please their particular temperaments to know that crime does pay someone. Their
own cut was, of course, forty dollars and a rope.

The movie is admirably plain and I almost said uncluttered—
a sick Freudian slip if ever I showed one. Outside of that slickest
of clichés, the splicing of sounds (door slam turns into roaring
motor, woman's scream turns into police siren, etc.), the director, Richard Brooks, has been at some pains to erase his own
fingerprints and to make his film artless, almost featureless.

The result is simple truth, something so rare and strange
in the movies as to be aesthetically thrilling. Anyone planning a
movie about homicidal punks will henceforth have to use *In
Cold Blood* as his standard. The speech patterns are right—
Capote's weird, gnome-like sensibility recorded the very thought
waves of his subjects and left Brooks a treasure trove. The
physical movements are right. Even the motions of violence,
which are as rigidly stereotyped on film as the dotted-line move-

ments of love, are freshly choreographed here. And they are not falsified by panting close-ups or look-ma-I'm-acting pauses. Hickock and Smith are not movie people at all, except in the sense that we are all movie people. They belong to the world of build-your-strength ads and add-inches-to-your-bosom ads, the world of lower-middle-class fantasy and withdrawal.

Unfortunately, the movie stabs itself lightly in the back in the last reel by tacking on a vague Civics I message about capital punishment. This serves to remind us that we are at the movies, after all. *In Cold Blood* is not really about capital punishment—equating the state's execution of Smith and Hickock with their execution of the Clutters is two-bit irony: the two crimes are quite separate and distinct, except for the cold blood.

The movie finally hasn't the outsize guts it takes to admit that it isn't about anything at all, in the usual sense: it is a straight rendering, à la Flaubert. You do not take sides, any more than you take sides in *Madame Bovary*. You may have been wondering about meaningless violence: well, this is how it works. And nothing for *you* to get righteous about.

Hickock and Smith are superficially just like everyone else; there is very little for our indignation to grab onto, except that the sense of unreality all of us bring to something—Vietnam, famine in India, whatever our pet turn-off may be—they can bring to anything. Murder is as morally neutral as whipping a prostitute is to one man or biting his nails is to another. There is no appeal against this fathomless indifference. If someone like that wants to kill you, Little Nell and Clarence Darrow couldn't talk him out of it. You might as well argue with the Pentagon.

Mr. Brooks conveys this so well in scene after scene that it is abnormally churlish to quarrel with his conventionally "thoughful" ending—which, thanks to the art that has gone before it, is completely tinny and ineffective anyway. To find two actors who look like the originals (Scott Wilson and Robert Blake) and then to find that they can actually act is the kind of luck that such virtue deserves. Perry Smith's fantasies are not always too convincing: the one where he plays his guitar to empty tables is trite and movie-ish. But outside of that, there is hardly a false note in more than two hours. The banality of evil has found itself an epic.

1968

7 / The Hippie Revolt / 491 /

The Stranger

RECENT BULLETINS ON TODAY'S YOUTH OUT OF
Sweden, California and Lower Zambesiland reveal him to be,
among other things, brutal, callow, cynical, trusting, lovable,
and desperately honest. It is good to know these things about
today's youth in case you ever actually meet him. You will
know right away to pull a knife and hand him a lump of sugar.

This year's stretch-your-mind-with-a-new-idea prize, be-
stowed for seizing every characteristic known to mankind since
the Flood and identifying it with modern youth, goes to a
breathy little item called *The Hippie Revolt*. This one will
certainly jerk you alert on your prayer mat: it shows scenes of
wild dancing, and body painting, and flower-picking, and peace
rallies as if they were all being done by the same kids on the
same day. A hectic schedule, this copping out.

Such giddy roundups are best left to the news magazines
where they are neutralized by the hopeless prose. Film impresses
without trying; and it is getting to be a bad joke setting the old
folk atremble once more with flashing images and howling sound
tracks. It might be explained that at least some of the kids in this
film are trying to get away from the noise the other ones are
making.

The Kingdom of Cop Out has many mansions, and it is

unclean billiards to lump the recluses with the exhibitionists, the nature crowd with the electricians, and then accuse them all of being conformists. You might as well say that Bertrand Russell and Dwight Eisenhower are typical examples of older men. On top of that, such socio-hokum movies tend to seek out the most cretinous spokesmen from each group and encourage them to mumble stray nothings about, you know, the scene and what's happening, baby, and the other chin dribble we've come to insist on.

The Scandinavian picture is, of course, incomparably blacker. The world's scurviest teenagers appear to cluster about Stockholm. The ones in *491* (a bad film to see but a good one to talk about) have incurable acne of the spirit. Where an American director would spend heap footage explaining how they got that way, a European of the old school will simply take them as read. Bad boys are a fact of nature; they come along every once in a while like tree blight, and have to be sprayed or burned out.

In *491*, a young social worker attempts something a little more personal, and gets eaten alive for his pains. He takes a bunch of delinquents into his house and showers them with Christian forgiveness and they wind up pawning his piano. It is the old story of the Christian getting his other cheek stove in, and it is told with zest and not much intelligence (Christ never commanded anyone to be a sap: to serve booze to alcoholics or leave the cookie jar open). But even when the Swedes are making exploitation films they seem to bring to them a certain gloomy conviction born of moral insomnia. The social worker is really being punished because he has kept one room of his house (soul) to himself. Then later, to redeem his piano, he takes money from a prostitute, willfully blinding himself to how she earned it. So he has not been a Christian at all and all bets are off. (Those boys would have got him anyway, even if he were a Moslem, but that's a different parable.)

It is interesting to find moral issues still dealt with in straight biblical terms in a frankly commercial film. It gives one a clue to the Swedish climate and to Ingmar Bergman's personal weather as well. For those with no patience for such guff, *491* also throws in a couple of the most sickening sex scenes yet filmed, including one not shown in this country in which a woolly dog is pressed into service by the fun-loving urchins and taught to turn a new kind of trick.

Final youth movie, before returning to our checkers over the cracker barrel. Albert Camus's *The Stranger,* the prophetic masterpiece about cool and honesty and all the other postwar surplus. Marcello Mastroianni is a mite old and shaggy-looking for the part of Meursault. But we have seen, since Camus started this particular ball rolling, so many burned-out, fresh-frozen late adolescents that it is high time they were played by older men. (Sir John Gielgud would make a much more convincing adolescent than most of the ones you see around these days.)

To match Mastrioanni's natural air of exhausted befuddlement, Luchino Visconti has reconceived all the book's main scenes slightly. But he has kept the two main things—the setting and the weather. A movie cannot show the inside of a man's mind, but it can show what he sees, and this can be decoded and arranged into thoughts. Meursault's indifference to what society assures him is important comes to us in the form of a weather report: it is a species of sunstroke. His refusal to pretend is partly a heat-drugged laziness, partly a bleaching clarity of mind, like the harsh whiteness of Moorish architecture.

Visconti has conveyed marvelously well, with splendid use of color and lighting, at least some hint of Camus's obsession with the Algerian sun. When Meursault commits his absurd crime, it is in a shimmer of heat. Languid, restless, hallucinating just a touch, Meursault empties his whole gun into the victim, where one bullet would have sufficed, or none. He does not know why. It was the sun, he explains. Society can make nothing of such answers, society doesn't recognize crimes of weather.

The courtroom scene is extravagantly ridiculous, but with, I believe, a possible purpose. A colonial courtroom has a peculiar unreality about it. Colonial institutions are usually parodies of the real thing, just as Colonel Blimp is a parody of an Englishman, or, as, let's say, a Philippine version of Groton School would be a monstrosity. An imported culture is a distorted one, and the courtroom scene is hardly more bizarre than a Pakistani talking BBC English. Furthermore, a colonial citizen has an absurd relation to government power. Meursault's judge represents a ramshackle society, held together with sticking plaster and menace. This is the society in which Meursault has been formed. Now it is come to judge its baby. This slightly overdone scene reminds us how hard Visconti had to squeeze the book to find cinematic equivalents for Meursault's sense of absurdity, and how shrewdly he has used what was there.

The chic thing now in movies is to show a man's interior by frisking the camera around like a puppy, as he walks, trots, or canters past buildings, blurred crowds, etc. *The President's Analyst, The Producers,* and *Sebastian* are just three recent examples of this pretty device. This does establish mood, often the wrong one, and sometimes situation, but no one ever got far inside a character that way. Visconti does it the old way with concrete scenes, and by using an actor with an actual face (Mastroianni) to help him along. The result is one of the best films of last year.

1968

8 / The Hour of the Wolf

To lay a huge flopping and kicking prejudice right out on the table—I do not believe that Ingmar Bergman can make a bad movie. If I see one I don't like, that's my mistake. Eyes need testing, lobes need tightening, all that. It has only happened once, but I can tell you, I was scared.

His latest, *The Hour of the Wolf*, is not so rich in ambiguity as *Persona*. Once you have cracked the code on the cereal box, that is all you are going to get: a short, sharp statement from the Chinese. Yet it is phrased as exquisitely as anything in the whole Bergman canon.

The subject, narrowly stated, is artists' wives—should they or should they not try to share their husbands' mental worlds? Should the sickness of creation be spread around, or should the artist have his shivering sweats alone? in the arms of women who don't understand, the Nora Barnacle Joyces, the thickarmed tough peasants?

The wife in *Wolf* tries to save her husband from insanity by assuming his obsessions herself. But, unfortunately, she begins to envy the obsessions instead—*because she finds she is not one of them.* This must be part of what Bernard Shaw meant by the eternal rivalry between the artist and the woman: he wants a wife and not an obsession; but she cannot bear that he be obsessed with anything more than he is with her. She comes out thrashing his dreams and memories, tearing the eyes of his muse, obsessed now as much as he is, but without his method of relief —creation.

What gives the movie especial interest is that Bergman includes in the artist's world not only his explicit subjects, but also his relation to the public: which becomes, after the necessary private distortions, a subject in itself.

The artist (Max von Sydow) is surrounded by a group of phantom parasites, the various aspects that the public takes in the artist's mind: the fatuous questioner, the put-down expert, the aggressive seductress who wants, in the phrase of a friend of mine, "a poet for Christmas": all the people who patronize and truckle, wine and dine an artist and send him home hungry, and generally sap his strength with every device known to necrology, one lethal group with a collective poison all its own.

In the movie, the artist has physically left that world and lives in solitude with his wife, on a stark, beautiful island. But he finds them there, waiting, trapped in his skull; and his wife is there too, arguing with them, shooing them away, treating them as rivals to the death. In a climactic orgy of imagination, he literally tries to shoot this good, interfering woman, to escape all the way into his own world and master it once and for all. His private and public obsessions assemble there for a jamboree: the bird-people he craves to paint, the old lady whose face comes off in her hand, the homosexual inclination that he tried to drown, alongside the grinning, parasitic faces of the patrons, the critics, the vampire fans. As he is about to make love to his ultimate vision, the gorgeous Ingrid Thulin, the laughter overwhelms him.

Not since *8½* have we seen on film the bone-crushing, mind-popping pressure that the artist feels himself to be under, caught between his dreams and the world's demands. Fellini's version was splendidly rich and vulgar: the artist as Jiggs and

Maggie, on top of his other problems. Bergman's is character-istically spare and excruciating. Where Fellini can end up joining the carnival, embracing all women, all pain, all memory in a crazy dance of life, Bergman can only wander off into the woods to die alone, like a wounded animal.

Yet these two directors tend in a curious way to appeal to the same tastes, a kind of Quixote-Panza partnership, the two sides of a single brain.

As for the old perceptual problem—how do I know I'm not dreaming this—Bergman is not the first director to understand that the screen doesn't care, it does not recognize these dis-tinctions, being unreal to begin with. But he is surely the best at sharing this convention with the audience and choking off peevish questions. Mental events and real events form a single weave.

1968

9 / *Thérèse and Isabelle* / *Young Törless*

To see how the sex and exploitation crowd are making out these days, I hied on over to *Thérèse and Isabelle*, the story of a schoolgirl crush. "For mature audiences," advised the sign outside: and a fine mature crowd we looked, my balding colleagues and me, as we adjusted our range finders and peeped around to make sure no one had seen us come in. Two hours later, we were older and wiser still. Because, for all our maturity, we had been had—just the way we used to be in the old days.

The big scene, the one they said couldn't be made, features two feet (or at the most, three) sticking out demurely from in back of an apse or chancel or whatever they call those things, while a slew of giddy subtitles fill in the rest. Anxiety over those feet caused me to take the words in rather randomly, but I'll swear I saw one line that read, "I groped for your mouth—in your hair, in your neck, in the folds of your uniform." Things are marching with difficulty back there, one conjectures.

The school where *Thérèse* takes place is absolutely tops in its field. The students all look like Goldwyn girls, achingly nubile, and the only class we are shown is some species of Biology I, with the teacher solemnly explaining how the sap rises through the stem—the last thing I would bother to tell these girls.

For a slightly more plausible school, and an infinitely better movie, you could try *Young Törless*—which looks from the ads as if it should be called Young Topless, although it is actually one of the more thickly garbed movies of recent months.

It is based, faithfully I gather, on a story by Robert Musil, written in 1906. The theme is the banality of bullying—and also the banality of being bullied. Three boys in an Austrian military school have decided to combine justice with pleasure. They have at their mercy a sneak thief, whom they ought to turn in, but decide to keep for themselves instead. Upon this boy's mind and carcass they proceed to play elegant variations in punishment, testing their sensibilities and his to the utmost, until the cause of the war is long forgotten.

The point is that they are not "natural" bullies, looking for prey. In normal circumstances, they would not have believed they had it in them. Like good little existentialists, they have become bullies simply by bullying; and the victim becomes a victim by being victimized. When Törless, the most sensitive of the inquisitors, asks the latter how he came to be such a sniveling coward, he is seriously perplexed. It wasn't planned, he just began acting like a sniveling coward one day, that's all. Nothing seemed to change: it was terribly easy. That, in fact, is the only thing that bothers him about it—how easy it was.

This is probably the exact truth about school bullying, and possibly about gas chambers as well. But it still has to be established dramatically, and here the movie falls just a little short of perfection. The victim (Basini) is fine. His descent into the comforts of submission, and even of complicity, is absolutely convincing. He would cooperate with his tormentors even if there was nothing in it for him: simply because embracing pain is less strain than resisting it.

The phenomenology of bullying is accurately laid out too, from humble beginnings through seasons of why-stop-now escalation, to the ultimate voluptuous orgy, when either the victim gets killed or maimed, or outside intervention enforces sobriety.

The only thing that does not quite satisfy is the development of the three torturers. This is a little stiff, and we more or less have to be told that it's happening. At the end, Törless gives a little talk about it that comes perilously close to a slide lecture. And then a pat little point is made, about how his mother might have become the town whore as easily as he had become the school bully—not a bad notion in itself, but you can't just leave it hanging there. Circumstance is not the *only* determinant of character. In the exact same situation, some will become bullies, and some won't; ditto victims, and ditto whores. The question, Why *these* particular boys?, is the one that the movie doesn't quite answer.

Which doesn't keep it from being an admirable movie: filmed with an elegant plainness and severity, and graced with three of the best young performers—Matthieu Carrière, Marian Seidowsky, and Barbara Steele—you could wish to see.

1968

221

10 / *Chicago* / *Weekend*

Every once in a while on this job it be-
comes necessary to thrust our pale thin noses above ground and
see what's happening out there—whether the people are imitating
the movies or the movies are imitating the people this year. You
will have read about Chicago by now (one had to scrape writers
off one's shoe out there before retiring), so I won't try to review
that again. But it did suggest a couple of cinematic points that
may not have been raised by the other reviewers.

1. The Chicago cops have been going to the wrong movies.
Bad middle-Cagney lines like "Yeah?" "Yeah." "Keep moving,"
and "Nobody asked you to come" have no place in the 1960's.
Nor is pushing cripples in the chest quite the thing any more.
On the other hand, their leaders show signs of watching their
Godard. There was a fine cop-induced panic on the night before
the Convention that no other director could have thought up. A
bunch of indolent overfed journalists were hustled off the
Michigan Avenue Bridge on the grounds that the gendarmes
were planning to open it like a medieval drawbridge (I don't
even know whether you *can* open the Michigan Avenue Bridge:
it looks pretty solid). We were pushed and chivied another block
for good measure and then five busloads of fuzz drove up and
confronted us solemnly, paws on night sticks, tiny eyes glinting.

"There's plenty more buses where they came from," warned a William Bendix type. The point is that there was not a Yippie in miles, nobody to overreact to but us writers, who in some mysterious way kept rolling up, in our own right, to form a small but ineffectual mob. Writers vs. police, with the middleman, or the criminal, completely eliminated. It was perfect *nouvelle vague* satire.

2. The pols should certainly lay off old Broderick Crawford movies for a spell. Quivering jowls are out. The Governor Shapiro model, squat and rubbery, is out. Hubert Humphrey is —well, what can I say? Mayor Daley, on the other hand, is slightly ahead of his time. The American family is not ready for that kind of language yet. Let His Honor ask himself this: would he want one of his cops to hear it? He complained several times that these daintily nurtured goons were subject to vile obscenities, which caused them to club people. They're only human, boasted the Mayor. Well, let him remember that Senator Ribicoff is only human too. And so are all those mothers out there in TV land.

3. Now, as to the protesters: I would suggest that we have here two types of movie creatures. One, the existentialists, or now-people, out of *La Chinoise* by *The Graduate*, led by the likes of Abbie Hoffman. "Revolution for the hell of it" is the password. They like the atmosphere of revolution, the luminous coblestones and crowd noises, the quick dash at the barricade, and the bandage round the head the next day. This *is* revolution. The rest is an effing bore for these children of quick cuts and trick photography.

The others, the classicists, get their kicks precisely from the sense of planning and purpose, like the thieves in *Rififi*.

In one sense they are the more old-fashioned, thinking in a straight line and all that. Yet I believe that they made converts in Chicago. Being beaten and tear-gassed is hot communication, hence unacceptable to the TV generation. My guess, talking from back in my movie manhole, is that as revolution becomes more specific and practical, the administrators of it will come to seem more romantic, the rabble-rousers less so; and that the next batch of movies on the subject will be cooler and quieter in consequence. *The Battle of Algiers* is the prototype—and who is to call that an old-fashioned movie?

Going a step further while the prophecy mood is on: as the New Left becomes more rigorous it will be more puritanical, and its weak links with drug-mystics will weaken still further. Just as the Irish Republican Army had to leave its drunken poets at home, so the New Left will have less time for people who crave a revolutionary high. The alliance, political and aesthetic, between the rebels and the freak-outs was always a marriage of convenience; and since the former tend to bore the latter and the latter to pointlessly endanger the former, their mutual dislike of the System may not hold them together much longer. A look around Grant Park showed how ill-assorted they already are, at least as a battle line. The cultural effects of this split could be interesting, and not only in movies.

The Chicago follies could also help to form an audience for more sophisticated political films, not Looney Tunes fantasies about the takeover of Fascism or teenagers or whatever spooks you, but movies with at least as much respect for reality as the gangster movies are required to show. After all, politics is just as much of a profession, and it has its rights.

It was Godard himself who said that "a tracking shot is a political statement." (Remember when they used to compare everything with sex? Ah, what Gaullism has wrought.) It's too bad Godard ever heard about Politics, because he insists on dragging it round with him everywhere he goes, like a dead cat, and it is stinking up some pretty good movies for him. (Unfortunately, Godard's political intelligence is of a type to make Abbie Hoffman seem like Bernard Baruch.)

Weekend is actually an extraordinary political movie, until

Politics gets into it. Godard's metaphor for the human race is the French traffic situation. By exaggerating this only slightly, i.e., by having the drivers actually get out and shoot each other, he brings it into line with world history. As evening draws on, the road from Paris becomes a graveyard of smoldering chassis and charred bodies, as from a fire-bomb raid. The hero stumbling among the smoking ruins inquires politely if there is a gas station around here.

It works, as few such satires recently have, because Godard has chosen the right institution to pick on. The lunatic hostility of drivers is only one step away from total war. And when the drivers do pull knives and guns on each other, our minds pass smoothly and without snagging to the larger forms of butchery; and the audience writhes in hysterical assent.

Eventually, Godard has to leave his cars, and one trembles. But he hasn't run out of gas quite yet. His hero and heroine stagger off the main highway and, in a series of elegant vignettes, encounter previous aspects of bourgeois culture—pastoral innocence, eighteenth-century rationalism, classical art—all dead of boredom or exploitation or some wild eruption of violence. We are running back through history, a path strewn with movie directors' bones, but Godard almost makes it.

Until, that is, he makes the mistake of looking back. At that point, he decides he had better tell the audience what they have just seen. So he embarks on one of those mock-readings in political science that finally made such a jaw-popping yawn of *La Chinoise*. If the lecture is funny, it is not funny enough; if serious, not serious enough. Is political science another burned-out bourgeois conceit? Would that Godard thought so. But even if he did, a long dull reading would not be the way to make the point. For a man so noted for cinematic sensibility, it is surprising how often he allows words to unstring him.

It is hard to pick up the movie once the director has put it down. But one must plug on. With capitalist society decimated

by its own machines, the survivors are taken in tow by maraud-
ing hippies, students of revolution. This gang then plunges
doggedly back through prehistory, to the birth of fetish and
taboo—thinly connected to present hippie practice by beads,
body paint, and such.

One might suppose that Godard would relish the downfall
of the bourgeoisie (now I can make my films!), but not a bit of
it. His Third World revolution simply takes us back to savagery
and cannibalism. The viciousness was not a capitalist invention
after all, but a human invariable. It is interesting that the National
Catholic Film Office, upholders of the Doctrine of Original Sin,
have denounced *Weekend* as too much, as having crossed the
line into anti-human. They are absolutely right.

This thoroughgoing pessimism might be impressive, but
Godard just seems to be playing at it. The last part is a charade,
a demonstration. His hippie-primitives are not derived from
real people as his ravening drivers were, but are a weird and un-
convincing composite of guerrilla fighters, freak-outs, and
Hottentots. At this point he is just being cute. What started
out as a majestic diatribe against humanity has become formula
satire, predestined to turn out the way he wants it to. Half a
good film was nothing to complain about in this particular festival; but the second half is so full of contempt, black nihilism,
and fascistic cruelty that one wished the director knew what the
hell he was doing.

1968

II / *The Birthday Party*

The BOOMLET IN HAROLD PINTER MOVIES IS HARD to explain. Since his little chess games do not exhaust even the resources of a small stage (most of them could be played out in an egg crate), they constitute a dismal waste of a wide screen. *The Caretaker,* currently revived after an earlier snub, achieves some small sense of motion, mainly by busting from one room to another and back, and even out into a hastily thrown-in back yard; but *The Birthday Party* scarcely moves at all, scarcely breathes. A spurious car scene and a vista of deck chairs do not a movie make.

Beyond that, one exposure to Pinter's obsession every three years fulfills most minimum adult requirements. After which you find yourself saying, yeah, yeah—nameless menace. *The B.P.,* one of his first plays, states more clearly than most what is on his nerves; the development of his art since then has consisted mainly of fuzzing his message and of burying it in different parts of the room.

The nameless menace this time around comes to you courtesy of an Irishman and a Jew: let's just call them the Judaeo-Christian heritage, shall we? The scapegoat is a would-be musician (Robert Shaw) holed up in a boarding house far from home—let's call him the artist in the modern world and be done with it. The story consists of a visit by the J.-C. establishment (they can always find you when they want you), followed by a harrowing initiation ceremony, at the end of which, in perverse imitation of baptism, the artist is born again as a brainwashed square. Hence the title.

So crass a use of symbols is not typical of Pinter. In fact, in his subsequent games of blindman's buff he has been known to leave the room altogether while the audience grapples with the grandfather clock. In his painful press conferences, alias dental extractions, he now insists that he has no meaning at all, no symbols, nothing, leave me alone. So although the movie is passing dull, it is useful to have this early leak, before his defenses were complete.

Try it this way. Pinter was a Jewish evacuee from London in World War II. This meant that he had to face the problem of assimilation, by himself, in a series of strange settings, at an age when most boys are concentrating on the best way to keep up their pants. English class apprenticeship is brutal enough if you are born to it. To an outsider like Pinter, it has the extra horror of meaninglessness. In *The Birthday Party*, he acts all this out. The nice lady who runs the boarding house sells him out; so does the girl lodger with whom he had enjoyed an infantile friendship. Well, he never trusted them anyway; translated into adult terms, the artist-scapegoat is a proud suspicious child. He builds no alliances against his masters.

The only hope he has is some crack in the Establishment. The Jew and the Irishman, brain and muscle, are joined only by panic and mutual necessity. It would take very little to pry them apart. But the victim does not have the key. Indeed, it is his presence that holds them together. That's how it goes with institutional life, from empires on down: the top people would probably kill each other if it weren't for the children.

It is not particularly effective to have all this worked out stiffly and laboriously on screen, despite good performances by

Shaw, Patrick Magee, and Dandy Nichols. Pinter himself has since gone further underground, where the self-pity is less visible, where you can't even be dead sure that he hasn't gone over to the master class himself. At those incredible press conferences, he is gnomic, supercilious, timid in such strange proportions that you can't tell whether he is picking on us, or we are picking on him. He is both the new boy and the upper-school tyrant.

Victims have always loved the stage; pity, terror, and revenge, and nobody knows it's you. Pinter was an actor before he was a playwright. It is no accident that his plays are written in code and that he denies to the point of tedium having any intentions whatever; it is as if some big boy's hands were on his throat. "Is this meant to be me, Pinter? Is this supposed to be *clever*, Pinter?" And perhaps it is no accident that for camouflage, and possibly out of admiration too, he learned how to empathize with the bullies himself. In *The Caretaker*, a much better play, the roles are optically interchangeable so that you scarcely know bottom from top. But this small man's judo had not been perfected by *The Birthday Party*, and the dramatic tension of his best work is missing.

1968

12 / The Fixer / The Charge of the Light Brigade / Greetings

If YOU HAPPEN TO BE A STRAY HISTORY PROFESsor, who yearns for a grant as big as a scientist's, it may be in your interest to harp on the ever-green relevance of history. But if you simply want to make good historical movies, it pays to remember that history is seldom all that relevant, except on a simple-minded Great Books level. At first glance, there may seem to be those uncanny parallels between, say, the Bay of Pigs and the Charge of the Light Brigade. But the closer you look, the less alike the two events seem. And by the time you really understand either one of them, the parallels have become the least interesting thing about them. "History repeats itself" is cant from the survey courses. Churchill was closer when he said: "Past experience carries . . . the drawback that things never happen the same way again." History must be loved for its own sweet sake, and not for the lessons it teaches, which are either trite or untrustworthy, or both.

The Fixer is stuck squarely with this problem. It is the story of an anti-Semitic outrage worked under Tsar Nicholas. And before you can get hotted up about that, you have to consider Tsar Nicholas for a moment. Can one make him the universal oppressor? Well, hardly. You don't meet too many Tsar Nicholases, unless your luck is absolutely atrocious. What about the Eichmanns who worked for him. All petty bureaucrats are alike, aren't they? Well, probably no again. Spanish ones hold your papers upside down and snort because they can't make head or tail of them. French ones send you off to the next department. English ones spill tea on your shoes. All three would probably draw the line at castration or shaving the heads of Jews.

Imperial Russia was a somewhat peculiar society, forged in absolutely unrepeatable circumstances. The filmmaker can ignore this, aim for the universal truths, and produce one more superficial costume drama testifying to the endurance of the human spirit. Or he can try to suggest the uniqueness of the occasion, and testify to the variety of the human spirit. This involves moving the audience into fresh imaginative territory, getting them angry over long-dead officials, barmy aristocrats, cavalry officers, etc., whose like we will never see again—a difficult task, but the only way to get at the grain of history. Otherwise, we get mad at the things we're always getting mad at, the Blue Meanies of our own time translated into pig Russian.

John Frankenheimer has used both approaches at once, with predictably mixed results. The Jewish victim (Alan Bates) presumably had to be universalized to justify telling the story at all. (This comes under the heading "Storyteller's Loss of Nerve.") Bates has to say things like "I am a man!" and "What kind of a man am I / I'll tell you what kind of a man I am." Standard Human Condition talk that hardly requires all those period costumes. Track suits would have done as well.

In this atmosphere of contrived uplift, the one point of universal interest—namely, that Jakov Bok does not even *want* to be a Jew, until persecution decides the question for him—comes through a little stiffly. Bok is going to prove a thesis about human nature if it kills him. Yet he and his persecutors are only partly unreal. At times they seem to forget the audience needs of 1968 and they joust with each other in terms of their own crazy times. It is a risk: here we were, feeling vaguely indignant about the Jew in history, and suddenly we are confronted with a piece of parochial foolishness that is hard to take seriously. Yet history is made up of such pieces, strung together, and in these brief moments *The Fixer* is a real historical movie. At others—the conversion of the jailer, the tear-stained meeting with the wife—it is as silly as any of them.

Of the actors, Ian Holm is the class of the outfit. Dirk Bogarde is, as always, ostentatiously sensitive. Bates works hard and now and then almost makes it.

The Charge of the Light Brigade wastes less time on the relevance question—what have stupid generals to tell us about modern America?—but trips heavily over a second hurdle: namely, that history is not always laid out in convenient dramatic form. If you have a stupid man as your central character, you should have at least one semi-bright one to offset him, right? But this was not permitted in the British Army of the period. So Tony Richardson has smuggled one in anyway, and then just left him standing there.

Because Richardson has also tried to stick to the main facts of the case, and his Captain Nolan (who isn't that bright anyway) had practically nothing to do with these. The real story concerns two epic dum-dums, Lords Cardigan and Lucan, vying with each other in feats of dumbness: not exactly a conventional movie script, but if you wanted one of those, why bother with authenticity in the first place? Why not remake *Gunga Din?*

Trevor Howard plays Cardigan so well that it might have worked as low period comedy, although his face keeps threatening to evolve into intelligence. And John Gielgud is splendid as the fuddled Lord Raglan, trying with Ike-like concentration to remember what the Duke of Wellington would have done. A short movie called *The Best of the Charge of the Light Brigade*, running about forty minutes, would be well worth seeing.

Greetings must be one of the first movies to take the graffiti generation for granted. Up to now, we have had speechless awe, mystification, and propaganda all banging away dismally at the same time. Now, at least, this generation is treated simply as what's there, not as some blessed state of transcendence, and in a spirit of good feckless gusto a little reminiscent of *Pull My Daisy* and the Beats.

The absence of self-congratulation is especially bracing. The three young men around whom the film jerkily turns are just as low-down and dirty as their elders, only a little less bashful about it. Their attempts to dodge the draft are as absurd as the draft itself. Never mind the holiness of their cause—they are willing to wear women's underwear, lisp, break their legs, anything to keep out of uniform. They do not reject America, they try to outwit it. And, more often, it outwits them. They are constantly being surprised, as neophytes should be, by furtive pornographers, Bronx secretaries, sex mystics, and their own base appetites, and constantly bouncing back like hard rubber.

Beyond that, their basic style is parody. They take the ponderous mumbo jumbo of, for instance, the Kennedy-assassination theorists and run screaming down the hall with it. Likewise, the cult of photography which has made the Vietnam War into a peep show and the sex act into a lab slide is treated with a wild-eyed derision. The things that adults take seriously become comic dances, festival masques. This is their America, they know no other, but they have turned it into a playground using the same materials we use for our funeral parlor.

Greetings rings true partly because it does have links with the past. There is a nostalgia about it, like good schoolboy fiction, even for those of us who come of age in the glum, knees-together postwar years. They act where we talked, they talk where we just thought. They are not some electronic concoction but college students whose scurviness has evolved to meet new challenges—and, of course, lose to them.

Greetings does not convey its exuberance with a bobbing camera and a garbled sound track. Brain de Palma and Charles Hirsch have made a solid, professional film of it, with obvious debts to Richard Lester *et al.*, but some good touches of their

233

own. I had been coming to feel that any allusion in film to the Vietnamese mess was a sure mark of charlatanism; but this combination of TV war and draftee's nightmare is a whole fresh contribution to international strain.

1969

PART FIVE

1 / *The Minor Novelist*

H<small>E WORKS WITH THE BLINDS DOWN AND HE</small> doesn't believe that James Bond is a spoof, or that Tom Wolfe is a spoof. He believes that they are nuncios from a world of speed and light and flashing colors, where men like himself are liquefied by deadly invisible rays.

He tries to keep away from Sunday supplements which discuss the death of the novel. He has a theory that it is bad luck to read more than three articles on this subject a week. He also steers clear of annual roundups. "A disappointing year for fiction"—that part is all right: but then his own book isn't even mentioned among the disappointments. He is one of those authors who mysteriously don't count. Maybe he should change his name. His present one is a mnemonic disaster.

It is entirely possible that he won't win the National Book Award this year. Possible that he will never be published in French or German. None of this would matter so much if the Novel wasn't dying. But it is curiously embarrassing to be a failure at something that is going out of business. Talk about integrating into a sinking ship!

At his best moments, he thinks of himself as the last of the old-fashioned craftsmen, turning out water clocks or filigreed sleeve garters. His store window, if he had a store window, would overflow with the very best pre-electronic devices, wind-up toys, stuffed divans, teapots. He should get out more and try to keep up. He can't afford to go abroad, but he could at least make it to a discothèque. Get out of the dead world of childhood and memory.

Instead, he reconnoiters the modern world through television. Batman, Bullwinkle and his friends, Soupy Sales. An assault course in irony. Later, when the children grow up, he hopes they will be told what the irony is for. Naturally, he takes all this personally. How can you write for people who start life like that? Everything will always be a gag for them. The twisted version will be the natural version. (A child's first words: "No, but I saw the parody.")

He doesn't want to get worked up about this, because anger pushes him further into the past. But these ironic, electronic children worry him constantly. They are being trained to move quickly, not to care. What kind of novels do you write, either for or about them? Anguish, loss, guilt are for the slow people. To feel these things, you have to have at least taken Batman seriously as a child. You have to have taken *something* seriously.

Newspapers are more reassuring. Newspapers are dying like novels. They resist streamlining, and continue to carry items about, say, heavyweight boxing as if heavyweight boxing still mattered. But the crackle of money in the sports pages is beginning to bother him. At this time of year, especially, it is like walking through an Arab bazaar. Willie Mays signs 150 G pact. Maury Wills holds out for 100 G. (Minor novelist holds out for two big G's, little hope seen.) The golfers are rated now on their money muscle; even the damn horses are referred to as top-money spinners, dollar-grossers, purse-grabbers. And behind that the cackle of the promoters, moving their franchises, signing their quarterbacks, cackle, cackle. It's almost as bad as the book section.

It all makes him nervous. A man without money is slightly

deformed these days. The fuel that keeps the new people moving faster than the speed of worry is money. If you leave a girl by jet plane, the speed whisks her away. Adultery ceases to count the moment you cross the International Date Line. Tragedy is just another name for slowness, for stagnation.

So how can a man write about the new thing when he can't afford to fly to Washington? How can he compete with the adventurer-authors who get paid like ballplayers? Well, that isn't his world of course. There are other worlds—poverty, for instance, for what that's worth. His kind of writing will come back. His editor says so every time they have lunch.

His editor believes in him, along with the reviewer from the Providence *Journal* and a select group of others. (If the club was any smaller, he would be obliged to leave the sinking novel right now. After six novels, he might find himself without a publisher.) The trouble is he has difficulty in believing in his editor.

Ed Filmore has a lot of silly enthusiasms and he has backed a lot of losers. He looks at the lunch bill closely these days, adding to himself, and they don't have brandy any more. Filmore is kept on a tight string by old mother publisher.

Yet the wretched Filmore can still generate little contagions of hope. During the incubating period, while the new book is in the womb of the publicity department, he can suggest phenomenal stirrings of interest. Louis Untermeyer loves it. Haven't heard from Robert Penn Warren yet, but it's just his kind of book. The United Hospital Foundation has ordered two hundred copies.

This ghastly charade still works every time. The ego is gently inflated until it reaches maximum distension and becomes abnormally tender. Filmore passes on nothing but good tidings until the victim is soft with good cheer. And then, bursting through Filmore's filter, come the real reviews, the bored ones, the ugly ones; or, as in the case of his last book, no reviews at all.

Ed Filmore reacts at first with baffled indignation, phasing

off into his own brand of wistfulness; then he seems to with-
draw distastefully from the whole project, as if even he did not
care to associate with such bold-faced disgrace. The lunches stop,
but the damage is done. Enough wind is left in the ego to make
one care about annual roundups, about National Book Awards
and the opinion of Robert Penn Warren that never arrives. Filmore in himself signifies nothing. The publisher shows what he
thinks of Filmore by tiny printings and minuscule advertising
budgets. Yet Filmore can still dazzle you, he has that small power.

Lesser people and hacks might be broken by all this. But
the minor novelist gets a certain sustaining pleasure from this
review of grievances. He has endured, and he has learned. (He
has learned, for instance, that you don't call a book *A Rose at
Dusk*, the title of his last one: it sounded unbelievably fresh and
vibrant at the time, but now it wilts sadly.) His books on the
shelf are like hard-won high-school trophies: the boy with
the flat feet who went out for track and didn't do too badly.

He doesn't *really* believe that the novel is dying. It is too
good for that. Maybe the *public* is dying, that's another story.
But he believes in the novel. When someone like Robbe-Grillet
calls for technical innovation, he doesn't know quite where he
stands. He agrees in principle, but he wonders whether these
people really love the novel as he does, that they should keep
wanting to mess with it. There is a contradiction here that he
cannot begin to resolve.

The odd and encouraging thing is that he knows he is getting better at the traditional novel. He is mastering his quaint
craft, book by book, all the better for being unnoticed perhaps.
He has strong views about the evils of early success, although he
thinks he is perhaps carrying this prejudice to extremes in his
own case. On his desk there is always a pile of papers to mark
and books to review. The books are possibly the greatest threat
to his integrity. It seems too much to ask of a man in his position
that he gratuitously attack, say, Norman Mailer and stir up a
swarm of unnecessary partisans against him. (And then again,

Mailer was nice to him at a party once and remembered his name.) All this seems very petty, and he pushes it sternly aside His fiction reviews are in fact rather notably vinegary, as he wrestles triumphantly with the demon of logrolling.

If he is low in his mind at the moment, it is partly just the time of year, and the pictures that come with it of the jet set sunning themselves, in the pages of *Esquire;* and partly the dying fall of his last novel. It always takes several months to convince himself that it will not live on in paperback, or win an obscure prize, or even be reviewed in the *N.Y. Review of Books.* Once vanity has been deflated all the way, he can start on another round. He is not a naturally vain man.

He wonders whether it might help to be just a mite sexier next time out. Publishers are too delicate to mention it, or even to think it, but he can tell a little horseplay would make them happy. He did try a couple of sex scenes last time, and they just sounded silly, and he tore them up. He has nothing against sex, of course, but it isn't everyone who can write about it. Make a note to try once more. If it arises spontaneously.

These regular poundings have toughened him in all kinds of ways. The really hard pill to swallow, once after each book, is the knowledge that his works will almost certainly be out of print long before he dies. The first two are out of print already. To see a chipped copy in a second-hand bookstore is like visiting your own graveyard. Or, to put it another way, the people in the next apartment still haven't heard of him and neither has his daughter's high-school teacher.

He recognizes a large element of fraud in his reasoning. One lobe of his brain indulges in stoic resignation; the other expects the old-fashioned novel to come back, with himself at the fore. It is not a bad working arrangement, so long as he doesn't allow Filmore to agitate it. But if the optimistic lobe goes up too high, it must later go down for a while, and a period of suffering ensues.

The one thing he has not learned is how to modify this ridiculous process. He has tried going away before publication; and he has tried leaving himself completely in Filmore's hands, reading only such reviews as Filmore chooses to send and trusting to the end in his editor's vaguely bracing reports. But nothing helps. As soon as the bell rings, and the first good word comes in from Louis Untermeyer, or from the girl who typed the manuscript, his ego goes berserk and starts to puff up uncontrollably; he believes, like Hemingway, that he is the champ; he crowds the newstands eagerly, like one of the boxer-writers, closing in for some unspecified kill. And he gets murdered every time.

Outside of that, he believes that his life is probably slightly happier than most people's.

1966

2 / *Private* CHAMBERS *v.*

Public CHAMBERS

A REVIEWER IS NOT, THANK GOD, OFTEN RE-
quired to judge an author on his legal merits. But the strange
warp of Whittaker Chambers's career insists that even a benign
collection of posthumous letters (*Odyssey of a Friend*) must be
read in the gloomy light of litigation. Never mind about his
literary virtue—would the writer of this prose lie under oath
or wouldn't he? When he testified against Alger Hiss, Chambers
went for good from the anonymity of a *Time* editor to a desk
in Macy's window where his words and his personality could
never be separated again.

William F. Buckley, who received the letters in the first
place, bows to the inevitable and introduces them as a character
reference. They are not a bad one at that: certainly better than
Chambers's own floundering attempt at one, the elephantine
Witness. It could be that the subject was more plausible in private than in public; and he was certainly more plausible by 1961,
when the collection ends, than in 1954, when it starts.

The Hiss case was largely a question of character even then
(to younger readers, that is all the question that's left). Long
before the investigation had passed from dentures and protho-
notary warblers to pumpkins and typewriters, the public had
chosen up sides on a basis of Which Kind of Man Do You Prefer.

Chambers knew his revolutionary politics and was able to trace that part of Hiss's support which came from Communist whispers. But, for several reasons, he was not up to date on American psychology, and never saw why at that particular moment a good many people found him hard to take, all on his own.

He was right about one part of it: people distrusted his religiosity. This distrust was supposed at the time to have something to do with the West's rejection of God. But if the Chambers of 1961 had reread *Witness* (he could not bear to see it lying about the house by then), he might have distrusted the religiosity himself. It is very much part of the period: the postwar spirit boom, when all kinds of unlikely people were hearing voices and receiving signs. Chambers himself left the Party because he heard "words," telling him to choose freedom—a motive which even religious sympathizers might now advise him to keep under his hat. And he rested his case against Communism entirely in theology, or holy-war theory, where secular readers could hardly be expected to join him. Later, Max Eastman was to lead a charge against compulsory theism for conservatives: but, at that point, the words atheistic and Communism were seldom far apart.

Curiously, in these later letters there is very little reference to God. Chambers presumably remained a religious man to the end, but the confessional fever subsided, as it did with other converts of the time, and his case against Communism became more earthly. "The West . . . has two main goods to offer mankind: freedom and abundance," we find him writing—a far cry from the days when it offered God, or nothing.

Chambers's religiosity was also served a poor turn by his conditions of employment. As a writer for a news magazine, he had taken it upon himself to reduce his spiritual gropings to simple big-picture terms: the West, History, Man's Spirit, the hundred great capital letters. Most intellectuals would have given up the struggle as hopeless. A news magazine is not obliged to cover the Mysteries. But Chambers had a mission to fight Communism, and this was the only way he could do it. He was shunted out of Foreign News, and anywhere else where he could attack the enemy head-on. So he took to plugging the Western Tradition in Dick & Jane terms in any department that would let him. I had assumed that the florid simplifications were foisted on him by the magazine. But it seems likely that he foisted them on the magazine. And several of the pieces that had one wincing the hardest (e.g., the Arnold Toynbee cover story) were among Chambers's special prides.

The democratization of great ideas was again part of the period, and perhaps it was snobbish to jeer at it. Anyway, people did, and it was part of the extra-legal case against Chambers, which he never seemed to fathom. For he found the habit hard to slip, and there are still great wedges of old-*Time* rhetoric in *Witness*, when he might have come on as the subtle and quite pragmatic thinker that these letters reveal.

For his pains, he acquired a reputation as a dime-store mystic, a *Time-Life* Dostoevsky, who couldn't see anything smaller than History: certainly nothing as small as a microfilm. The narrative parts of *Witness* are reasonably sober and convincing: working on a news magazine is not all bad. But then he would blow it with garrulous metaphors about Western Man struggling up the Cliff, metaphors which he seemed unable to turn off. And the credibility of the quiet parts was seriously damaged.

The rhetoric gets a few brisk airings in the first letters to Buckley: "I never really hoped to do more in the Hiss case than give the children of men a slightly better, only slightly better, chance to fight a battle already largely foredoomed," etc., etc. A fine way to write to a friend. At this point he was still half in public, displaying his wares: the mechanical inflation of everything, the trademarked pessimism, the gaseous abstractions. Just when you're used to thinking of yourself as the West, you find

you've become the children of men and Mr. Chambers is giving
you a second chance. It took no Communist plot to make this
seem tiresome.

But this changes quite sharply as we go along. Occasionally
the rhetoric is challenged into life by some threat to make him
public again. But his usual tone is not only moderate but scrupulously sensible. Hissites will no doubt find stray evidence of de-
rangement, as when he writes seven-page letters and burns them
(Chambers was a great burner), and then writes to *tell* Buckley
he burned them; or when he doesn't open letters he gets himself.
But this jumpiness seems normal enough, unless one disbelieves
Witness altogether. Chambers may or may not have been in danger of murder when he left the Communist Party, but he surely
had reason to think he was. The fact that he was theatrical about
it doesn't mean that it didn't happen. (Theatrical people are always being persecuted.) For a year, he worked at night with a
gun on his table, not knowing whether he was important enough
for execution; not knowing in his bones whether the people he'd
worked with *did* things like that.

This uncertainty accounts for a certain fantastic quality
whenever he discusses revolution in the letters. The American
party was trying to import a European religion, in which assassination was certainly part of the ritual. But had it survived the
journey, the way the Mafia had? Or were the American Communists partly playing at it? Chambers writes about their fanati-
cal dedication unto death. But when a party member came looking for him after his defection, said member gave up after a
nervous glance: with the best will in the world, this pale literary
agent could not make himself into the Mafia type. At that same
time, the period of the Moscow-German pact, European de-
fectors were being gunned down as far west as Paris; but Americans had to imagine themselves into European situations to feel
the same fear.

246

This was not difficult for Chambers, whose mind was always set toward Europe anyway and who was taken for a European by his Communist contacts. His hunters may not have known their roles, but he knew his. These letters long after the event are still packed with anecdotes of gallant European Bolsheviks showing excruciating dedication under fire. It is hard to feel this way about Elizabeth Bentley. But Chambers did his personal best to translate the atmosphere to America, and to incarnate, in himself, the stoic, world-weary Communist he believed in so ardently. Cut off from society, a hunted man in Baltimore, it was not hard for a gifted writer to imagine himself in St. Petersburg.

With so much of the revolution going on in his head, it is not surprising that he jumped when the postman came. A Hissite would no doubt press the point and say that Chambers was a role-player to the core, a cardboard revolutionary living out a dream. A Hissite would also dig out the familiar memory lapses —Chambers could not remember whether he had ever written about a particular man in *Time*, astounding in a writer—and the desolating melancholia, interspersed with skittishness.

Still, the letters would disappoint him, I think. Chambers's role-playing, if that's what it was, included a respect for the small facts, whether as spy or farmer. He took himself deadly seriously in the role of witness and was sometimes unintentionally funny about it. (For instance, after quoting a passage Trotsky wrote in 1902, he pauses to say, "I was then one year and several months of age." Or discussing Randall Jarrell, he says, "Jarrell is as certain a sign of the end as I am." Such portentous self-insertions pop up *passim*.) But in practice, as opposed to talk, he was pretty sensible about it. He declined to become a cocktail-party witness, or a lecture-circuit witness, and he didn't set out his shingle as a permanent oracle. Murray Kempton has pointed out that he did like to suggest mysterious private pipelines when the mood was on him and to become the old revolutionary who knows what he knows. But he also admitted that he was nearly always wrong about American politics, and he indulged in free-wheeling guesses without pretending they were based on any post-1938 party secrets. (Checked out from our present vantage points, they certainly weren't.)

In another respect, these letters clarify Chambers perhaps a little more than he might have cared to be clarified at the time. There are two sides to every revolutionary, and Chambers had chosen to show the visionary, garment-rending one to the secular public. But now he was writing to a Catholic romantic and a change of tactics was called for: the pragmatic, so-what, does-it-work? side, which had nailed Hiss, rhetoric notwithstanding, surfaces all the way for Buckley.

In *Witness*, he had still been facing toward the Communists, barely aware of his own allies. These were just the simple people who phoned and said "God bless you" in the middle of the night; honest, unintellectual folk who understood life's processes. (He was particularly charmed by a gun salesman in Baltimore who recommended aiming both barrels at prowlers and "Fay-ya-you-well.") He did not yet understand that it was his allies who frightened people the most. Cultural wars, quite outside his Communist closed shop, were in progress, and his case managed to land plumb in the middle of them.

After the case, he had more time to look around at his new friends. The first thing he saw was Senator Joe McCarthy, and it was like a convert finding his first difficult doctrine. Swallow as he could, it wouldn't go down. He hadn't given up Communism to range himself with Yahooism. It might even have occurred to him at this point that simple people who call in the night are not necessarily well-wishers.

Next he found Mr. Buckley, and that worked out much better. These two devotees of the simple folk were able to swap high culture and enough good argumentation to keep an ex-Marxist sharp. The intellectual training of Marxism can make the Right a lonely place, and a man who knows his St. Thomas is a windfall. "You are articulate (rare on the Right)," he says. No matter what you think of pink professors and the like, it is always disconcerting to find that your side is dumber than theirs. "Think of it," he groans. "In this great power, the Right can find no voice to speak for it except Senators McCarthy and Knowland."

Buckley also offered him two attractions of which the Right has its own versions: agrarianism (at least, one assumes the silent partner was interested; he certainly got an earful) and Europe. Chambers moved from a Europe-centered Left to a Europe-centered Right. Among all the German tags and Russian fables, I could barely find a single reference to American culture, except a slighting one to Elvis Presley, a stilted one to Rocky Marciano "(if that is his name)," and some praise for Randall Jarrell. In a passage worthy of Graham Greene, he says that Alger Hiss "looks like the American boy . . . clean-cut, 'nice,' probably played basketball . . . America is dying of the American boy." His goodhearted admirers might have been startled by this. They could hardly have supposed that America was dying of the American boy.

There wasn't much else that was congenial over on the Right. He underwent one of his formidable soul-searchings as to whether to join the *National Review*, but he seems to have spent a lot of time heckling it. He could see no earthly reason why Alger Hiss, or anyone else, should be denied a passport. The number of spies who traveled would be trivial. That wasn't what the fight for the West was about anyway. He abhorred wire tapping and believed that conservatives should take over the cause of civil liberties. As the cumulus of rhetoric lifts, it is harder and harder to see what he has in common with his new side.

Mournfully, he runs his knife down the pasted-over area on the American Right. "A capitalist cannot be a conservative." There is no greater agent of change than a capitalist. Yet Chambers prefers him to the woolly machine-haters who grind their own burlap, and while protesting that money bores him, he goes on about his own investments at some length, in a tone of strenu-- ous whimsy ("We are heavy people," says Esther Chambers). One senses by now that it is an effort to don the metaphysical robes. He chides the Right for its impracticability, even as a liberal might. And in a final whittling down of his past, he even appears to give up on Nixon, his first and last ally on the politi- cal Right. "We had nothing to talk about," he says. The old subversive will not be taken for granted by anybody.

The neutral good sense of these criticisms does much to bolster his credit, retroactive to the Hiss case. Buckley has al- lowed a few good shots to be taken at his own positions in order to rescue a friend. Liberal readers will likely agree that whoever wrote these last letters could have been a reliable witness and what they took to be hysteria might have been an extreme case of cold-war fever (or frostbite). As that let up, so did Chambers. His tone is so different by the end that it might be a different man—except that, at his worst, one still felt he could turn his mysticism on and off at will.

His critics have sometimes applied more rigorous tests of sanity to Chambers than they would to most writers. A bad poet should be allowed his licence too: and Chambers's worst flights strike one now as nothing more sinister than failed poetry. He was, incidentally, quite a good prose writer. But his most per- nicious dream was that his sensibility was poetic; and he paid and paid for it. A dedicated witness should sacrifice such talents. As it was, the people who knew him and worked with him be- lieved him in impressive numbers, but people who only read him had trouble.

Of course, to believe him is not necessarily to like him. His devotees still push him a bit too hard, accepting his own estimate of himself as somebody pretty damn important over whom one must choose sides. (One's response to this is apt to be surly.) In the flesh he seems to have affected people violently, but in his letters he simply doesn't have that kind of voltage, except in the context of his case. He obviously had a gift for what the Jesuits call "particular friendships," but outsiders are not warmed by this as much as the particular friends always seem to expect. Several times he tells Buckley that only thrice in his life (biblical sonority) has he had such a good friend as Bill—a bit hard on the particular friends he had over at *Time*, and elsewhere. But one assumes that he made them seem special too, at the moment.

Chambers also worked strenuously at maintaining his friendships, and while the flow of gratitude and apology makes for occasional sticky reading, it also suggests, in line with Buckley's purpose, a character that would not betray a friend like Hiss for the sake of showing off. Fair enough. But I believe what bothered St. Ignatius about particular friendships was the question: where do they leave the rest of us? Chambers was undeniably clique-y, as Great Friends tend to be, and he divided Buckley's *National Review*, as he had *Time-Life*, sharply into the Good and the Childish (a favorite term of opprobrium) or the historically irrelevant. There was no malice about it, but a good deal of condescension.

And what was this West that he loved so much? On a trip to postwar Europe, he managed to despise both the locals, for exploiting the tourists (which was not unreasonable of them at the time), and the tourists for being exploited. His West seemed to contain precious few living people, outside of a few heroes and cronies. Its main virtue was that it was not the East, which he really loathed. Chambers had a generous spirit, for those close to him, and for a few symbolic figures in the distance, selected peasants and old revolutionaries; but it could only work by choosing and discarding, by drawing a circle around what he liked and anathematizing everything outside it.

Yet perhaps a man who enrolls in college at fifty-seven is not to be judged too easily. The growth and change recorded in these letters is surely exceptional in a man of his age. It is a pity that we don't hear the other side of the exchange, because Buckley also changed during those years from a one-sided point-scorer to a man who understood his opponents' ground increasingly well; and Chambers may have had something to do with it. This could just have been the changing times, Chambers's beloved History, that sweeps us all along, journalists in front. But reflecting on the sober sense of the later letters, one wonders whether Chambers, having whipped up so many Furies on the Right, did not help a little to calm them down and give us that brief interregnum between paranoias that seems now to be drawing to a close.

1970

3 / ALBERTO MORAVIA:

The Lie

Apathy, indifference, the image of death in sex—these are Alberto Moravia's major and minor interests, and they constitute rather cramped quarters for such a restlessly prolific writer. Admirers must sometimes wish that Signore Moravia would swing out a little wider. Yet he keeps bounding back to his negative themes like a retriever who knows that they conceal something more significant. And such is his conviction, skill, and curious air of gloomy authority, that readers continue to bound along with him to see what he comes up with next—to the point where Moravia may soon achieve the difficult double of a Nobel Prize (he is rumored to be in line for the next one) and a solid popular following, without ever quite having told all he knows.

In *The Lie*, Moravia continues to scratch away at his blank patch of ground. This time it is harder than ever to tell whether he has found anything, because the book may be just what it calls itself. Or it may be the truth masquerading as a lie; or something in between. The novel is written in the form of a diary, by a character who may easily be a lie himself.

Francesco Merighi is a journalist who has spent the last ten years on the road, ostensibly because he finds his marriage "ungenuine." His wife belongs to the working class, which he once considered the very repository of genuineness; but he sees now that that was rather ungenuine on *his* part—the poor are as unreal as anyone else, they just budget it differently.

After ten years of jet-propelled apathy, Merighi decides to reinsert himself into the family circle, in order to extract a quick novel from it. His plan is to keep a diary for two months which will be a genuine account of his ungenuine life, and will serve as chrysalis for the novel. The latter is not to be one of those flashy novels in which things actually happen, but a drip-by-drip account of daily life, in which nothing happens at all.

But events conspire against him by happening anyway. The moment he involves himself in the family, he discovers that his wife has become a procuress in his absence and has tried putting her daughter (his stepdaughter) to work for her. This is unforgivably dramatic and will never do for his diary-novel. He must play it way down in his account, de-dramatize it—rather the way Moravia might (Merighi is, of course, a name not altogether unlike Moravia).

Not only do events betray him, his imagination turns treacherous too. It begins heightening scenes, even inventing them, in order to make things livelier—and less genuine. The diary cannot wait to become a novel, but sets to work distorting, enlarging, suppressing everything in sight. For instance, it begins to seem possible that Merighi really knew ten years ago that his wife was a procuress, and that his diary simply does not care to admit it. It even appears possible that he has really come home to make love to his stepdaughter and not to keep a diary at all. Or is that his imagination heightening things again?

In short, this is one of those books where the author has placed mirrors facing each other, so that you can't be sure which one you are looking at. This may not be altogether a new trick, but Moravia plays it with great virtuosity and a real novelist's interest in knowing what the mind does to truth.

The diary gradually becomes, by a feat of dexterity, a character *in* the diary. For instance, Merighi writes a scene in which he seduces his stepdaughter, in order that he will not seduce her in real life. This is the diary as safety valve. He abstains from certain other actions because the diary wouldn't like it; i.e., he wouldn't want these actions turning up in his novel. This is the diary as conscience. Finally, he refrains from confronting his wife and salvaging his stepdaughter, because that would ruin his story altogether. This is the diary as monster.

It is doubtful whether anyone has ever performed more double jackknives than this with the old diary-novel form. Through a prism of hints, fantasies, and evasions, Moravia manages to suggest a tragic story—his best story: social corruption as reflected in and through the lives of women. But with characteristic coolness and flatness, he keeps the reader from getting too worked up over this, from thinking that the book is bigger than it is.

If you like Moravia, you call his deflating tendency integrity; if you don't like him, you call it a crippling limitation. It could be that his own tortured quest for "genuineness" is precisely what causes him to tone down his colors in this way, and that *The Lie* is a rather elaborate apologia for his own methods. The mind falsifies everything, all novels are lies. But perhaps his are less so than some people's, perhaps drip-drip is always truer than splash.

In any event, after a long career which spans and obliquely records the ungenuine Fascist years and so much other unreal history, Moravia continues to move around vigorously in his strait jacket and redecorate his cell. If this vision sometimes seems as stagnant as the life it reflects, his art continues to live and grow. And *The Lie* is certainly one of his most intriguing, intellectually entertaining, and artistically adventurous books.

1966

4 / S. J. PERELMAN:

Baby, It's Cold Inside

Wʜᴀᴛ ꜰᴏʟʟᴏᴡꜱ ɪꜱ ᴀɴ ᴀᴄᴛ ᴏꜰ ʙʟɪɴᴅ ʜᴏᴍᴀɢᴇ. I cannot be the only writer in America who learned half of what he knows—the good half—from S. J. Perelman. While the fit is on, let's say that Perelman did for American humor what Joyce and Proust did for the novel: he carried it to a point where it could only survive by becoming something else. Perelman doesn't write humor any more, and neither does anyone else. His descendants write surrealist collages or introspective novels or blackhearted satire. The straight spoofy skit that he took over from Leacock and Benchley is dead as vaudeville.

All the wires of comedy that crackled through New York in the golden 1920's met with a bang in Perelman. This included the Benchley preposterous, the Jewish hostile, and even the rustic anecdotal. Stage comedy was in gorgeous sunset, and Perelman was a man of the theater. *The New Yorker* had brought streamline economy to comic phrasing and Perelman wrote for *The New Yorker*. And those period divinities, the Marx Brothers, had made a distillation all their own, literary ("I am about to have a Strange Interlude") and street Arab and deadly nightshade, and Perelman wrote for them too.

He was not, of course, the only humor conductor in town. The great James Thurber, for instance, was fusing Benchley's tricks with the deadpan Western storytelling tradition. George S. Kaufman was running guns between the literary wits and Broadway. Every Golden Age is a hybrid. But what distinguished Perelman was an unrelenting bookishness, a direct assault on culture. Where the older men were still fencing with their landladies or getting trapped under the bed, Perelman was tackling language itself, experimenting with it and mocking it, and using it to flay the barbarian enemy: the hucksters and hacks, the beaming empty face of commercial society.

Perelman was a broader social critic than the others, but almost entirely on the level of language. It was his special pleasure in the thirties-forties to take some inoffensive professional manual by the scruff and wring from it every drop of false feeling or slovenly thinking. Perelman is essentially a dandy, quick to take offense ("Which was it, a tooth or a yellow shade? Do you ever take a drink in the daytime, Doctor?") and even quicker to fall asleep: many a story ends with the master dozing moodily over some outrage.

Having left the dentists and bookkeepers for dead, middle-Perelman turned on the popular novels and movies of his youth with a fond snarl. If his mind is a trifle twisted, blame it on Valentino and Elinor Glyn. But already one senses that just being funny does not interest him very much. His style becomes denser, like the later Henry James, and more turned in on itself. A comic has to keep working, but his mind seems to be on something else.

By the time the later Perelman takes to the road, to give the back of his hand to other nations, his baggage contains much rage and despair and a fastidiousness as highly mannered as anything in James. Although the work is technically funny, laughter hardly arises any more. The incomparable comic gifts are used entirely to convey a point of view. His present persona, spatted and caned, ferocious and bemused, whips through the bars of Singapore like someone out of Conrad; is ever likely to have a moustache-bristling scene in Shepheard's Hotel or the British Museum; is manhandled by sadistic Dublin tailors. It is funny all right, but the look in the eye is flinty and unamused. *Baby, It's Cold Inside* is an honest title, things being as they are.

Perelman's famous brother-in-law, Nathanael West, once came unstuck trying to imitate S.J. (in *A Cool Million*). The imitation might have gone better the other way. Perelman's dark and quirky imagination, plus his quite freakish mastery of language, make him a writer who has to be read seriously. And from the beginning.

1970

5 / CHESTERBELLOC

Every good name dropper has a vested interest in how his names are doing, their current exchange value, and the likely quotation when memoir time comes around. My own best coins, Chesterton and Belloc, have, alas, devalued steadily. Strictly speaking, I didn't see that much of either of them in the flesh—Chesterton just once at my christening when I disappeared into his lap (sorry to sound like an English lady diarist, but that's the way I heard it)—but they filled my childhood like Mardi gras balloons. I dimly remember Belloc advancing for Sunday dinner, behind a barrage of telegrams: "Belloc five miles away," "Belloc getting closer"; finally turning up with a ham under one arm and a lettuce under the other, his diet of the moment; lustily polishing off both and eating the meal we were serving as well; all the while rolling his r's ferociously, like a stage Frenchman. I'm told I later chased him around the garden with the branch of a chestnut tree, and I can almost believe it: he provoked that kind of response in many people.

My meetings with Chesterton were more spectral. My mother was working on his biography from roughly my seventh to my thirteenth year, a strange way to encounter someone. I knew his letters and unpublished drawings before I exactly knew who he was: a bit like knowing a man's galoshes and the smell of his pipe tobacco, but never quite seeing his face. Chesterton, I understood, was simply what the word "genius" meant: a spirit so huge and fertile that it could grow poetry, novels, detective stories, turnips and mimosa all at once. I'll swear I grew up thinking that physical fatness had something to do with it.

At fifteen or so, I waded through his books on my own and found to my surprise that the estimate held up pretty well. It seemed to me that any writer combining imagination and good sense at that level of intensity could accomplish anything he wanted. So, when Lionel Trilling placed Chesterton's social criticism on a line between Cobbett and Orwell, I agreed; when Jacques Maritain, the Thomist, called G.K. a better natural metaphysician than himself, I only wondered at the understatement. I even thought that a short essay of his on dreams knocked Jung out of the ball park.

Larger than life, I suppose. No one is that good. Taking the lowest possible consensus, Chesterton was a brilliant philosophical journalist, who wasted too much time cutting up other journalists and journalistic ideas, and an inspired dabbler in other forms; Hilaire Belloc was a grand master of language, so willfully cranky in its use that he seemed to *demand* a minor place in letters. Still, they towered over the hedge at our place; and to write about them now, with all the fake judiciousness that follows, seems dizzily unreal, as well as something of a betrayal.

Chesterbelloc was, I believe, a word coined by Bernard Shaw, in order to have a bigger and clumsier target to his right. If so, the old stage manager was being his usual shrewd self, because the two reputations have long since sunk of their combined dead weight, where either might have survived on its own. Potential Chesterton fans were always put off by having Belloc move in with them, while Belloc's particular delicacies were lost in the noise that seemed to be coming from the pair of them.

Modest, independent salvage work has recently been attempted: W. H. Auden's *G. K. Chesterton: A Selection from His Non-fictional Prose* and Herbert van Thal's *Belloc: A Biographical Anthology*. But both will need much more than one book. Chesterton resists collection maddeningly since he seldom wrote anything hopeless and he never wrote anything perfect. Mr. Auden's collection is pretty good, although leaning a bit heavily on Chesterton's later wheezing period, when I gather he was so bored with writing that he dictated everything and rarely bothered to proofread. His famous word-play was mechanical and compulsive by then, an old music-hall turn. Yet even limiting oneself to his very best years (say, 1900–1914), one finds Chesterton's virtues so prolix and slovenly, and so enmeshed in his vices, that there is no way of squeezing them into a single book. (On the same principle, his wife allegedly despaired of getting him into his clothes, and wound up buying him a cloak.)

Belloc contrariwise was extremely even in quality, so that a reader who supposes he's getting the best might be disappointed, but a reader who knows he's only getting the average might be more impressed. Mr. van Thal's recent collection of Belloc conveys nothing more powerfully than Belloc's eerie equilibrium: his 1891 style barely distinguishable from his 1936 style, either in prose or verse; and both so classically pure and stiffly graceful that they are almost outside time altogether—an effect more French than English. Where Chesterton was like a workman who wouldn't clean up, but served you plaster, drop cloths, and all, Belloc was neat as a pin.

A matter of very different backgrounds, household gods, self-images: Belloc was halfway into the English upper class, but also just French enough to want to be more so. His father, a French painter, died when Hilaire was a child, and his boyhood was largely spent in England: hence he was able to study "Frenchness" in platonic abstraction, and become more French than de Gaulle. This meant things like lucidity, straight roads, military discipline. Chesterton was a middle-class Londoner at a time when Dickensian "character" was much in vogue, with its burdens of eccentricity, vagueness, improvisation. "The rolling English drunkard made the rolling English road," he wrote. That these two writers, straight and rolling, could be mistaken for one suggests how much play-acting went into both of them, and perhaps how much of the other each contained.

The toughest chain binding the dead men is undoubtedly their combined reputation for anti-Semitism, and this might be a good place to start separating them. Auden himself was put off by it, but finally blames the whole thing on Belloc and on Chesterton's brother Cecil. There is some historic verification for this. Belloc and brother Cecil staked their good names, or at least that of their magazine, *The New Witness*, on exposing the Isaacs brothers in the famous Marconi scandal of 1913.* In the eventual trial, Cecil floundered badly on the witness stand (Belloc having vanished to France). Gilbert underwent some kind of nervous crack-up in November 1914, brought on, so his wife believed, by the strain of the trial and the onset of the war, leaving his stormy brain catatonic for some months. In 1918, Cecil died in a British Army hospital, and a week later Gilbert wrote an open letter to Rufus Isaacs—"Daniel, son of Isaac, go in peace—but go," an act of feverish vengeance for his dead brother.

Rufus Isaacs had gone with Lloyd George to Versailles, "the chief Marconi Minister as our Chief Foreign Minister":

* In 1912 the British government signed a contract with Marconi Company of London, of which Godfrey Isaacs was managing director. Before this was publicly known, three cabinet members—Lloyd George, Murray of Elinbank, and Godfrey's brother Rufus (later Lord Reading)—bought shares in the American Marconi Company, whose value might be assumed to increase indirectly as a result of the contract. The ministers were slippery under questioning, maintaining that they had no shares in "the Company," not specifying *which* company. But *The New Witness* went beyond its evidence in accusing Godfrey Isaacs of bribing ministers. Godfrey sued and collected £100 damages. The story, like many jokes of the period, contained a Scotsman, a Celt, and a Jew.

presumably to sell out the cause Cecil had died for. The anti-Semitism—and there really isn't that much of it—all seems to date from that period. One chapter of *The New Jerusalem*, 1920, and a couple of cracks in *The Superstition of Divorce*, also 1920, are about the sum of it. Somehow the issues had become briefly jumbled in G.K.'s mind—his patriotic brother humiliated, the wily Jews running England: and, of course, Belloc with his theories.

Yet an explanation that blames it all on someone else bothers in its own way. Chesterton was in other respects a thinker of visibly painful independence, an arguing machine, who dearly wanted to agree with everyone he wrote about, but just couldn't. Why did he swallow the Belloc line, even under stress? On the purely personal side, and particularly with his own stage sets around him, Belloc is reputed to have been a hypnotic personality, in strange parts formidable and reassuring: "There entered [the room] with him the smell of danger," wrote Chesterton—a smell to which he had dubious title in any literal sense, but what a creation!

Belloc was also a virtuoso at playing the wise older man. His brief training in the French artillery (according to his biographer Robert Speaight, eight lonely, wretched months) had made him an expert on military affairs. He later won a seat in Parliament which taught him who ran England and how. His performance in these respects was a work of art compared with, say, Hemingway's, and it gulled a better type of friend—no Leonard Lyonses or Gary Coopers in his set. "There is great psychological value in a strong affirmation," he once said; and Chesterton for his part later claimed that he himself joined the Catholic Church for the sake of "Authority"—the exact thing Belloc seemed to offer so abundantly.

Soulmates, then, up to a point. This was the seamy side of their partnership. Chesterton had apparently doted on his younger brother and his brother had always been the real Chester

THE MORNING AFTER ❧ V

in the Chesterbelloc. With Cecil gone, along with some of his own incredible vitality, he fastened on certain Bellocian positions out of simple loyalty, and with less of his early skepticism (he had always feared that his hairshirt itch to question everything might lead to madness; Belloc's affirmations were an antidote). It could be that anti-Semitism was a small part of the package: although small to vanishing as his mind regained its strength.

Yet even this is misleading. Chesterton probably trusted Belloc as much out of laziness as anything else (he was always happy to have someone else go to the library); but he would have picked Belloc's general philosophy to pieces in five minutes if it hadn't paralleled some thought-out position of his own. Although his anti-Semitism (which he preferred to call Zionism —i.e., get them out of here) differed from Belloc's in quality and stress, both were based on a doctrine of place: in Chesterton's case a real place, the London of his childhood; in Belloc's, a memory and a yearning.

Chesterton's ruling political passion was always for local control—a passion which used to be considered reactionary once upon a time. His prophecy novel, *The Napoleon of Notting Hill*, 1904, foretold that London would eventually (1984, by one reckoning) break down into separate kingdoms: a medieval notion which Mayor Mailer later tried to bring to pass in New York under a more-or-less radical banner. Local control, whether from left or right, often tends to anti-Semitism—as though the one thing that keeps a community from being itself is its Jews, a wildly unhistoric notion; it sometimes also tends (the Chesterbelloc might have considered this a different type of question) to anti-Catholicism, when the frenzy for self-definition gets out of hand. Anyway, Chesterton's quarrel with the Jews was of this fuzzy kind, a distrust of their alleged universalism as Belloc gave him to understand it: that is, with a people who maintained their own identity at heavy cost, but seemed bent on persuading other people to blend theirs.

"It is strange that the Jews should be so anxious for international agreements. For one of the few really international agreements is a suspicion of the Jews." That chapter in *The New Jerusalem* is pretty rough stuff. It is also the only place I know of where Chesterton talks of "my friends and I"—as if he were writing one last editorial for his brother's magazine. In fact, it is almost written in his brother's voice, which had a brutal swagger to it. "If England had sunk in the Atlantic, Disraeli would not have sunk with her, but easily floated over to America to stand for the presidency." I.e., a Jew cannot be a loyal Englishman or a loyal anything else; if they insist on running other peoples' countries, let them wear Arab robes, to remind us of their inexpungible Oriental origins.

He never, to my knowledge, used this voice again, or these opinions. But one thing remained constant. The Jewish problem was that the Jews lacked their own land; they must be given a real nation and, if necessary, cantons in other nations. They must become farmers as well as lawyers. No word comes off a Chesterton page with a heavier sneer on it than the word "cosmopolitan."

Hence, his quarrel was never solely with the Jews. He also took on the British Empire, Prussia, and American business. And, as we know, local control can cut in small cruel directions as well. (After all, Populism and States' Rights gave us the K.K.K.)

In an early untypical essay, Chesterton talks of Chinese workers descending on England and being laughed at for their yellow skins—correctly, he says, because color is a more human criterion than economics. To choose local option is to accept its tastes. Elsewhere he attacked the idea of race vigorously ("an attempt to explain the things we are sure of, France, Scotland, Rome, Japan, by things we are not sure of at all, prehistoric conjectures, Celts, Mongols, Iberians"), but he did talk of a nation as a club of friends, and you know who keeps trying to get into clubs. This was a predilection for Belloc to play on later. But it began as an unexceptionable concern for small communities and their integrity. He actually demonstrated in the streets against English intrusion in the Boer War, getting into what must have been the funniest-looking fistfight of all time with a passing Jingoist. He had, to a metaphysical degree, an Englishman's passion for "home," and thought it caddish to blunder into other people's.

It was a hard dream to cling to in the years 1915–1936, and it gave this kindest of writers some bitter moments: imagining in his fever not only that Rothschilds were manipulating the Great War from both sides but that Oriental quacks were blurring the lines between individual souls (if he had a truly peculiar dislike, it was for Islam), and that Americans with their parched, empty souls were bent on flattening the countryside and making the motorcar king. And he kept looking for faces behind the Change, rejecting like the Devil words such as "progress" and "evolution," which suggested there were none. For that brief, crazy moment the faces may have been Jewish, but much more often they were masks of boredom: the faces of rich, restless people, tinkering with customs and beliefs as if they were lawn furniture. Change for its own sake was fatigue, and a rejection of life. Boredom was the sin against the Holy Ghost.

"One must choose sides," were Chesterton's last words, and they speak for a violent side of him, which was usually, but not always, alchemized into humor. It was not just the fat, jolly man turning liverish—though there was some of that—but a gaudy, slashing cast of mind that shows especially in his drawings. His obsession with swordplay, and with the word "sword" itself, which had seemed part of his famous innocence, could turn to something a little uglier when his mind darkened. "Of myself and those I know best I can answer for the vision that made surrender in WW I impossible. It was the vision of the German

Emperor's face as he rode into Paris . . . I am quite content to call it hatred." I am more inclined to call it the calculated effect of wartime propaganda.

But this violence had always been implicit in his carefully chosen parochialism. Boundaries must be cut and ideas must be died for (incidentally, he once wrote an essay about "insufficient martyrdom" which might apply nicely to cases of insufficient police brutality). Even a romantic fantasy like *The Napoleon of Notting Hill* had to end with killing: the sorrows of life would sometimes make it real blood. Yet his addiction to paradox permitted him to love his enemies, as Belloc could not. In the novel *The Man Who Was Thursday* his dreaded international spy ring turns out to consist entirely of good men spying on each other. He loved the idea of masks—even being Chinese was a mask, even being an enemy might be a mask.

In this he differed decisively from Belloc. For Belloc the spy ring would have been a real conspiracy, and the police would have been another, the whole combine to be run by Satan himself, in sardonic comic guise. "May all my enemies go to hell, Noel, Noel, Noel, Noel" was his Christmas message one year. Chesterton might play at this with him, but Belloc really meant it.

To his last days, and after several strokes had smashed his mind into brilliant fragments, Belloc talked incessantly about how the fellows of Balliol "had decided I should not eat," because they had denied him a fellowship in 1896. The value of the fellowship was about £300 a year. Noel, Noel.

And these were not the only enemies. As a boy at the fashionable Catholic school, the Oratory, he is said to have stood on the railway platform, with tears in his eyes, as his classmates piled into the first-class carriages. Family gossip also has it that he was turned down by an aristocratic girl, before finally marrying, of all things, an American. His lifelong obsession with money ("My children are howling for pearls and caviar") bespeaks the agony of upper-class connections without an upper-class income. Later he got even with the rich in some splendid poems and broadsides (some not so splendid, just dull with hate). And he got even, too, with the "official historians" who sneered at his research; and with the parliamentarians who didn't welcome him into *their* club; and he was even heard to say in the very last days of all that Sir Duff Cooper was a far greater man than Chesterton. Noel, with a vengeance.

This was the man who undertook to instruct the likes of Chesterton about the Jews. And the surprising thing is how reasonable and in some strange way compassionate his book *The Jews* is—much more so at least than anything he wrote about the English rich. He explains their persecutions, with unconscious irony, as he might his own: Jews are unassimilable outsiders, and the outsider will always be persecuted. Belloc, a Frenchman in England, an Englishman virtually unknown to the French; also a Catholic with one foot in a Wasp establishment, sneering from the doorway at Parliament and the Academy—he understood these things very well. Chesterton, who reputedly felt at home everywhere, must have just taken his word for it. (Incidentally, H. G. Wells claimed to have once surprised Belloc with the question "Are you one-quarter Jewish or one-eighth?"; to which Belloc answered, "One-eighth." But that may just be a story about H. G. Wells.)

Belloc's second case against the Jews is, not surprisingly, that they are natural conspirators who change their names even when they don't have to. He says that no one dares discuss the Jewish Question frankly for fear of reprisal (being rejected by Balliol? Now mind you, I'm not saying it's so, just that it's possible—a typical Belloc proposition). He admits that they, unlike the English rich, have been driven to secrecy by their history. Therefore, like G.K., he champions Zionism and wishes it well. In short, he is begging one of his conspiracies at least to come out in the open.

The Jews is an interesting footnote to the history of anti-Semitism. It conjures a period when brutal remarks were made, absentedminded as belches, at overblown dinner parties, and when red faces reddened slightly further at the thought that so-and-so might "be one."

Belloc, with his many identities, seems to be asking the Jews to declare themselves, and spare themselves this humiliation; and yet, to be among the jeerers. He urges Jews to stop changing their names and hiding their identities; rather quaint advice today. In theory, I suppose he would be delighted by the present openness of Jews, particularly in America, and with their public exploration of their tradition; yet I'm not sure he would be. He would, though, have grasped the joke that the Wasp oligarchy conforms much closer to his detested kind of secret society than the Jews ever have; and that his accursed bankers exclude Jews like the plague.

I believe this is about the worst that can be said for either man on this score. These were games Edwardians felt they could safely play, even when the Edwardian age was done. For both, the Jew was primarily an agent of change: both, I'm convinced, would have been horrified to find these agents of change being liquidated in Prussian gas chambers; both, in fact, hated Germany, and only distrusted Jews. The irony almost hurts one's tongue: they thought (with Rothschilds on the brain) that the Jews might some day sell England out to relatives in Prussia. Otherwise: Chesterton was a cartoonist both in words and pictures, and race was one of his occasional comic properties. I have seen an unpublished drawing of his that might, in these tenser times, seem to be jeering at the blacks. Cartooning is the most extreme form of cruelty allowed in civilized countries. But his basic gag, as for any cartoonist, was humanity itself; and to look for consistent prejudice in his work is like looking for it in David Levine's.

As to Belloc, his attitude toward the Jews is mainly interesting as a gateway to other corners of his soul. Partly, it was just one unassimilated man sticking out his tongue at another—with a special taste for exposing Jews who had gone further in government and journalism than he had. But, partly, it was one of those fixed positions on which his amazing equilibrium depended. His peace of mind seemed to require certain reiterations. For instance, in his fine word-paintings of French revolutionary figures written in the 1890's and reprinted by Mr. van Thal, we are told in litanous refrain how each subject felt about the Catholic Church, even where this is of no apparent relevance; and again, in his study of Oliver Cromwell, written thirty years later, we are plunged straight into Cromwell's feelings about Rome—relevant this time, but not *that* relevant. It begins to seem like an author's tic, and we dismiss it more sweepingly than we sometimes should.

Belloc felt that he had a mission to defend the Faith at all times. He once explained to my father that his line "nor even in my rightful garden lingered" did not refer to his choice of England over France, but to his choice of prose over verse—because he could defend the Faith better in prose. Yet it is a funny kind of defense. These nagging Catholic intrusions could only serve to make the Church tiresome—like a crank handing out pamphlets at a football game. Belloc loved verbal fighting, but it looks as if he did it principally to annoy people. At least, his method of persuasion is peculiar: it comes down to exaggerating repeatedly the size of his army and telling the enemy to come out, they're surrounded. Very few enemies believed him.

It is sometimes argued that Belloc's real motive was to strengthen the confidence of English Catholics, after centuries of second-class citizenship, and perhaps it was: some were strengthened to a pouter-pigeon arrogance, like the late Evelyn Waugh; some were embarrassed and wound up trying to hide

Belloc under the rug (a Catholic history student at Oxbridge usually denied all knowledge of Belloc—a mistake in some ways); some no doubt advanced under the Master's smoke screen, as moderate Negroes advance under Panther rhetoric. But, finally, nobody got as much confidence from Belloc as Belloc did himself.

For some reason, buried deep among his social and geographical dislocations, Belloc simply had to see the world his way: and not just the past, but the present and future as well. This meant somehow shuffling things so that he was at the center and the others were outsiders. It also involved taking a Sleeping Beauty view of Christendom; i.e., maintaining that there was still a Catholic Europe as alive as ever, kept in thrall by mischievous gnomes, shufflers and cads, bankers, publicists, and Oxford dons.

Thus, between the wars, he could maintain (and with him the good-natured Chesterton) that a strong Poland was the key to Europe. The secular jackals had succeeded in dismantling Austria at Versailles—Austria, which had been falling apart like an old wedding dress all their lives—but there was still Poland, and the sturdy French peasantry, and the silent majority of Englishmen ("who have not spoken yet"—Chesterton), all as strangely untouched by time as Belloc was.

For relative unreality, it does not compare so hopelessly with Shaw and Wells on Hitler and Mussolini (as to Adolf, the Chesterbelloc at least knew a bounder when it saw one). It was hard for the prewar sages, who had lived by their wits and what they read in the papers, to cope with postwar change. During the thirties Belloc became profoundly melancholy, even by his standards, believing that the next war would truly be the death of Christendom: but perhaps also understanding from events that it was already dead, that his myth just wasn't working.

The collapse of France was by far the worst of it. The old artillery man had invested more of himself in this than in his other stories, and his old age and final loss of equilibrium came a year and a half after the fall of Paris, and just after the United States had taken over the defense of Christendom. He had always seen the French Revolution, Napoleon, republicanism as all somehow confirming and redirecting Christendom, not weakening and derailing it. The French Army would defend it yet, like Roland against the Moors—unless the French Army were betrayed from within, by a shuffler or cad.

The Dreyfus case occurred just at the time when this romance raged highest in Belloc. And, worse still, it directly concerned his precious French artillery: Dreyfus was trading the very cannon that was going to defy the Prussian infidels. Belloc always remained shifty about the facts of this case, maintaining that there was doubt on both sides (one would have to have been in court and familiar with "the most technical terms in gunnery" to form a judgment). But, on its impact, he had no doubts at all. "It is to the Dreyfus case that we owe four years of war, 1914–18: for it destroyed the French Intelligence Bureau and so permitted the German surprise on Mons and Charleroi." This is Belloc at his gargantuan worst, from the Dean Rusk apologetics (gunnery terms indeed) to the incredible explanation of World War I. It also says the final word on his anti-Semitism: he got it from the French Army Officer Corps, the one group whose contribution to his unhappiness he had mysteriously forgiven.

Belloc's hatred of change gave him a sad old age. After his wife died in 1914, he refused to have anything in the house changed, and to the end there was no electricity or telephone, and the low beams menaced anyone over five foot six or so (his own height). He even gave up shaving and changing his clothes, but sat in his old black suit, by now gray and stiff with candle drippings, "contemplating my own vileness."

Yet even then, as I found him in 1950 dozing and scowling by the fire, he would suddenly tell a joke or sing a song, reminding one of what sweet art had once come from this melancholy. His love of Europe was not just a neurotic evasion but a genuine vision, of a kind glimpsed only by artists, and that briefly. His masterpieces, *The Path to Rome* and *The Four Men*, convey a version of Europe too good to be true perhaps, but too vivid and robust to be called exactly fantasy. He had seen it somewhere, sometime, and he kept it steadily before his eyes: inns, songs, an open road so scrupulously guarded that, at an age when the Kerouacs have long gone muttering off to their corners, he could write a book called *The Cruise of the Nona* expressing all a young man's passion for movement and surprise.

An artist knows what he has to do. Defending the Church and the Europe that went with it was one way of paying his dues on his vision. Writers have done worse things for trashier muses. As to his politics—probably any time a writer calls on these to protect his world, the result can be grotesque. Belloc's never-never land seems relatively harmless, compared with, say, Ezra Pound's—at worst gallantly futile; at best, surprisingly sharp, as when, in *The Servile State*, he sees some ultimate government-business combine as a more likely tyrant than World Socialism.* Belloc's temperament was in an odd way less physically belligerent than Chesterton's: much more bluster than bloodshed. When he wasn't beating off his enemies with his tongue, his mood was often eerily gentle; and it is easy to forget how funny he usually was about it, even on the attack. Humor was actually the strongest link between him and Chesterton, not any kind of prejudice, and an account that leaves that out reminds one, for earnest foolishness, of the new revisionism on the Algonquin wits.

Oddly enough, no one ever talks about the influence of Chesterton on Belloc. It could be that the latter simply would

---

* It is the Devil's own damnable task, as he might have said himself, to place Belloc's politics. He hated the English two-party system, would not have trusted a theocracy, called himself a republican. One knows precisely where he would have stood in 1793.

not submit to influence; but there may have been some anyway, of a subtle, personal kind—G.K. raising his friend's heavy spirits, sharpening his comic gifts, maintaining a schoolboy atmosphere in which a middle-aged man could still enjoy writing light verse. The influence the other way is superficially obvious. Chesterton's political instinct dozed, and this great quintessential Cockney even wound up joining an unassimilated international organization, the Catholic Church. He defended Belloc in his fight with Wells over evolution, and even backtracked slightly on the Dreyfus case.

Yet Chesterton's own philosophical trajectory remained true enough. As a journalist, he had to keep all his horns blaring at once, and he was probably tempted to leave some of it to Hilaire. His main line of interest in the last years was the religious experience of mankind, and the paradoxical nature of Being itself, and on this his thinking proceeded vigorously on its own way, even when one feels he was too written-out to get it down right or scrape off the fat.

The Everlasting Man, 1925, marks a spurt of energy and contains some religio-historical insights of genius. After some playful journalistic slaps at Wells and the pop evolutionists (unlike Belloc, he didn't really care a fig about pre-human evolution, or whether "creation came about quickly or slowly"), he gets to such questions as why one society worshipped the Sun and another one (old money-mad Carthage) sacrificed babies; and in each case what it *felt* like to be a character in Fraser's *Golden Bough*. But his kind of writing required constant energy, with every sentence a fresh battle, and after how many million words, he probably felt he'd had enough. If at this point he seemed to echo Belloc—well, somebody had to man the trench, and Belloc hadn't aged a day.

The main part of his story, though, can be told without reference to Belloc. The range of Chesterton's talent was almost alarming, like a glandular growth, and the area he shared with

Belloc was comparatively small. And I think he shared it because he wanted company. His wife had removed him from
London (one always blames somebody else for Chesterton—
perhaps his one great flaw) to get him away from his drinking
friends; so he had to assert his solidarity in print. Also, he must
have been one of the rare geniuses with absolutely no taste for
the part, no wish to be unique. Artistic perfectionism was too
pushy for him, wisdom too pretentious. The spillover of his
thinking leaves us (if anyone can find it) a body of aphorisms
universal enough to belong to literature—Shaw looks like an old
newspaper in comparison—yet he did not set up as a sage. His
Cockney soul wanted, even intellectually, to be one of the boys, a
comrade in battle line and pub. And as if to prove it, he accepted
equal billing, and a few ideas, from a man of lesser intelligence
and dramatically lesser wisdom, Hilaire Belloc: as he had once
accepted ideas from his loutish young brother, Cecil, whose
death was such a brutal turning point in his life.

1971

6 / KURT VONNEGUT:

Slaughterhouse-Five

KURT VONNEGUT WAS PRESENT (SO IT GOES), as he would say, at the Dresden fire-bomb raid in 1944—possibly the greatest atrocity ever committed by Americans and certainly the quietest. Most of the public hadn't heard of it until well after Nuremberg. Vonnegut says it took more than twenty years to write his novel about it; and, in a sense, he hasn't written one yet. As though blinded by the glare of the fire bombs, he has turned his back on the raid and written a parable instead.

His hero is called Billy Pilgrim—who represents the kind of pilgrim we are down to by this century—on his way from Dresden to whatever heaven you can still believe in after Dresden. Billy is World War II's Sad Sack, with all the comedy carefully drained out of him. (A funny Sad Sack takes the curse off war and Vonnegut wants it left on and doubled.) Billy is not even the universal victim, who testifies to the human spirit, because his spirit is long since broken; he is a vegetable, he is below the human requirements for pity or laughter. He is not even a "character" any more. A pilgrim of the period was moved along by someone else's boot, so did not need to be.

We first stumble over Billy wandering vaguely behind enemy lines, numb with pain, finding "no important differences between walking and standing still," with a heel missing from one of his shoes. Vonnegut is, of course, an expert comic writer, and a word from him would have us howling like children at Pilgrim's predicament. But the author fixes us with a liverish eye and the word never comes.

To his apathetic relief, Billy is captured, kicked around like a rag doll, stuffed into a tiny overcoat—all the makings of a Christ-figure, except that he is a vegetable and doesn't qualify. His colleagues watch him like rats, beyond compassion or instruction, kept alive and warm by dull animal hate. His captors despise him. It takes all the fun out of war to find you have been fighting such wrecks as this. Vonnegut will have no Christs giving value to Dresden, any more than he will have clowns.

As Billy bobs along like garbage in a sewer, beyond ridicule and pride, wishing only for a place in the dark to move his bowels, the city is hit. The incident is almost casual. After the Goya-like feast of human depravity, what did you expect? A strategically meaningless obliteration of an open city seems the most natural thing in the world. Up to now, the reader may have been consoling himself that Vonnegut was overstating the moral squalor of war. But suddenly you understand that decisions like Dresden and Hiroshima can only be discussed in the context of moral squalor. A fable worthy of Dresden requires characters out of a bestiary. The enlisted men must be brought down to the level of the brass, and the brass down to the level of the atrocity. And if you say, but they're sub-human, you've got Vonnegut's point about Dresden precisely.

How does the human soul recover from having been a rat or a vegetable, an aggressor or a victim? The rats have it easy. They join rat races, become respectable citizens or old soldiers who write histories of gallantry. Pilgrim later has a son, who starts off delinquent but straightens out and becomes a rat for his country, in another war.

But peace is hard on the vegetables, because their minds froze during the nightmare, and they are forced to remember it without anesthetic exactly as it was. Pilgrim is doomed to play his humiliation over and over in his mind; and it is so glued to his nerve ends that to remember is to reexperience totally. His vegetable passivity recorded all the things that the rats missed or forgot or lied about later. And civilian life will never be more to him than a shadow, or cheap imitation, of war after that.

Pilgrim's solution is to invent a heaven, out of twentieth-century materials, where Good Technology triumphs over Bad Technology. His scripture is science fiction, man's last good fantasy. He imagines that he is whisked off to a planet called Tralfamadore, where suffering and death are trivial. "When a Tralfamadorian sees a corpse, all he thinks is that the dead person is in bad condition in that particular moment"—but there are plenty of other moments. The past is as real as the present, and you just pick the tense of your choice.

This does not cure Billy of the war. But now, when he returns to it, he can take his Tralfamadorian wisdom with him to cushion the pain; and he can even make believe he had this wisdom all along. He pretends that he had visited the planet back in 1944, although we know he read about it some time later during a delayed nervous breakdown. He now imagines that, as he was walking his Calvary, he already had visions of heaven to sustain him—a benign lie of his own about war.

This gets Vonnegut into some delicate time-switch writing, which would have many writers wheezing—a character remembering a past in which he foresees the future—but he does it with splendid art and simplicity. *Slaughterhouse-Five* is written with nerve-racking control: a funny book at which you are not permitted to laugh, a sad book without tears, a book of carefully strangled emotions. A tale told in a slaughterhouse.

Vonnegut will probably get a lot of mail saying that it wasn't like that, that there were many acts of nobility among the seediest war prisoners, and possibly even that the people who decided to bomb Dresden were deeply troubled men. He does admit, in a curiously mannered introduction, that he is not going to give the war-lovers a chance. "There won't be a part for John Wayne."

But beyond that, he says only, like Pilgrim, "I was there." It is a fiction of witness. This is what it felt like to be on the ground that day. This is what the human face looked like by firelight, specifically the American face. Billy's rat-like companions are not so much people as moral equivalents. Vonnegut does not theorize outside of his parable. The Tralfamadorians (who sound like American technocrats after a course in Zen) expect more wars, and so does he. He just wants you to know how it was in Dresden.

So—war drives people crazy; or at least, craziness may be the most honorable response to it. And craziness has its compensations. Pilgrim, the all-American escapist, demonstrating human love techniques to the Tralfamadorians, with the aid of one Montana Wildhack of Hollywood, winds up the happiest man in the book.

1969

7 / WILLIAM GOLDING:

The Pyramid

W<small>ILLIAM</small> G<small>OLDING HAS MADE HIS MARK AS A</small>
concocter of desolate fables about people at the end of their
ropes or just beyond. *Lord of the Flies* gave us a herd, or sloth,
of schoolboys marooned on an island, reproducing in miniature
most of the mangier horrors of human history; *Pincher Martin*
shrank the nightmare sharply to one man trapped on a rock, or
in his own head, whichever is worse, and enduring what sounded
like the world's worst hangover. (That wasn't the alleged subject, but you can't fool me with those symptoms.)

So, in *The Pyramid*, it is disconcerting at first to find Golding resting up for now in a comfy English village full of quaint
characters who call each other things like "young Oliver" as
they bicycle past on the way to the apothecary—one of those
placid, teeth-grating places that seem to settle like layers of
green mold on English detective stories. Not even the promise
of Peyton Place doings behind the vicarage can lift the gloom
of this dismal setting.

Until, that is, we realize that Golding finds it just as nerve-
racking as we do and just as bleak as one of his desert islands.
The name, and nature, of the place is Stilbourne. The neighbor-
ing cathedral is called Barchester, which, along with a barmaid
called Mrs. Miniver, serves notice that Golding is writing a

parody of genteel novels in general. The English village, with its crystal pyramid of class, is like a glass tomb. Golding's mission is to show how love and hope are buried and mummified in the pyramid.

He does it in the form of two lengthy anecdotes, with an intermission piece thrown in mainly for entertainment, showing how culture gets its lumps at Stilbourne. In the first episode, an upper-class boy makes total use, and a middle-class boy makes partial use, of a lower-class girl.

Their relative positions make real love quite impossible—corpses must not fraternize up or down in the pyramid. But poverty is worse than just a bad mathematical position. We discover in the end that the girl has been deformed by it before her betters ever laid a glove on her.

In the second anecdote, the punishment is delivered upward instead of downward. A lady patronizes a young garage mechanic out of wistful, harshly repressed sexual attraction. The mechanic, a cool, new-breed Englishman, calmly whips out a wife and child he has been concealing, moves the family in with her, driving her inch by inch to one of the most spectacular breakdowns you could wish to see.

The penalties of a class system are thus exacted by anyone with the wit and brutality to use them. The narrator himself, who is the middle-class seducer of the first episode and a helpless observer of the second, leaves Stilbourne with a frozen, muddled heart. His parents, themselves zombies, have fussed over him long enough, worried about his bowels and his music lessons, to segregate him from life forever.

Golding's pessimism is his greatest claim to importance. It is thoroughgoing and much deeper than a light reading indicates. In *Lord of the Flies* he showed how people go to hell when the usual social controls are lifted, on desert islands real or imaginary. But here he turns on the social controls themselves and withers them. The structure that keeps us from devouring one another in public does not, in his version, keep us from nibbling away on the sly.

The book is set vaguely before World War II, so that it might be taken for an attack on the old order. But when the hero returns for a last look, things have not improved much. The village is built up, modernized, not so much a pyramid now as a cement mausoleum. The garage mechanic is King, and the old lady who put him there is dead and gone. Meanwhile, the narrator is as cold as ever.

Golding's writing is not ideally suited to a social novel—it is angular and ugly and the dialogue occasionally sounds amateurish. He has much more authority when he writes about real jungles. On the other hand, he retains his gift for grinding life into fables, of reducing social situations to the single man chained to the rock. In real life, Golding has been a teacher of Greek and Latin, and his approach to fiction is closer to classic Greek drama than almost any other novelist's I can think of: humanity —one man or several—writhing in invisible torment under a curse of its own devising, and in the background a chorus of woe.

1967

8 / NORMAN PODHORETZ:

Making It

Bᴜᴛ ᴡʜᴀᴛ ᴅɪᴅ ʏᴏᴜ ᴅᴏ ɪɴ ᴛʜᴇ ʙᴏʀᴅᴇʟʟᴏ, ᴍʀ. Fitzgerald?" Scott, in the famous story, had been trying to shock Edith Wharton with tales of his early days in Paris. Mrs. Wharton was, at best, politely curious. So, too, with readers of Norman Podhoretz's much self-acclaimed book *Making It*.

What does Mr. Podhoretz do in the bordello? Simply sits up there and purrs, as far as we can make out. His ruthless confession must rank with the great literary teases of all time; or with the fake pornography they used to fob off on teenagers in the bad old days.

"It is better to be a success than a failure," it says on page one. See the unveiling of Little Egypt, gentlemen. One thousand breezy photos. But "being a success," as Chesterton pointed out years ago, is one of the most meaningless phrases in the language. It may get us into the tent, but it is no substitute for a real bump and grind.

This is the first impression of *Making It:* that of a burlesque queen solemnly striding up and down to the strains of "Temptation," and nothing coming off. Hour after pitiless hour. Norman likes money (tiny bump), Norman likes to be well-regarded (desultory twirl of tassel). Sorry, men, no refunds. It is only on the way home that we realize that we have seen a rather dirtier show than we thought, and that Norman has shown us plenty.

The theme of the book must be familiar by now. Podhoretz's life has lacked specific content as perhaps only an American life can. For example, he was raised as a Jewish boy simply because his unbelieving father wanted to keep him unassimilated. At a Jewish seminary college he consumed enough Hebrew lore to become class valedictorian without ever supposing that any of it mattered. By the time he got to Columbia University, he had apparently severed the act of learning from its natural objects, and was free to concentrate on such phantoms as pleasing the teacher, getting good grades, and being in the intellectual swim; at the same time, he found himself being pressed into Wasp gentility, an ideal as attenuated and irrelevant as his father's Jewishness had been. A Jew and not a Jew, a Wasp and not a Wasp, scholar and operator: all set now for "Making It," "traveling first-class," and all the other empty cans we append to celebrity.

Pleasing his elders for rather obscure objectives seems to have been Podhoretz's story all along—somewhat like the man in *H.M.S. Pinafore* who "polished that handle so carefully that now I am the Ruler of the Queen's Navee." First a platoon of doting relatives, then a Dragon Lady schoolmarm. Next Lionel Trilling at Columbia, followed by F. R. Leavis at Cambridge; a short ugly interlude in the army, with no parents at all; next, Elliot Cohen, his patron at *Commentary* magazine; and then a whole host of elders, veritably a faculty, the Family of New York intellectuals, who made him their ultimate pet. Home again, safe and sound.

Now, as editor of *Commentary*, with no more elders to conquer (except the American Jewish Committee and Group Captain Norman Mailer), Podhoretz asks himself what it all means. But instead of drawing at least one obvious conclusion—that a career founded largely on showing off to the grownups is likely to result in a fairly infantile version of success: comfort, admiration, power, for their own sakes, the baby's triumvirate—he has decided to celebrate both the career and the success, and to elevate them to the rank of universal desirables. His theme is that the intellectual community is as greedy as the next fellow, but that our author is the first one honest enough to admit it. Courageous in a way—suppose he turned out to be wrong? Suppose he really was the only greedy one? Henry VIII grunting over his chicken bone. But Podhoretz takes no chances on this. He absolutely insists on sharing his vices. As in his famous essay "My Negro Problem—and Ours," where he botched a useful mini-confession by demanding, in effect, that everyone else sign it, he again inflates himself to the size of a Significant Social Index. When Norman sins, *everybody* sins. Which means, of course, that nobody sins.

No doubt, he is just right enough. Every intellectual is a little bit greedy; some more, some less. Podhoretz calls this a "dirty little secret," but for all that, I cannot imagine any intellectual claiming, "I do *not* want money, fame, or power," even if it were true. The dirty secret cuts both ways. No one admits to greed, but no one denies it either. The rules governing self-display, both one's virtues and vices, are quite ambiguous and a good deal more interesting than you would ever guess from this rather simple manual.

Ambiguity is totally alien to Podhoretz's book, which has but one gear and one track and rolls down it like a *Daily News* van. For instance, the dirty little secret of sex has been unveiled for some time, yet we still frown on people who boast about their sexual prowess as much as we frown on people who boast about their money. Envy? (but our own prowess may be even greater). Squeamishness? (but our conversation may be a solid stream of sex or money in other respects, and nobody minds that).

A tradition of conversational manners is a complicated affair devised originally to ward off dullness and pain, although sometimes used perversely to cause both. Podhoretz's revision of the code would surely do so. People sitting around discussing their success, even their success at Columbia University, would be as inspiring as executives modeling long johns in the locker room. Civilization has its reasons for keeping such talk to a minimum. Mr. Podhoretz, who tells us that he has made the upper middle class (you can tell it by his clothes: no more colorful folk costume for him), knows this quite well. Hence his reticence. He does not really talk about his success.

At certain points, the book turns the reader off quite primly, shuts the porter's gate on him. How does Norman make it with servants, other children's parents, rich bores? Can he join any club he wants to? Does he ever find the whole thing a bit stuffy? Before we go haring after him, we would like to know about these things. But the upper middle class doesn't tell.

We would also like, since this is presumably a full-blown investigation of the subject, to hear some case histories besides his own. Are other Family men and women snobs and climbers? and if so, which ones? The names come tumbling out like clowns from a circus car. Mary and Dwight and Philip—but then he gets stuck. A gentleman doesn't rat on his friends. He simply uses them to pad his index.

An anatomy of *Making It* should not bog down on the first navel it comes to. Why have we been brought here, anyway? Anyone who has paddled about in these literary wading pools knows at the very least that George Plimpton looks over your head and Podhoretz looks under your armpit and that Macdonald looks you periodically right in the eye. (Our bad luck that the armpit man wrote the book.) Podhoretz is mildly informative about the structure of the literary establishment, but only mildly, and his lack of social observation is blinding. How does an establishment man furnish his house? Whom does he marry and why? Podhoretz thinks the novel is on the way out— but a novelist could change Philip Rahv's name and tell us something about him. Podhoretz can only take this liberty with one person—himself. And even his one big scene, his Eliza Doolittle debut into the Family, is flat and unevocative, for want of other actors.

But the real point of the book is not to describe a scene or even himself, but to rationalize and justify his own living standard. It is as if he wanted the reader to say, It's OK, you can keep the money. He is demanding, through bluster and wheedle, some kind of open-ended absolution. The words we might use to condemn him have all lost their jurisdiction overnight: from arriviste to apple polisher to sellout. So uncompromising is he that we can't be sure whether those words could still apply to anybody; whether there is any mode of progress so self-serving that even he would condemn it. (From his upper-middle-class aerie, he knows that there are such modes, because —another garment that fails to come off—his own rise is shown to have been remarkably clean and disinterested. Only his thoughts are impure.)

Podhoretz's Damascus occurred during a jamboree on an island owned by Huntington Hartford, when Norman, frosted glass in hand, looked around him and saw that it was good. One looks despairingly for irony in this scene. Podhoretz to cover himself puts a tiny twist in his voice, but nothing like enough. Finding happiness in one of the less poverty-stricken corners of the Caribbean is no great trick. Religious creeds are more convincing when uttered in adversity, and Norman's doctrine of self-interest would ring more commandingly from a hovel in Trinidad than from Mr. Hartford's spotless beach.

No one demands of a left-wing writer (Podhoretz claims to be of that persuasion) that he turn down luxury. It is good practice for going to prison, but that will not arise in Norman's case. American writers don't have to keep in training like their Eastern brethren. It doesn't take much wind to sign a petition.

But we do still have our little problems in the West, and it is mildly surprising to find so little allusion to these in *Making It*.

It may be all right to have your tabs picked up by some chuckle-headed tycoon, or even by Mr. Hartford. But this can lead to certain bad habits. It becomes a drag having to look into how the tycoon got his money, his labor practices, and so forth, and now on top of that, one has the further nuisance of worrying about the C.I.A. and such. Jason Epstein has noted in the *New York Review of Books* that, since the cold war began, certain types of thinkers have enjoyed more winter cruises than other types. The success that Podhoretz talks about always has to be paid for by someone. The complexity of Foundation living has made it hard at times to trace that someone.

In other words, a modicum of training is still useful. The conventional wisdom about ambition which Mr. Podhoretz revises so airily has always known this. It is based not so much on Christian asceticism as on a determination to function when the patron dies or turns ugly. (A good deal of Christian asceticism is based on the same thing, but that's another story.) You don't function so well when you, or your wife, or your in-laws have become used to silk sheets. One apologizes for the truisms. But in his lightning survey of Western thought on the subject (two credits, freshmen) Podhoretz seems to have overlooked them completely.

Mr. Podhoretz's own prosperity is probably built on air and luck like most people's. The magazine he edits is subsidized by a most benign master, the American Jewish Committee. He is allowed at present all the freedom an editor could want. But suppose his bosses change their minds? He could always find another job: either a smaller one with the same freedom, or a bigger one with less. In either case, he would be joining the rest of the human race, with its familiar discontents. And no more talk about making it.

That a man with such an Ayn-Rand-and-water program should call himself a man of the left is symptomatic of the fifties and sixties. Podhoretz has given us some intellectual history here after all—his mind moving, with the rest of the salmon, to pro-

Americanism and back, but his tastes moving steadily to individual profit, and winding up somewhere to the right of Horatio Alger. This means that his left-wing opinions are just talk. And talk is cheap.

Podhoretzism is a baneful doctrine for any writer anywhere. Twentieth-century politics aside, one never knows when any writer will be called on by some private or public reverse to double as hero or saint. A diet of guilt-free softness will not help. And beyond that, self-satisfaction is every artist's enemy. The ego that sets you to writing in the first place hangs around like a great swollen, sensitive fool, demanding an impossible payment in flattery and love: do not hurt me, it screams to the world. My master thinks he wants criticism, but don't listen to him, listen to me.

It might be argued that this is the state of the insecure writer, and not one who has been taking Dr. Podhoretz's success medicine and learning to love himself as he deserves. But even if the medicine worked, vanity would still be the writer's enemy, for it maketh him sloppy and humorless and it dimmeth his wits. See *Making It, passim*. To advise writers to wallow in their occupational disease rather than fight it is, to put it temperately, mischievous.

But besides this seedy moral and professional manifesto, Podhoretz has written a personal story of a slightly more touching sort. He suffered from a brutal case of precocity, a disease which can make both childhood and adulthood wretched, with just a few good years in between. Norman grew up in Brownsville, a tough neighborhood to be precocious in. And he must have exerted, even overdeveloped, his political gifts trying to be one of the boys. In *Making It* he assures us that he succeeded; but in "My Negro Problem—and Ours," he gives some hint of the anxiety underneath it, his fear of the colored marauder and the fragility of his own confidence.

Having learned more or less how to make like a tough guy, he then had to unlearn it at Columbia and Cambridge. At the former he was resented as pushy; at the latter he is under the impression that he wasn't. His experience there also gave him a notion that class in England is quite different from class in the United States, that it has nothing to do with manners or dress. I have heard Englishmen make the same point over here. It takes time and much observation for a foreigner to learn what is actually going on.

Anyway, those were the golden years for Norman, and he lovingly records every A plus as if it had happened yesterday. At that point in time he was ahead of the field, and he wants it on permanent record now. Since then, a lot of people have caught up and passed him. Boys who were making C's and waitresses, while Norman was busy imitating Professor Trilling's style, have straightened out and made their moves. And Norman is no longer a boy wonder, no longer the promising young man that all the older men are gruffly impressed with, but another thirty-seven-year-old writer who didn't do anything last year or the year before: a good enough position to be in, but not if you've tasted glory; not if you ran the hundred in 9.5 in high school.

This subject could have made a good book—has, in fact, made many good books. Romantics like Fitzgerald and Connolly have done fine things with it. Podhoretz's trophies carefully lined up for inspection are like old dance programs, or like Fitzgerald's overseas cap never worn, genuinely touching mementos. But what Connolly and Fitzgerald never did was to pretend that things are just the same now: that a nice apartment and being on some damn presidential committee and affording a smart school for your daughter are valid extensions of the old dreams. In his late thirties, Fitzgerald was writing *The Crack-up*, a study of encroaching middle age, of a sensibility dwindling and cooling, and of a break with his past self that could not be mended. Now, more tragically, Podhoretz comes bounding along to tell us how well he's still doing—first, A pluses, and then, lots of money. Great territory, you should move there.

This is the sense in which the book is revealing after all. Podhoretz would rather show himself to be a crass operator (well, at least I'm honest) than an anxiety-ridden failure counting his assets and looking prosperous for the sake of the customers. Of course, he is not really a failure; he is a good editor and an adroit essayist; but no one could ever be the success he felt like at twenty-one. And second best is a hard pill to gag down.

Thus, we get this book instead, which refuses to face the fact, to say the words. It must be hard for a man of Podhoretz's intelligence to be so obtuse, but self-respect demands it, and the big fool Vanity says go ahead, we'll make a mint. And we get these terrible flights of self-congratulation that have made the book funny to so many people, but could just as well make them cry.

"I toyed with the idea of doing a book about Mailer that would focus on the problem of success," but he decided to make it a book about himself instead; as if to say, I was going to write about Rockefeller and money, but decided to write about the local branch manager instead. The book is to be a "bid for literary distinction, fame, and money all in one package." A great economy offer that only lacks a set of dishes. The precocious child cannot just write a book like other people and take his chances; he must write a *great* book, nothing less will do, and ram it down our throats.

In this mixture of complacency and agitation, he has written a book of no literary distinction whatever, pockmarked by clichés and little mock modesties and a woefully pedestrian tone. There are one or two shrewd observations—for instance, the distinction he makes between jealousy and envy, and some of his remarks about the writing process: in particular, that people take up this career because they find they do it well, and not because they have something to say. But they usually do get something to say eventually, or else they give up. Podhoretz has been rummaging among his belongings and come up with this. One can't imagine what he keeps underneath it.

Meanwhile, mediocrities from coast to coast will no doubt take *Making It* to their hearts and will use it for their own justification; they will prate about power and honesty and add another wing to the game room. In the present condition of our society and the world, I cannot imagine a more feckless, silly book.

One last note might be added, because the matter comes up a good deal in conversation and not, for obvious reasons, in print. It has been suggested that Podhoretz also implicates Jewishness in his peculiar syndrome. I do not believe he does this: Jewishness is part of his story, but a coincidental part. He could just as well be an Irishman. The book could simply be titled *America 1967;* slickness, shallowness, and the flight from pain and death and art—all in one package.

1967

9 / GIUSEPPE BERTO:

Incubus

From VERGIL TO DANTE TO ANTONIONI, ITALIANS have excelled at representations of hell. There are probably good reasons for this. It takes a rich sensibility and a complicated conscience to do justice to hell; or, in Freudian terms, a frisky id and a bizarre superego. And these by-products of sensuality, stern religion, and high civilization might be expected to flourish preeminently in Italy.

In *Incubus* the locus of hell is the narrator's stomach and immediate environs. Within an area reaching from the duodenum to the southwest kidney he suffers the tortures of the damned. His own explanation is that his father, who has recently died of a revolting stomach cancer, has decided to haunt him. But this does not quite satisfy the modern half of his intelligence, so he sets out on a low-farce pilgrimage to have the old man exorcised scientifically as well.

Simply as a saga of male hypochondria, *Incubus* is a comedy on the heroic scale. The offending stomach is taken to every specialist in Rome, each of whom, like a baffled garage mechanic, finds something fresh to tinker with. The stomach is opened and closed, kidneys are shifted hither and yon, his skin is acupunctured. Even the X-ray machines seem to be quacks, turning up new findings for their masters to exploit.

When the reader has had his fill of intestinal disasters, the trouble shifts to the hero's nerves. This switch opens up a whole new bag of fantastic speculations in the hero's ancient-modern mind. He fears that deadly chemicals are assailing his nerve ends, that his prostate is somehow linked to his ears, but always that his father is punishing him—for deserting the paternal deathbed and other nameless offenses. This calls for a whole new team of specialists, even zanier than the stomach men. But at last the hero comes to rest on a psychoanalyst's couch, and the novel expands into something beyond a first-rate satire on Italian medicine.

The analysis is a routine Freudian one, and it is disappointing at first to learn that the sprite in our hero's stomach and nerves is just a common, or garden, superego. But said hero manages to outflank Freud by turning the superego itself into an incubus, or unfriendly spirit. It seems that the layers of civilization which are piled up in the Italian psyche, from early pagan to high-and-low Christian to *dolce vita* modern, are not to be flattened out so easily. The hero will keep all his totems—gods, devils, saints, superegos, Alfa Romeos—all gurgling round in his system. If the superego is indeed man's mechanism for adapting to civilization, the modern Italian version must be one of the most complex and overloaded in history.

And this is what the novel is finally about. The father fixation is well drawn, especially the hero's childhood recognition of his father as a disembodied moustache, as a head without features, as a vague figure of power, but there is more in his stomach than just a dead father. There is also Fascism, the collapse of the monarchy, the queer disheartening war experience, the ambiguous relationship with Catholicism, and much, much more. In certain respects Federico Fellini explored the same phenomenon, less profoundly, in the film *8½*. (The hero of *Incubus* is, incidentally, a film writer: the representative Italian hero is apt to be connected with movies these days.) The same harassed middle-aged Italian wrestles with the same neo-baroque conscience; the unresolved moral questions, which he has lazily postponed or evaded, have backed up on him, and as he sits down to the feast of postwar plenty, he finds that he has a vicious case of indigestion.

Giuseppe Berto is an unusually sly novelist. His narrator (who has no name of his own) talks like a man trying to explain himself in a bar, in long self-qualifying sentences, adopting, when necessary, the slightly buffoonish manner of a Poppa Karamazov, to make you like him and perhaps to take advantage of you. But under cover of this ingratiating garrulity, Berto has written a somber, carefully constructed book. In the end, conscience, the past, "father," overwhelm the hero; he is cured of his neurotic anxiety—and with it goes his will to live. The moment he is free of his father, he embraces him in a dead-man's grip; indeed, he *becomes* his father, to escape the oppressive stimuli of the modern world, the movie world, the sex world.

Without any obtrusive use of symbols, and without violating his story with look-at-me metaphors, Berto has done two things: described the onset of individual middle age, and silhouetted this against the aches and pains of an old civilization trying to act young with an old man's heart and an old man's nervous system. People who wonder what "the novel" is still good for might ask themselves what other art form could do so much so well.

1966

10 / IRIS MURDOCH:

The Red and the Green

Iris Murdoch, the English novelist, is one
of those permanently promising writers. After each of her books,
great things are confidently expected—of the next one. And
perversely, almost coyly, Miss Murdoch delivers a little bit less
each time, until it is no longer quite clear what it is we are
waiting for.

Her new book, *The Red and the Green*, not only establishes
her one more time in the ranks of the promising, but may also
help to explain what she has been up to these last few years.
(Incidentally, Miss Murdoch writes like a dynamo and can run
through four or five phases while James Gould Cozzens, say, is
plodding through one.) In her recent books, Miss Murdoch seems
to have been burrowing deeper and deeper into a private world
where it is difficult to check her progress one way or the other.
A Severed Head and *The Italian Girl* could be described as
Freudian fantasies with a Plasticine base: the characters are so
malleable, so little bent or hardened by actuality, that the author
can manipulate them at will, to make any point she likes. She
appears to be using them to satirize something—but what?

Her new book constitutes a serious attempt to escape from
this private world and into a "public" novel. Her setting is
Dublin, 1916: near in time to James Joyce's Dublin. But you'd

never recognize the place, for this is the Dublin of the Anglo-Irish ascendancy, of horse shows and fox-hunting weekends and dilapidated country estates—the far side of the tracks from James Joyce and his cronies.

Her subject is the famous Easter Week rising, in which a group of heartbreakingly optimistic rebels attempted to bring England to its knees by taking over the Dublin post office. *The Red and the Green* anatomizes the responses of Anglo-Irish Dublin to this incident. In affairs of this kind, most people find their responses chosen for them by a pressure of interests and loyalties, but Miss Murdoch's Anglo-Irish characters are as free as gypsies. They have no real connection with either country, and can be English or Irish, red or green, as the romantic whim takes them. In the course of the book, they do make passionate choices—but rather as one might choose a baseball team or a favorite historical character.

As the novel creeps closer, as novels will, to other Murdoch novels, it becomes clear that these semi-detached Anglo-Irish types are strikingly similar to the plastic people who have been causing all the confusion in her other books. They are basically the same emotional acrobats, forever trying on new masks, new styles, even new sexes, constantly defining and redefining themselves existentially with a freedom that doesn't arise for most people, and with a flippancy that is peculiarly Anglo-Irish. (It is probably no accident that some of the most dazzling poseurs of our time—Wilde, Shaw, the later Yeats—have come from this same social situation.) If we take it then that Miss Murdoch has been writing about the Anglo-Irish outsiders for some time without acknowledging it, the point of her satire becomes a little clearer.

Another puzzling aspect of Miss Murdoch's recent works is also given a setting for the first time in this book. This is her preoccupation with family liaisons which, if not outright incest, are the next thing to it. Here the author unveils her all-time champion, one Aunt Millie, romantically entangled with (a) her half brother, (b) her nephew, (c) her half nephew, (d) her sister-in-law's husband, (e) her half sister-in-law's brother (unless my charts deceive me on this one)—and all this, not successively, but more or less simultaneously.

One's first reaction, bearing in mind the author's escalation in this area, is to wonder what combinations are left for next time. Even if Aunt Millie is meant to be a metaphor for Ireland, loved in different ways by different people, a metaphor must make sense on the literal level, and Aunt Millie is just too much.

But as a metaphor for a congealed society, where a small group conspires to act as if nobody else existed, Aunt Millie begins to make a little more sense, as indeed does Miss Murdoch's whole, strange, marooned world, where relatives fall in love randomly, homosexually and heterosexually, up and down and across generations, because there seems to be no one else available.

Iris Murdoch was herself born in Ireland, and refers to it as "somewhat of a dream country." It does seem to have taken a curious grip on her imagination and to have conditioned her basic view of mankind. The labels that are most often attached to her books—that they are intellectually brilliant and witty, but also cold and unreal—have been attached to other Irish "outsiders" from Swift to Shaw and Wilde. *The Red and the Green* is far from the best of her novels (she is a wobbly technician at the best of times, and this isn't the best of times) but it may be one of the most illuminating; it places her at least part way in a tradition, and makes her other books seem more interesting, and even more realistic, than they had before.

1965

11 / *The Writing Condition*

To BEGIN AT THE BEGINNING: THERE IS NO WRIT-
ing for glory any more—not great big glory, anyway. Outside of
English Departments and the publishing warrens, only about
three American writers are widely known by name—and, of
those, at least two are famous for non-literary reasons. And I
don't see how any writer, even the phantom three, can now
expect to outlive his own lifetime. There is enough doubt about
the future of print and of a recognizable human race to make
such speculation pointless—one still indulges it occasionally, but
weakly and foolishly, out of professional habit. If print does
survive, the swelling volume of world literature and improved
access to it will diminish individual names to pinpoints.

Two conditions spring from this, which more or less cancel
out. First, one is disinclined to gamble everything on a masterpiece. Ten years is too long to spend on a book that will live
less than one. But while there is no immortality, there is still a
limited flashbulb fame, so one is tempted to angle for that instead; the quick killing, the season in the sun. The syndrome of
"making it" is directly connected with the loss of personal
immortality.

On the other hand, now that you are down in the company
of poets, you might as well write a masterpiece. You're going to

impress only a few people whatever you do, so you might as well impress hell out of them. And please yourself too, if you can.

The consequence, as in poetry, is the limited masterpiece, the one that doesn't take too long or wear you out too much. The charting of a great book like *Ulysses*, the careful burying of one city under another like the layers above Troy, is beyond most writers, even the ones inside the Academy (they're nervous too, and so are their publishers). But the perfect lyric is still in reach, the book that can be written in the summer and pay expenses—with a scream for quick attention often inserted somewhere.

Why do we do it? Ask a bathtub tenor why he sings. Once upon a time, we found that we could. To people of my age, a Jack Benny thirty-nine (we didn't exactly have a generation, there wasn't one at the time), the novel was still king. There had to be a great war novel, even if it meant throwing 100,000 young men into the breach. And one had to be a damn pussycat not to try a novel oneself. I have a few more reasons now, generated on the job, but it began with naked competitiveness. One would need a better motive today. Or, to put it another way: a young Mailer would *start* with movies now.

There are blessings to having apparently outlived one's Form. Since no one is now demanding any kind of novel at all, we suddenly have the run of a huge empty house. The bedroom, the nursery, set up shop wherever you like. We have been granted the recklessness of minor powers, responsible to no one, and it would be a dirty shame not to enjoy ourselves. There are plenty of grim French nannies around to tell us what fiction can and cannot do any more, and they are probably right. (That's a fight I'll duck for now.) But what fun is decadence if you can't do as you please? Robbe-Grillet will be just as dead as we are when the old house caves in.

The above might be termed necessary sophistry. I would

probably write the same way whatever the state of fiction. It takes a deal of energy to write a whole book, and you can't work effectively against your own bent for that long. I know people worn to a shadow trying to devise a fiction for the sixties or the seventies, because they feel they ought to: it is finally as taxing as trying to smile all day, and they often collapse into short stories or silence.

At the same time, old-fashioned characterization, scene-setting, well-made plotting, etc., do reek of artificiality by now, and even a more-or-less traditionalist must scavenge among the New to find how these can be got round. Books like James Merrill's *The (Diblos) Notebook*, James Salter's *A Sport and a Pastime*, Susan Sontag's much maligned *Death Kit*, and numerous others, all make interesting compromises with the French nannies while retaining old-fashioned, even journalistic, qualities. This amount of experimentation will soon, if it doesn't already, seem quite routine, and us bumbling eclectics will practice it as a matter of course.

However, I believe that, so long as consciousness conventionally conceived dominates the rest of our day, it will continue to dominate our fiction. The old categorization of events and people may be quite arbitrary and false: yet it is what we still bring to our politics and our affairs in general—and even to our analysis of the New. A Richard Gilman can write brilliantly of the revolution in consciousness, in a style worthy of a nineteenth-century divine. And Miss Sontag's language clashes even more spectacularly with her message. In general, I don't push this point too far. It is a cheap crack to accuse a McLuhan of needing books to tell us that books are through (he only needed the books to get on television and really tell us). But so long as we still write non-fiction the old way—and talk and think—most fiction will be written that way too.

More sophistry perhaps. I know that, for myself, experiments in the new consciousness would be as blind as Ptolemy's

map-making. I can render a fractured or disordered consciousness, but not one that receives basic data radically differently
from my own way. I admire writers like Donald Barthelme who
can jumble impressions prophetically, as it were, *creating* a consciousness proper to our present and future nightmares. But
Barthelme is still recognizably one of us; he is improvising on a
sensibility we already know. The new consciousness, if it ever
arrives, will be less elegant, less emphatically literate.

The demand for formal innovation is no stronger, and perhaps weaker than it was when I began writing. Much of what
passed for innovation in those days appears now a series of one-
shot tricks, with no particular aesthetic force. Important changes
in art come when they are ready, and you can't just make one
because you feel like it. As to the fatigue of established forms:
I believe it is only the uncreative who say that all the songs have
been written. I have never fully understood why Joyce is supposed to have ended the modern novel (and just when it was
getting interesting, too). If a young writer of the necessary
talent wished to write a Dickensian novel about New York, I
would hate to tell him it was too late. Of course, such writers
are theoretically extinct, but sometimes they don't know it.
When Luis Borges came to New York last year, he told a small
group of writers that Robert Louis Stevenson was a far greater
writer than Wilde or Shaw, and possibly even greater than
Chesterton. Left to themselves, writers feed from strange
sources.

Anyway, if linear fiction really is dead, what could be the
point of non-fiction novels? Is the interposition of real names
and dates enough by itself to bring the old form into the
seventies? In the past, it was understood that the author made up
the names, because he could say more about his people that way,
and made up events, because the truth wasn't always good
enough. The thrill the reader gets from knowing that he is
getting plain gossip instead of heightened, selected, imagined

gossip is a cheap, regressive one. Plutarch represents no artistic advance on Henry James. I am willing to go all the way with Robbe-Grillet; but in that case, Truman Capote goes too. If our sensibility has moved beyond *In Cold Blood* with fictitious names, it has certainly moved beyond the book we got.

Armies of the Night is only a slightly different case. It benefits from Mailer's status as a serial character, an intellectual Lannie Budd. So by all means, use the real name, as authors have done before. It is especially interesting to see the author re-creating himself to fit the occasion. But if he had called himself Rojak or Shaughnessy, we would have known whose sensibility he was talking about. If Robert Lowell had become Waldo Cabot, and Dwight Macdonald, Sandy McGregor, we would have spotted them eventually. Mailer would have been accused of writing an old-fashioned *roman à clef*, instead of a breakthrough. The book's true originality would not have been affected seriously.

The imposition of private sensibility on public subject matter is hardly new to the novel (see Tolstoy). The ultra-private fiction of the forties-fifties, and the self-absorbed life it spoke for, was bound to spark a reaction. Writing whores pick these things up fast and, yes, I am planning to bring politics into my next novel. By, say, 1974, we will have discovered that public events are only private relationships writ large and dirty, and we will beat it back to broken marriages and unhappy childhoods again. Politics is frustrating, and heartbreakingly boring, and the creative temperament can't stay with it very long—certainly not long enough to understand it. Anyway, a writer cannot afford to take these fluctuations too seriously or he will snap his neck off and never write again.

The probing of individual consciousness (the only kind we've got, condition it how the crowd may) can go on indefinitely, so long as we don't run out of contexts. In this we have an edge over those arts in which formal exhaustion can be a statistical fact. Homogenization of global life, private and public, could eventually deplete the stock of contexts, but I doubt it. If it didn't happen under Eisenhower, it will never happen. Leisure and all that crap will produce more bizarre life styles, not fewer. The kick of having Charles Manson actually called Charles Manson may or may not abate—a twitch on the libel laws could change the face of naturalistic fiction. But there will still be things to say about Manson that can only be said in fiction—lies, conjectures, superimpositions of the writer's own evil self. It is interesting that several of our jauntier new journalists (Wolfe, Breslin, Hamill) have been trying a furtive hand at fiction. Hard-nosed Seymour Krim finds this discouraging (he would scream if they tried poetry, the goddam sissies). But I like the thought that even the writers who have driven journalism through flaming hoops, and have made it do everything but sing and drink a glass of water at the same time, find something still to say at the end of the day's flailings. If this keeps up, the only people left writing the new journalism will be old novelists.

The one condition that could kill fiction stone-dead (and I don't take it lightly) is the one that would kill writing altogether: the blurring and slurring of consciousness, the conquest of pain and time, Nirvana.

1970

...AND LONG AFTER

1 / WILLIAM BUCKLEY:

The Killer with a Heart of Gold

Writing a biography of William F. Buckley is somewhat like trying to play a serious part in a Marx Brothers movie: you're not going to get a lot of attention either way. So let it be said right off that John B. Judis, in his *William F. Buckley, Jr.: Patron Saint of the Conservatives*, seems to have done a better job than I would have thought possible at this stage. It takes tact to perform an autopsy on a live body, but Judis has done his work cleanly, without either breaking any bones or leaving out anything important. The controversies on which Buckley feeds are all here, laid out with admirable lucidity and, what is more unusual, so is the atmosphere surrounding them. And now, back to Groucho.

On the face of it, William F. Buckley has lived a very proper conservative life: which is to say, he sowed his intellectual wild oats while young and has since mellowed into a tactician, or statesman, as you prefer. The fact that the oats happened to be conservative ones is neither here nor there. Buckley is to conservatives roughly what his father, a wildcat oil man, was to the Forbes 500. And besides, being a radical youth would, in those days as in most, probably have seemed rather too conventional for such a gifted showman. Everyone knows what to say to a radical youth ("just wait till you're older," of course), but what precisely did you say in those days to a conservative youth, after you'd said "welcome

307

to the bank"? Before Buckley came along, there was no model for the conservative *enfant terrible*; now of course there are scores of them, but even today his imitators never seem to get it quite right (smugness is not enough).

Not that Buckley's conservatism was ever anything but totally sincere. But if one views him as being at least as much an aesthete as an intellectual, his choice of cause was, to borrow his own words a moment, "insanely felicitous" and, as ever, beautifully timed.

No one who wasn't there can imagine the wave of sheer niceness that swept the country in the wake of World War II, of a kind you might effect for a returned veteran (make sure his room is just as he left it). Although offstage a record number of divorces were recorded, you'd never have guessed it from Hollywood; and as for a ditto of labor strikes, the mass media simply did not register friction. There were no satirists in those days, unless you count Bob Hope, no McLaughlin groups, not even a lonely Mike Wallace to puncture the stillness: it was as if we had been put on a bland diet of everything.

Upon this self-conscious idyll, this jittery Eden, young Buckley burst like a combination firework and stink bomb, in the grand Irish manner of Wilde or Shaw (and if he seems like an untypical Irishman, so did they). His thesis, as it came to me secondhand (we didn't exactly *read* Buckley in my set, we were content to sneer, as he might say, pre-emptively), amounted to perhaps the first full-scale assault launched on what would later be called the secular religion from the angle of those who actually pay for it: namely, in his first brief (*God and Man at Yale*), the woolly old alumni of Yale, who, as he saw it, were spending good money to have their sons taught that one way or another daddy was all wet and wrong about everything, a doctrine that, to this day, has never made a professor unpopular.

Nothing could have sundered the postwar concordat more dramatically. In whatever kind of peace treaty a nation makes with itself, academic freedom had somehow sneaked its way into being a cornerstone and an absolute. And then—there was the way he said it. Perhaps nowadays, young Buckley's rather special brand of polite impertinence would get lost among all the coarser varieties—irreverence is a debased coin—but in the early fifties, Buckley carried, *mutatis mutandis*, some of the same postwar surprise value as a Marlon Brando or Jack Kerouac: his defense of such hopeless cases as Joe McCarthy and those incredible alumni seemed almost wickedly perverse, not to say deliciously embarrassing, in one so obviously intelligent.

But more daring even than this outrageous flirtation with "American boobism" (to use Mencken's old phrase) was his manifest willingness, verging on eagerness, to be hated. On television we watched professional wrestling back then in which contestants willfully set out to be villains so that Americans, in their prison of politeness, would have someone (besides phantom Communists) to hiss, while in college auditoriums, people filed in to watch Buckley: and although, unlike the wrestlers, he usually confounded their wishes by winning his debates, it was all right with us, because he was wrong—wasn't he? I mean, those positions were so preposterous.

It is now history how, in this semi-comic guise, he stole the liberals' pants and Pied Pipered just enough of their youth away to form his own movement. And now, of course, he is stuck with them. His wild oats eventually became commitments, as wild oats will, and his disciples expect him to go on leading and inspiring them indefinitely even if he feels like doing something else. Even the liberal Mr. Judis rather wants Bill Buckley to return kicking and gouging to the ring, as certain atheists wish the church to go back to the old ways.

So although Buckley's politics were always a sort of antipolitics, aimed at someday releasing mankind from its perennial obsession with legislation, he is as much bound by them as anyone. Never mind how many books he writes celebrating all the things you can do with life besides politics—his friends and his enemies dismiss these books with stern impatience, and demand the Act again, as they might classic Coke.

Where, then, did the Act come from and where, if it has gone, did it go to? From Mr. Judis's account I would guess that the youthful Bill began, like many of us, myself certainly, as in some sense his mother trying to be his father. Aloise Buckley was, it seems, an extremely *gemütlich* character, endlessly friendly and welcoming, which Bill still is (in fact, he has the personality of a Dickens ending) while father Will was more reserved, ironic, and if it came to it, combative. Will Buckley, Sr., was not, however—and this is important—authoritarian around the house (only his opinions were), but quite a seductive father, the kind you *want* to please all life long. Nobody, one likes to think, could have browbeaten Buckley into sharing that particular world view, or any other, but perhaps he could be enticed. And Buckley, Sr., rewarded him handsomely with the kind of unreserved approval that might almost make a young man cocky.

Of this world view, perhaps the first thing to be said is that no Buckley could ever have founded a magazine called *Commonweal*, because the word itself was too alien. As Irish Protestants by ancestry, the family had a long history of outsideness, but also of *above*ness, which is not such a bad location if you have the vitality to enjoy it, but only a so-so place to pick up a burning sense of the Public Interest. Mr. Judis stresses the part that circumstance played in the Buckleys' ubiquitous apartness, but in every case, whether as northerners in the South, or as the wrong kind of Catholics in the North (too rich to be Irish, or too Irish to be "accepted," or something), it seems that they actually preferred to stress their differences rather than settle them, as if the differences themselves were some precious source of energy, and nothing to snivel about. Even in Sharon, Connecticut—and surely if one can't make one's peace there, one simply isn't trying—they seemed, to the neighbors at least, to be too proud to feel at home. Will had spent his glory years in Mexico, and he may have passed on to his children a sense of being foreigners everywhere, even—and this is what kept them from being just awful—among the rich, their natural allies. Although to the plebian ear, the Buckleys may sound like the last word in Blue Bloods themselves, no one has done more than Bill and his movement to dispossess the real ones of the Republican throne and replace them with sunbelt cads and adventurers.

It was this last quirk that made them truly eccentric, and original. Like the Kennedys, whom they resemble in no other important respect except numbers, the Buckleys were not even going to take a chance on being snubbed by older money. Instead they formed their own little renaissance garrison, an upper class with one family in it, and rejoiced in each other—and Bill still shows the unmistakable signs of a happy childhood.

As the family genius, he had probably enjoyed himself the most, but also absorbed the most, so that by the time he hit the outside world, he was the very quintessence of Buckley, and no compromise was possible. A certain comic pathos ensues in Judis's pages as young Bill brings the family ideal banging against the heads of his new chums: so far so good in the primary grades, where you can barrel right through on *hauteur* and courage, but strangely painful by mid-adolescence, when so many things are painful anyway.

Buckley seems to have entered prep school and the army as a rather lonely young prig, still trying his formidable best to feel superior, but not, in his own *gemütlich* soul, content to be quite so unhappy about it or so at odds with his *new* families. So he began perhaps for the first time to listen to someone besides his father; and such are his gifts that he went on to become one of the world's finest listeners, thus launching a mighty second career, as the editor who discovered Garry Wills, John Leonard, and Joan Didion among others, and as an interviewer-debater who allows himself dangerously close to his opponent-subjects' flame. If ever he does lose the Faith (a cold day in hell anyway you look at it), it will be because he has simply listened himself out of it, over hundreds of hours with the brightest liberal spokesmen he can round up for his "Firing Line" shows.

It seems possible that this second side of him might never have developed so satisfactorily if he had gone straight from home to Yale, because at a university an entertainer of his quality can always find admirers, regardless of his likability. And it was at Yale that Buckley the *enfant terrible* really came into his own, but with the invaluable difference that he now knew pretty much what he was doing. If the old preschool and army brattiness "played" here, he would use it to advance his otherwise very serious beliefs, but with an adult's hard-won sense of when to turn it off and charm his way back into favor, and if the crowd wanted Amadeus along with his music and surely that is what the whole postwar brashness movement, from Brando to Punk Rock, is about—well he couldn't quite give them that, but he could give them the next best thing, a role he probably learned in England, that of the make-believe brat who, for a few stagey moments, wields his precocity like a cut-throat razor, in the interest of flaying you alive, before buying you a beer. And if you found his weird invocations of, say, catechism morality a bit perverse or childish, you were always free to discuss it with him afterward, if you thought you could go three minutes with the Champ.

Buckley's sheer openness then and now dazzles like a smile, and I was reminded of how little it had changed when I noted in Mr. Judis's acknowledgments that the subject had offered his complete cooperation to the author, to a stranger, that is, with opposed political views. When, in our crabbed times, did you last hear of anyone offering his *full* cooperation to anyone?* All of which puts Buckley in the painful position of being an open book to whom people look constantly for guidance. Suppose he does change his mind about, say, Reagan? Well, he can always change the subject,

---

* This was written in 1988. By 2001, one sometimes finds oneself praying for a little *less* cooperation. But whether the new cooperation is always full "till it hurts," or just till it tickles, can be hard to say. Buckley remains very unusual.

but even that tells a tale in a man who has lost all the privileges of inscrutability.

It's important, in assessing Buckley, to note that he has been operating under this kind of anxious observation for a long time; which means that he can never quite be himself, because in all his public emanations, he tends to have something more pressing on his mind.

For instance, Mr. Judis reports that on the air Buckley continued for an unseasonably long time to take the most outrageous positions he could think of in order to fill the house, even at the risk of caricaturing his own cause. But in his magazine and with his own right and left to consider, he became quite early on something of a voice for moderation. For instance, as far back as 1956, we find the *National Review* advising its zealots not to get their Irish up over a U.S. invasion of Hungary: we weren't going to do it, and it was silly to pretend we were—a position I can't remember his airwaves persona urging on anyone.

Perhaps as a result of these and similar calculations, Barry Goldwater found himself in 1964 fronting for a conservative movement which had evolved a defiantly bizarre façade all but obscuring a somewhat more solid interior, and he was, of course, hung from the façade. And then at some point after that (1968 might make a good date for it) Buckley may himself have begun to feel that conservatism had become a little too serious to need a Jersey wrestler shilling for it any more, and Battling Bill, the Eli Phenom, went into a slow fade from which he has never fully recovered, and to hell with the ratings.

I pick 1968 because that was also the year of his mini-blood bath with Gore Vidal: a curious little replica, staged in an ABC booth, of the hatreds raging outside in the streets during the Democratic Convention that year. "Queer" said Buckley, "crypto-fascist" said Vidal, and then and there Bill may have decided that this stuff wasn't fun any more. To put the matter Christianly: if he no longer felt playful about it, and if the faces he was making had turned into real faces, it was time to get out. (In such circumstances, catechism morality would demand no less of any of us, even critics on the day that they find real blood on their typewriters.)

And who knows? Perhaps on that same night or some other like it, this very decent man may, just like that, have wearied of being hated: Lord knows, he had held out long enough. And this late-blooming mellowness may have added yet another imponderable nudging him to hide his cards, namely a more intense regard for personal loyalty. Although he has always been a byword in this particular virtue, one always felt up to now that it could be overridden fairly lightly by concerns of state. Now those concerns might have to be a little more pressing.

I am thinking in particular of President Reagan's recent visit to Moscow which Buckley, unless I missed a column, chose to ignore completely, at least in his Epistles to the Pagans, thus creating a somewhat eerie journalistic vacuum. It's possible, of course, that since all his silences are pointed, Buckley may feel by now that the point on them is all the weapon he needs. And it's also possible, as one gropes for tortuous *raisons d'état*, to imagine him giving his old friend Ron the edge of his tongue in private and leaving it at that, on the principle quite new to him that there's no point arguing with a *fait accompli*, and that his influence may best be exercised in private anyway. The Jesuits had young Bill for a year (1938–9), and as usual probably have a lot to answer for. But in this case, something also tells me that he wouldn't have done the same for Richard Nixon.

All of which still leaves him some distance from E. M. Forster and his famous saying vis-à-vis the relative merits of betraying friends and countries (although I've always felt it should be noted some place sometime on old E. M.'s behalf that a Cambridge Communist wouldn't even have seen the point of the distinction: you betrayed whom you were told to). The change, if any, in Buckley would be in the direction of his mentor, Whittaker Chambers, who had once turned his friend Alger Hiss over to the state, but with a heavy, complicated heart. Since young Bill was not born with a great gift for complexity, Chambers must have come as a godsend, with his melancholy subtleties kept barely above water by rather freakish high spirits. Chambers added much specific gravity to the highflying Buckley, and helped to shade-in his private self, if not always his public one.

For all his brashness, Buckley has never resisted education from others, and Mr. Judis records how aptly he put himself to school to the two wise men of the *National Review*, Chambers (who never quite seemed to land on the magazine, but always hovered), and the foxy James Burnham, exchanging friendship for wisdom back and forth with each in the ancient Greek manner. Burnham's sly prudences in particular arrived ready to go, after a stint with the CIA, and were packed straight into editorial policy; Chambers's influence is more elusive, and probably belongs more properly in a spiritual biography. But both would undoubtedly have suffused the major book that Bill never wrote.

As for that alleged book, waiting for it, as I gather some disciples still do (every American is supposed to write one), seems by now rather like waiting for Norman Mailer's Big Novel, or even a Teddy Kennedy presidency. The world is full of major books, but this one, even supposing that Buckley could have written it, would have come at the cost of just too many good sideshows, of a sort that no one else could possibly have staged. With such careers as Buckley's or Mailer's, the action may not even be in the main tent anyway: simply sit back and enjoy the circus.

In the bubbly personal journals that crown Bill's smoking-jacket period, he has been accused of enjoying his money just a little too much, but it's my impression that he is barely aware of the stuff. Some of his pleasures are expensive, and some are not, but I couldn't swear that he knows the actual list price of *any*thing: if he is celebrating something these days, it is the freedom not to care, and to enjoy one's blessings with a glad, unquestioning heart, as God presumably intended.

This insouciance can produce comic effects. As I recall, he once set out to do some columns on the minor inconveniences of life, and his first one concerned the infernal difficulty of mooring his boat in some country or other. Although he had invited his readers to chime in after that with their own matching peeves, it seems that none of them really felt up to it, and the series died right there, with Buckley still baying at the harbormaster.

In real life, his unearthly detachment may make him at times an unreliable guide to things like socialism (honestly—who needs it?), (then again, who needs another guide to it either?), but it also makes him—the virtue that dare not speak its name—a model of personal private generosity for his fellow millionaires to emulate if they ever get round to it. If there's one thing about money that he *really* enjoys it is giving it away; and insofar as he occasionally likes to think of the world as the Buckley family writ large, he has a vested interest in believing that this impulse is universal. In a particularly poignant passage, he once noted that the trouble with the rich was that they weren't as good as they ought to be (or words to that effect), and I remembered thinking, whoever expected them to be?

Well, to every man his own Utopia, I suppose. To my mind, the vision implied here of a Daddy Warbucks (or even a Ronald Reagan) world, serene in its benevolence, seems as farfetched as any liberal meliorism: but then Buckley's political philosophy might seem a cold little thing without it.

But, of course, I can already imagine the old gunfighter rising wearily from his barstool to answer this, and that's the last thing I want at this point. For one thing, the man has surely earned his rest from *Commonweal* Catholics by now, and for another, there comes a time (quite early these days) in everyone's life when an ancient enemy becomes a more welcome sight than a new ally. "Is Bernard Shaw a coming peril?" Chesterton was once asked (and I quote from wobbly memory). "No," said the great man, "he is a vanishing pleasure."

Mutatis mutandis one more time (no Buckley piece would be complete without it), I couldn't put it better myself.

P.S. (I apologize for the number of parentheses in the above, but for some reasons I can't begin to explain, Mr. Buckley seems to call for them.)

1988

2 / There Goes the Judge

W<small>HEN THE SECOND AND FINAL PURGE OF THE</small>
Book-of-the-Month Club judges occurred in the summer of 1994,
it was no big deal. "Are they still here?" one imagined people
saying. The practice of hiring outside "judges" to pick one's prod-
ucts had seemed an anomaly even in the age of flagpole-sitting and
six-day bike racing when it began, and its survival into the beady-
eyed eighties could only be justified by unbroken success. The
moment it faltered, it was gone.

Thus, when it *was* perceived to falter, in the fall of 1988, with
the summary firing of three judges in one swoop, there wasn't a
thing the king's horses could do about it. Although the fallen
judges were swiftly replaced by three equally distinguished others,
the new panel might as well have been called the Other Shoe
Court. When it finally dropped, not a creature stirred in the forest.
By then, it was just another personnel shuffle in just another business.

"They don't make bloodbaths like they used to," thought I,
as a proud member of the class of '88. But in truth, words like
purge and *bloodbath* still sounded so alien that I couldn't associate
them, then or ever, with the venerable firm I'd signed on with
some fifteen years earlier.

My fear when I was first asked to be a judge had actually been of choking to death on sheer Gentility and Niceness. Dozens of Helen Hokinson cartoons—or the same one dozens of times—flashed before my eyes, full of the dim suburban matrons who would henceforth be my prey. Since real writers are anything but Nice, I assumed that book club judges must be the ultimate cads—stage literary-men, with a pipe in one tweed pocket and a rare book in the other in case anyone wanted a photo; book-bounders and library lizards who sidled up to strangers offering unspeakable middlebrow delights. "Have I got a book for you—genu*ine* literature, the way you ladies like it."

Did I really want to become one of those? Didn't you need white hair or something? On the devil's side of the argument, the job *was* a sinecure with a real medical plan, and maybe my friends wouldn't hear about it. By an irony that haunts me still, I had just been offered an almost irresistible job at *Time* magazine—but who could tell with newsmagazines? Here today and gone tomorrow. The Book-of-the-Month Club was obviously built to last, at least as long as middle-class insecurity lasted. The two men I had my exploratory lunch with seemed as solid as Lloyds of London and Pan American Airways rolled into one. Indeed, Chairman Axel Rosin and his sidekick Warren Lynch could have passed for the kind of jolly businessmen who show up on page 1003 of a Dickens novel to wrap up all the orphan's problems over plum pudding and brandy.

Awash in *gemütlichkeit*, I just said yes—a contract would have seemed crass—and the deed was done. "How does it feel to be a judge, your *honor?*" asked Axel roguishly, in his slight German accent. And right then it felt like the best reports you get on drowning; that's to say, surprisingly comfortable if you don't dwell too much on the implications.

And it remained that way until the manuscripts started arriving. Mother of Bookstores, I had never seen such manuscripts, bombing in by Special Delivery at all hours of the day and night. Had books always been this *big?* These were not bound galleys, or galleys at all, but raw manuscripts with the author's last-minute thoughts stuffed into the cracks, in what appeared to be Cyrillic lettering.

My plan to cut corners by reading a key page here and a key page there got me nowhere in those trackless wastes. One just wound up with a floor full of paper and a sense of being lost in the snow. Another thing that had to go was any hope of reading these things in the bathtub. Especially with a lit cigar.

It was, in sum, a desk job like any other, or a very sloppy armchair one. And my last hope of turning it into a sinecure anyhow died in my first months too, when a novel showed up featuring a villainous walk-on character named Wilfrid Snead somewhere around page 900. Old Snead had it all—bravado, cowardice, stupidity, even a pigeon-chest (that one hurt)—but he was on and off stage so quickly that if I'd blinked I'd have missed him, and management would have *known*.

But by then I was hooked and would have read the books anyway, because whatever these may have been like in the Hokinson era, they were good books now—at least as good as the ones the best editors in the best houses got to read—and if we didn't like them, we could holler for even better ones. The Club issued excellent reader's reports on everything published in America and we had only to whistle to receive the book of our dreams by return post, and usually get the club to buy it, too, if not feature it.

Later there would be an unexpectedly harsh difference of opinion as to whether judging was a full-time job, but unless you truly hated reading, you soon filled it yourself, if only to improve your chances of beating the pack to the next Balzac. Then again, the more you read, the more there'd be to talk about at lunch and the longer that amiable meal would last.

Fortunately all hands agreed upon the desirability of this. When I finally met my colleagues, I realized at once that this is precisely what they'd been hired for—not their salesmanship or their conspicuous "literariness" but their sheer lunchability and voluble congeniality in a small space. It was as if they'd already been road-tested over miles and miles of lunch—first, no doubt, to make sure they could talk and eat at the same time, but then to check out whether they could also listen, and laugh at other people's jokes, and not get too mad or stubborn over lost causes. (This incidentally would be the hardest discipline of all: to know when and how to quit on a book you believed in, without sticking out your tongue—or telling the author about it later, if you ran into him or her someplace.)

As the last group to sail out under the old understandings and bearing the old memories, the judges I first met seem like mythical characters to me by now, like the crew of the *Flying Dutchman*. We certainly won't see anything like them again. That day, their ages were sixty-seven, sixty-eight, and sixty-nine in no particular order that I can remember. Contrary to legend, Clifton "Kip" Fadiman was perhaps the closest thing to a house-highbrow, although we would take turns at this. After losing what was known in those days as the "Jewish seat" on the Columbia University English faculty, Kip had sailed into the next pond and become King of the Middlebrows instead. But he was still the judge who talked longest and best about the likes of the early Salman Rushdie, Thomas Pynchon, Günter Grass, whatever.

Gilbert Highet was a (retired) pop-academic of a kind more familiar in his native Britain than here—the sort of chap who can run you up a comparison of the Peloponnesian War and Vietnam, or of toga lengths and miniskirts, in a jiffy to the sufficient entertainment of students and radio audiences alike. And John Hutchens was simply the quintessential book-and-newspaper guy, smacking of city rooms and secondhand bookstores and late night book-talk in smoky taverns.

In my dreams, Fadiman is always the Host as he had been on radio's "Information Please," and Highet is the Actor, leaping from behind a curtain to show how an *assegai* is really thrown or drawing on some top-secret intelligence work he did in World War II to snap out "Negative, old boy," or "Sorry, can't comment on that" when the spy talk turns too sensitive. (The Ultra-Secret is still safe with Gilbert, wherever he is.)

Hutchens is an Uncle from somewhere else, ideal for changing the subject or getting a new angle on an old one. John is also the most likely of us to have read the paper that day, and seems perennially amused by something he has just learned. I am an Audience, conscripted, I deduce, for my flaming youth (I am forty-one at the time) and refreshing illiteracy. *Someone* has to represent the public.

All that was missing now to make this a perfect lunch club was some actual food. Despite the high styles of Kip and Gilbert, which seemed worthy of at least a baronial dining hall, à la Blarney Castle, the humble truth was that we had all our lunches sent up from a diner-type restaurant nearby, which specialized in overdone hamburgers and whatever the plural is of "BLT down" (academics—our closest natural relatives—will put up with just about anything).

Enter, thank God, our next two members, Lucy Rosenthal, who simply by being a woman subtly altered the atmosphere of guys munching sandwiches in a locker room, followed by the Canadian novelist and bon vivant Mordecai Richler, bearing boxes of Canadian cigars made in Cuba that, as he pointed out, fairly cried out for a counterpoint of great brandy. And since, by happy chance, Mordecai himself was twice as good a judge with a little brandy inside him, we found ourselves confronting yet a third innovation, wit *after* lunch, a period previously devoted to locating galoshes and stuffing manuscripts into briefcases.

Before Mordecai was obliged to take the next and final step of bringing our food down as well, packed by Maxims of Montreal, the Club gave way and got itself its own kitchen, and a chef, and a new building to go with both, and let Kip Fadiman loose on the wine selecting, and we entered our Lucullan phase.

The first years in our new house seemed to pass in a dream, of the kind Puritans expect to pay for and Cavaliers don't (bet

Puritan on this one). What kept the work from anything like monotony was its gambling aspect. Every year offered exactly sixteen major slots to fill and a million books to fill them with, some of which were available right now and some that were due any minute now—maybe. And they might be great—perhaps. Meanwhile you didn't want to fill your slots too early and miss a masterpiece, or too slowly and have to fill up with junk.

So we scanned the skies and rolled the dice, and sometimes we left it too late, but sometimes we made a killing, and either way, we'd had a good game to lighten the burden of brooding in one position too long and of carrying out mounds of wastepaper afterward.

The only faint shadow on the dream was cast by one Ed Fitzgerald, our businessman-in-chief, who'd joined the Club shortly before I had and was rumored not to believe in the independent judge system (no businessman ever did, especially not one who'd worked, as Ed had, at the no-nonsense Literary Guild).

But a glance at Fitzgerald told you that his shadow was as unreal as everything else here on Gingerbread Lane. Ed was simply too nice a guy to fire anyone he knew personally and too sentimental to end a tradition, even a goofy one. Like the hard drinker he later revealed himself to be, our pet executive seemed a touch too twitchy to sit through our meandering, spitballing lunches, but he did like to pop in for a cheery minute or two, at which point we'd invariably ask him to explain the concept of "loss leaders" (whereby you make money while losing it—I still don't get it), and he'd happily haul out his yellow legal pad, and you knew that no harm could come of this man.

Later Ed's drinking and his sentimentality would both play a slightly less benign role in this story, but for a short eternity the equilibrium held, with Ed's blood sugar hanging at par and the rest of us sitting down to lunch every third Wednesday spouting opinions and small-talk to an audience consisting mostly of Axel Rosin, Warren Lynch—until he died, suddenly and shockingly in

1977—and a crony of Ed's, from *Sport* magazine, named Al Silverman.

Everybody liked Al on sight because he so manifestly liked them back even faster. In fact, the whole liking transaction was absolutely central to Al's nature and his style of doing business, which would one day make his fate at the end of all this the most purely *embarrassing* of anyone's, as his business friendships found themselves on a collision course with his real ones and Al found himself trying to hang on to both, like Buster Keaton in a windstorm.

But as long as the dream lasted, Al's charm and his excellent feel for books made him the perfect go-between with the publishing world. "I guess you know Al Silverman, huh?" were the first words a publishing type would say to you, after which he'd sort of purr. Isn't it grand that we both know Al? And business positively hummed.

Hummed so sweetly, in fact, that when Axel Rosin suddenly announced his wish to sell the operation (also in 1977), nobody gave it a second thought, let alone blamed him for anything. It wasn't as if the Club were losing money—it just made, as I recall, a bad fit in Axel's portfolio, a predicament that apparently loomed as large in his world as an unfortunate necktie or calamitous pair of spats in Bertie Wooster's.

So be off with it, by all means. For fourteen years or more, Axel Rosin had been a good and conscientious caretaker of the club his father-in-law, Harry Scherman, had founded, doted on, and bequeathed to him, but there's only so much you can ask of a son-in-law, and we all fell to work cheerfully helping Axel decide who should own us next.

Among the contenders, I remember the name General Mills coming up, I guess because it seemed so strange, but a mild consensus quickly formed in favor of Time Inc.—for a reason that now seems quaint. Time, we figured, was in the word business, too, and would know enough to leave us alone. It, too, had arrived at a version of editorial independence, which it called "the Separation of Church and State," and this meant, with them as with us, that the business side had to keep its mitts off the product no matter how great the temptation. Done and done.

So Time it was, with or without our advice, and after basking briefly in his role of Lame Duck, Axel Rosin left us to our fate, disappearing up the steps of his club never, or hardly ever, to be seen again. And we went on with our lunch.

And (lowercase) time went back to standing still, too, jarred only by the occasional warning shot. The first of these was the displacement of Lucy Rosenthal as our fifth judge. Lucy had been perfectly qualified for the job in all but one respect. She wrote splendid reader's reports, was eminently lunchworthy, and had her own area of authority—women's fiction, of which she brought us several choice specimens. Nevertheless, she *did* come from within the Club, which meant that the principle of the Distinguished Outsider was being suspended for the first time in our history. Which was okay this once, but watch it.

As it turned out, though, the next two judges after Richler—Gloria Norris and David Willis McCullough—would also be Club employees, and although both would soon establish their independence, the subtext should have been clear by the third time: *we don't want any more outsiders* around here, distinguished or otherwise.

And we don't want any more judges we can't get rid of either. Clearly the displacement of Rosenthal was a trial of their strength and our weakness. Since they were still feeling their way in the bloodbath business, they gave Lucy another job right away, with a vague title that sounded important. But the subtext of the subtext now read "Who's afraid of the big bad judge?" Not so long before, Axel had talked about the judiciary "allowing" management to sit in on its meetings. Now the word was "we made you and we can break you." All of you. Today Lucy Rosenthal—tomorrow Gilbert Highet!

Warning shot no. 2 came from the direction of the Literary Guild, which had decided to muscle in on our turf by making huge bids for serious books. The result was a furious little arms race with the two superpowers trying to spend each other into the Stone Age while a few authors got implausibly rich. A crisis point was soon reached when we stepped aside like Sumo wrestlers and allowed the Guild to have Arthur Schlesinger's vast scholarly book on Bobby Kennedy for a mere million and a half or so, the loss leader to end loss leaders.

One more such victory apiece and *both* sides were ruined. So the Guild eased off showing how rich they were and took to stressing how fast they were instead. "If you don't buy this book by 3 P.M. tomorrow," one imagined them growling into the phone, "you'll never see it again." At that time of day, the BOMC judges would presumably still be floundering between the late-lunch toddy and the afternoon nap, and completely out of it judgment-wise. So the terrified publisher really had no choice.

There were two things wrong with this scenario, both of which we were delighted to demonstrate immediately. Contrary to legend, the judges never had to wait for our famous lunches, or even till nightfall, to make our decisions. We could dial telephones in a twinkling and we knew each other well enough to hold our talks in shorthand. Even in the computer age, there's a limit to how fast *anyone* can master a book. But if the Guild wanted a contest, fine with us. Anything you can read we can read faster. It actually added some spice to life, and I can't remember losing anything we really wanted in the speed-read period.

Fallacy no. 2 in their strategy was so obvious I'm not sure why we needed proof. The truth was the publishers *wanted* to hear from as many book clubs as possible and stood to lose a bundle over these crazy deadlines. "You missed a great auction on your book," I said to an author I knew. "We were planning to bid for it, but we never had a chance." This germ was planted at a Saturday night party, and by dawn on Monday the author's publisher-in-chief was on the phone, first defending himself and then apologizing. "We won't let it happen again," he promised—and he spoke for a very large company.

"We have some power, too," I said to Al. "Why don't we use it?" But so far as I knew, we never did, and the myth of judicial slowness lived on stubbornly to the end, if only on the tongues of management, because it provided the perfect excuse for downsizing us out the door if the time came. "Publishing has moved on," they would intone, and no matter how fast we moved to keep up, we could never outrace our image of hippopotami in labor.

Consulting the notes I meant to take, I find that the argument from judicial rigor mortis began to dig in about four years before the end. It's not quite true that nothing happened in the real-life "1984"; at least two small things did that shook our little cabbage patch to its foundations. Clifton Fadiman had a birthday and the Club got a new president. From Time Inc. itself.

If this story were a musical, Kip Fadiman's eightieth birthday would undoubtedly be the Act I closer. It was a blowout, the closest the Club could come to a stomp scene, and in retrospect, it has "end of an era" stamped all over it. I myself contributed a heartfelt, two-handkerchief toast to Kip, and incidentally to "Information Please," on which I'd been raised and which I now saw as all that was best about America in the 1930s and 1940s: it was the Algonquin Round Table boiled down to a quiz show, Art Deco in words, Fred Astaire in the form of a question. Also the Tower of Pisa, the Mona Lisa, and Will Durant.

The tension of public speaking may have heightened my sense of what followed, which is of wine flowing and cigars glowing and people hugging and smiling as if we'd just won a war. And someplace in the revels, Ed Fitzgerald, our pseudo-shadow, came ambling up to Mordecai and me and said as soberly as only a practiced drunk can say these things, "These jobs are yours as long as you want them," thus blinding us to everything that would follow.

From now on, no matter what *seemed* to be happening, or how close we personally appeared to be to liquidation, our jobs were *safe*, guaranteed in tears by Chairman Ed himself. And as if to prove it, I fattened myself further for the kill by adding an extension to our house and our mortgage, while Nemesis licked its chops in the wings.

One other thing happened at that party to reinforce the *Goodbye to All That* motif. Warren Lynch's widow, Fran, came storming up to me early on, before the goodwill had set in, to protest our adoption of a Robert Ludlum novel as a main selection. "What is this club coming to?" she demanded.

This wasn't such a serious charge as yet, just an ominous one. We'd always picked a few page-turners per annum, and the basic Ludlum book wasn't that bad the first time you read it. But when the, I'll swear, exact same book came around soon afterward with a new name, and management suggested we take it again, I wondered if Fran hadn't been on to something; and when it popped up a third time I knew she was—because this time management announced that they'd already bought the damn book and suggested most warmly that we make it a main selection yet again— that is, a trillion dollars is a lot to pay for an alternate choice, you dig?

Maybe the author wasn't even Ludlum by then but someone from the school of Ludlum or the studio of Stephen King. The process seemed to degenerate very rapidly. The meetings would still start normally enough with Al casually reading off the new titles. But then, at what seemed like every third or fourth lunch, he'd come to the hot potato du jour and tell us with just a hint of embarrassment that "we had to pay a *lot* for this one, so we certainly hope you can see your way to making it a main selection."

It was like dancing the limbo and wondering how low they'd ask you to go. Okay, we haven't reached the floor yet. "But don't you think we ought to read it first?" "Well," pause. "The thing is, *nobody's* read it yet. The author has only written five chapters so far. But he's *very* high on them. He thinks they may be his best yet." Also his editor is high. And his agent is delirious.

So that was it now. Small wonder we were too slow. They wanted judges so fast they could decide on books that hadn't been written yet. And if we couldn't, please get off the track. The arrival of our new boss, Larry Crutcher, in December signaled that it was time to get things moving. "Larry was a numbers man before there *were* numbers men," a friend at *Time* told me, and he hadn't been sent here to preside over an organic evolution. The eighties were afoot and several fat cats were already glancing slyly at Time Inc., as Time Inc. had once glanced at us, as a nice little dessert to take over hostilely—unless the dessert moved first.

Yet Larry Crutcher, as he first shuffled into view, was the last person you'd associate with speed. With his long body and extra-long face, he looked every inch as Dickensian as his name. One could easily picture him perched on a high stool in the counting house scratching away at his ledger, pausing only to prime the goose quill and chuckle over a mistake in arithmetic.

This was the wave of the future? Using the old-fashioned gauge of conversational hipness, I'd say that Kip Fadiman's mind moved a good five times faster than Larry's (or most people's). But nothing could be more irrelevant now. The project was to "grow" the company every which way, offering everything but a seat on Air Force One to new subscribers, the way new magazines do in the hysterical phase.

And membership obligingly swelled, for a while, before subsiding to normal. It's the easiest thing in the world to get people to join book clubs; the trick is to keep them there. Experience suggests that there's a natural size for these operations, and certainly our attempts to stretch the BOMC had led to similar boomlets and bustlets in the past, as the rascally public snapped up the door prizes and vanished into the night. But new money likes to invent its own wheels, and a period of intense optimism ensued. Maybe they'd even leave the judges alone.

Fat chance, of course. As Father Time paced the floor waiting for its deal with Warner Bros. to be born, it would reach out mechanically to straighten things and make sure all its sales figures were shipshape for the new arrival. So for the first time ever, we began to be confronted with quarterly statements of earnings. "We really bombed with the Nadine Gordimer, but thank God for James Michener, as usual." At which we could only blink. Weren't we supposed to bomb with Nadine Gordimer? Wasn't it the best book available that month?

What made the mid-eighties so excruciating was that no one ever told us *not* to judge books on merit. They just read these statements mournfully and moved on. "Our main selections have been disappointing," they'd said neutrally. But so what? We had our own version of loss leaders, I remember arguing. People *liked* belonging to a club that takes the odd Nobel Prize winner, so long as they didn't have to read the book themselves. But nobody asked me to explain this theory on a yellow legal pad, and the question "So what do we need judges *for?*" continued to hang just above our heads until we got our answer in 1988.

Meanwhile, perhaps the quarterly reports had been introduced to teach us a little humility. With such a sorry display of fiscal muscle as ours, we should be grateful for the guaranteed bestsellers that management brought to our attention, no? Somebody had to pay for our effete hobby. The argument must have impressed *them* anyhow. "We're pretty sure you're going to like the new such and such," Al would say, ever less apologetically, "because we bought it, sort of on that understanding."

"I think perhaps that should be a management decision," Kip would suddenly pipe up, striking a brand new note. "Let's leave that one up to management, shall we?" "Why on earth should we do that?" Mordecai and I would bellow innocently. But Kip obviously knew something we didn't, and was still there ten years later, and we were not.

Even without Kip's pipeline, though, it was obvious that something was slipping out swiftly from under us. Our names began to appear in smaller and smaller type under our book reports, and we weren't called judges anymore but "members of the BOMC editorial board," which sounds pretty disposable. Also the company newsletter seemed to have a rule against ever mentioning us, however wild our adventures, and we were no longer invited to the author lunches either, unless we heard about them independently and said "pretty please."

In fact, if it hadn't been for Ed Fitzgerald's pledge of tenure, I'd have sworn they were trying to get rid of us. But Ed was a gentleman, and when he was replaced as CEO by Al Silverman, that was even better. Al was one of us, a working stiff who'd supported his family for a stretch writing sports books and even using the Authors Guild health plan. So he clearly wasn't in thrall to worldly goods.

That such a one might someday be tempted to take a spin as a good company man didn't seriously occur to me—and I still don't know if that's what happened. All I can say for sure is that Al or no Al, the Club continued to close in on itself tighter and tighter, with the rest of the world well lost. Small example: one week, a review I'd written appeared on page three of the *New York Times* Sunday book section, which is actually published on the previous Tuesday; yet eight days later, on the following Wednesday, no one at the Club had yet seen or heard of my piece. *The BOMC News* was now the paper of record, just as the weekly in-house editorial meetings were the hot center and place to be, with the judges out someplace among the lesser nebulae.

As if to confirm this new order, Al invited each judge to attend one of these sizzling in-house meetings (which were exhilarating in a Stock Exchange kind of way), shortly after which we were flown in a body to the BOMC printing and distribution plant in Camp Hill, Pennsylvania, to meet the rest of the mighty machine of which we were a small part. It was like being shown an instructional film. Welcome to the Romance of book-binding, shave-tail. And how about those hundreds of addresses! Isn't it amazing?

Like Alice biting into the wrong cake, I had a definite sense of being downsized by now. Yet in retrospect, I'm not sure that Al wasn't actually trying to save us that day, the only way he knew how. If Time Inc. didn't want independent judges, what about semi-independent ones? *Distinguished* cogs in the wheel? As we've since learned, our hash was already on the verge of settled, and our geese cooked. But maybe Al still hoped to keep his pals around on some terms or other.

Precisely how long we lingered on Death Row, a judge would be the last to know. In 1986–87, a young professor named Janice Radway began researching a book on the Club (it finally came out in 1997) and was specifically asked *not* to interview the judges because their position was "indeterminate." And our latest editor-in-chief, Nancy Evans, who'd blown into the Club in December 1984, blew on out again in February 1987 because, as she later told me, she'd learned that the jig was well and truly up with the old ways.

So the knowledge was all around us. But every now and then, someone would lob some sand in our eyes and blind us all over again. For instance, a Time Inc. executive came to one of our lunches and seemed mightily impressed by our dialogue: he didn't use that many words in a *year*. And as an ongoing tease, Al Silverman took to dangling some raises we'd requested a while back under our noses. Our salaries had been becalmed for an ominously long time now, so Al's murmurs of "any day now" and "maybe next month" were moderately reassuring, not so much in terms of money but as proof of our existence; and he kept us on this mild tranquilizer almost to the end.

What were they waiting for? According to Evans, she and Al had done their damndest for a while to defend our quaint customs to the human adding machines on the other side of the net. But the simple fellows just couldn't get it, any more than they would have gotten it in Harry Scherman's day. Of the two Time executives on the case, their tough cop couldn't see what on earth the judge system had to do with Synergy, his one and only idea. (Spin-offs from Nadine Gordimer? Get real.) And the friendly one, who'd come to lunch that day, turned out not to care *how* loquacious we were. The proof of the pudding was in the balance sheet for him too, and this we flunked almost by definition.

So Nancy had pulled out—in the direction of a most excellent job at Doubleday—and Al had stayed on. But the argument was over so far as I can make out. All that remained now was to implement phase two, the execution of the judges, as smoothly as possible. Of the old brigade, Gilbert Highet had already died bravely, of colon cancer, and perhaps John Hutchens would be retiring soon. If so, that might be a good time to strike, even if it meant delaying things a little. In the meantime, Al's job would be to keep the remaining judges calm and functioning—and, above all, in the dark.

Unfortunately, Al's genuine gift for friendship would render him the worst possible choice, next to maybe Maxwell Smart, for any mission that required the faintest subterfuge. In hindsight, it seems clear that he was bursting throughout to tell us everything, the whole story, out of sheer good nature, and the effort of suppression caused him to dither and frown so much that I feared he might be on the brink of a small breakdown. "Did you get a chance to look at such and such a book?" he would ask on a Tuesday, forgetting that he had asked the same question on Monday, when the answer was also "yes."

One of the keys to Al's likeability was a most human awkwardness, beautifully typified by his odd habit of rising to speak at our authors' lunches at the exact moment the entrée arrived. I can still picture John Fowles, frazzled and red-eyed from his book tour, lowering his fork incredulously and staring into his gravy as his praises were sung. So even the most routine cover-up must have seemed booby-trapped with embarrassment, and our actual firing a torture of sorts.

At any rate, it was clumsy. After a frantically busy spring of 1988, new books mysteriously stopped coming, and one summer meeting after another was canceled on these improbable grounds. "Still no books," Al would exclaim like the Ancient Mariner, "no books at all." But because this unprecedented drought was confirmed by neither *Publishers Weekly* nor one's friends in the business, something tricky was obviously going on in the Club, and why in Hades weren't they telling us about it? If a whole season was about to be wiped out, it would be mortifying not to have known it.

By good chance, publishing in America hadn't quite ceased after all, and an absolutely average spatter of books arrived in time for our September lunch, which even before we got there was surely the fraughtest and least digestible meal any of us would ever taste. Was Al planning to announce our fate over drinks or wait until dessert? As we waded schizzily through our chores, I began to feel as if I were eating stage food in a Harold Pinter play. We had another new editor-in-chief now, Brigitte Weeks of *Book World*, whom we'd met in the spring; but I'd missed a couple of lunches, and all I remembered about her was that she couldn't abide cigars and that you had to make appointments with her secretary to talk to her on the phone. (Definitely a Pinter play.)

So maybe today was simply "get used to Ms. Weeks" day, and I'd worried over nothing. This wasn't quite so hallucinatory as it sounds, because Gloria Norris and I had both just been instructed to go see our new chairperson in her office after lunch, and surely nothing very fateful could come of that? I'd recently given up cigars myself for health reasons and was all in favor of stamping out the beastly things, if that's what she wanted to talk about.

But I'd reckoned without Al's epic clumsiness, which was shambling inexorably toward its High Noon. To cut a long nightmare short, it turned out that poor Brigitte Weeks had indeed been handed the revolver and told to dispose of us herself as part of her new duties. Just Gloria and me that is; it seems that Al himself had already done the deed with victim number three, Mordecai Richler, over drinks in a bar, as one old friend to another. But I, who had worked and played with Al for fifteen years, had been incorporated into Weeks's freshman hazing instead.

This smarted, of course, but it was worse for Weeks, I think, being asked to dispatch two grizzly judges in their lairs, before being sent to find a left-handed encyclopedia or whatever. I sympathize with her retroactively, though less so with the young hotshot from Marketing whom Al had sent along for moral support. Him I could have done without, even retroactively.

It was soon clear that all Brigitte Weeks wanted to do was

recite the words of the firing ritual as fast as the law allowed and be done with it. Times had changed, she informed me—although nothing about her genteel self, or Al's jittery one, suggested that they had kept up with them any better than we had—and the old way of doing things no longer worked, our record profits not withstanding. Also, as our new editorial chief, she felt that she had a right to her own team—a concept that Al would repeat mantrically when I saw him afterward. "Brigitte needs her own team."

And with that phrase, our era ended. The judges had never been part of anybody's team before, and if we were now, what was the point of calling us judges any more? Why not assistant bookpickers or preliminary page-turners? The word *team* belonged to the business culture anyway, not the world of books. And a "team of judges" also sounded suspiciously like something you'd expect to hear in Mayor Daley's Chicago.

But maybe that was the point. The Club still needed judges the way Hizzoner did, for the sake of appearance. Someone might have whispered to Crutcher that judges were good for business. But they didn't have to be real judges. As I've recently learned from Janice Radway's manuscript, even Harry Scherman hadn't originally planned for the judges actually to choose the books—and no one was more surprised than Harry when the mannequins had proved so good at playing their parts. So why not just revert to Scherman's original plan and stuff us back in the store window?

Would we have gone along with this? "They didn't even ask us if we *wanted* to sell out," said Mordecai laconically. But we probably wouldn't have been much good at it, after the glory we'd seen, and anyway firing us was surely what this was all about in the first place. With Hutchens now indeed retired, Mordecai and I embodied two-thirds of all that was left of the judges' ancestral memory and simply *had* to go.

The other one-third, namely Kip, they felt they could keep, on grounds of sheer venerability and manifest willingness to play ball, while McCullough they kept, too, on grounds of *juniority*—perhaps the lad was young enough to forget the old ways on Animal Farm. Norris got fired to provide, I've always supposed, cover for the assault on Club history and thus received the rawest deal of all, losing both her judgeship and her old job at the Club in the interests of realpolitik. But fortunately she's done fine ever since as an author-agent-book person.

By five minutes into that Afternoon of the Long Knives, I began fervently to wish I were rich enough just to march out proudly, thumbing my nose at everyone. But I had to hang around for the humble details, most of which were just details. We'd stay on the medical plan a bit longer, but we'd lose our life insurance. Stuff like that. Once you've had tenure, any settlement seems rotten.

Fortunately, I still had a possible ace in the hole, a pension plan Ed Fitzgerald had rather grandly introduced a few years back. But something told me I didn't want to hear about it just yet. Let me go on dreaming I'm Steve Ross for just a little longer, with a golden parachute lined with diamonds parked outside the window.

"Wake up, private!"—there was no avoiding it. Our pensions turned out to be so small that Mordecai burst out laughing when he heard the number. So—maybe we were stage literary men after all, working for scale. Still, it seemed an undignified way to end a system they'd once made such a fuss over. "Did you have a contract?" various lawyer friends would ask me later, and I remembered that dream lunch years ago. "No, just a gentleman's agreement," I said, and these, for perhaps obvious reasons, are not valid in the State of New York.

If Mordecai laughed that day, he must have howled when the Time-Warner merger was consummated and we learned of the megabucks the real players were getting out of this. It was like a cartoon in the old *Daily Worker* featuring strangers in shiny top hats making off with the gold bricks while the workers are paid in company scrip. Later one executive who'd allegedly messed up during the early stages of the merger was given millions just to go home and forget the whole thing. What was his trick? Did he lock himself in his office and refuse to budge until they'd met his terms? Would that have worked for us? With our luck, they'd have come in after us with tear gas and mace.

It was the first time I'd ever encountered a real economy-of-scale in action, and I doubt I'd survive another one. (Literally so: the next crew of judges would receive no benefits at all—a priceless saving to pass on to Steve Ross.) The bruises were obvious and plentiful, but did they serve a purpose? Would a better and finer BOMC emerge out of this reign of terror?

As I tottered out of my interview with Weeks, dragging my tin parachute behind me, Al beckoned me at last into his office, looking appropriately rueful but bracing. "God bless the good ship *Time*," I snarled, "and all who sail therein." "This had nothing to do with Time," said Al quickly. "This decision came from within the company"—thus discharging his last duty to the firm without quite telling a lie. Larry Crutcher was in the coop all right, but he was no chicken.

But hey, don't go away mad. With his will to like and be liked still miraculously ticking, Al had managed to convince himself that we would take all this like good sports with no hard feelings whatever, and he even barmily proposed that we continue coming to the lunches for three more months while Brigitte's team was phased in. "Is he crazy?" asked Mordecai. But with the mellowness of time, I see it now as a last piece of clumsiness to remember him by, like Nixon tripping over the hat stand on his final way out.

More to the point: getting mad at Al now was like bawling out the waiter for the sins of the chef, and I imagine that the poor fellow received an earful in the weeks that followed. No sooner had he delivered his official speech about the Club "positioning itself to meet the demands of the future" than the world began to answer back, commercially in the form of numerous canceled memberships and privately, one imagines, to the tune of friends in the business asking what the Hell happened?

In its aggressive insularity, management had obviously imagined that if they shrank the judges sufficiently, they'd become invisible. But it turned out that the public still kind of liked the judge system. Best-sellers they could choose for themselves, at better discounts than ours, from the new chain stores. What the judges had provided was the equivalent of advance word-of-mouth from old friends. And the flimflam of replacing us with new friends, new judges, didn't fool anyone. The Club had simply changed over-night, and for good, into a typical, poll-watching, "bottom line *über alles*" operation, of which there were more than enough in real life.

So our new masters had given away the Club's one big edge over the competition, because they still didn't get it and never would. But Al Silverman *did* get it and had only to sniff the wind to wake from his trance and become, I'm told, a mordant critic of the new order, a "loose cannon," as somebody called him, and in no time he was out of there himself to become editor-in-chief at Viking, one of the last great traditional houses.

As for the judges, one of Mordecai's and my first moves was to send word to Crutcher and Co. via our ad hoc lawyer Charles Rembar that we were both *writers* who might publish our own hilarious version of events any day now. So they sent us another half-year's salary just to shut us up, which was fine with me because I hadn't planned to write anything anyway. If we couldn't make a fortune refusing to leave the office, we might as well make a few bob for not writing, and besides I really didn't want to pick on the Club just now. I still had too many friends there.

Thus, tongue-tied by our own conniving, all three of us had to sit still for an article about the Club in *The New York Times Magazine* that contained several bursts of the management side of things. Our vow of silence evidently didn't cut both ways, and an anonymous spokesman was overheard to suggest that (1) the judges had lately become more interested in their own books than in other people's (would that we had) and (2) that we went to the lunches principally for the great food and wine, not the work.

That last crack almost jerked a response out of me, vow or no vow, to wit, "I eat better at home!" which was and is absolutely true. But what was instructive about both complaints was the way we'd gone from being strictly "part-time advisers" when they gave out the pensions to full-time gluttons and layabouts when they talked to the *Times*. And as if to verify the greedy-judge version, the spokesman plumped up our salaries to somewhere "believed to be in the high five figures." (So we finally got that raise! And then some.)

But why were our salaries *believed* to be anything? What was the big mystery? A spokesman at the Sheed household would have been all too happy to give them the exact figure, along with the hot news that, right to the end, we went to the lunches because we liked to talk about books and bet on them, and were actually on a modest roll when the drought came that summer and cut us off in mid-sentence.

By then I had come to enjoy the work so much that I foolishly asked Brigitte Weeks on the way out of that last meeting if I might stay on as a sometime consultant. That was one question she knew the answer to frontward and backward. Definitely not! Some people just can't take a hint.

But they did let us go on judging for the last three months of that year, which we did, and lunching, too, which we decidedly did not, despite our alleged devotion to that meal. Already the atmosphere of the place had changed from cozy to ice-box cold. In the manner of pretentious businesses everywhere, they had just installed a new telephone system (press button three to reach button two), which added a good ten minutes to routine calls, which chills you off right there; and when you did reach employees they sounded as if (1) they've never heard of you and (2) they shouldn't be talking to you right now, whoever you were.

And Time Inc. seemed to have changed, too, at least from where I stood. Over the years I'd known a raft of people over there and written a bale of stuff for their various publications. But all my old friends had been on the editorial side, I realized, and calling one of those now would have been like calling a writer in Hollywood, charming but pointless.

My most relevant buddy over there, Ray Cave, had actually

gotten fired, too, as editor of *Time* magazine before I could reach him. Ray, like us, smacked of an *ancien régime* when editors still called at least some of the tunes for business-people. Not that Henry Luce's famous wall of separation didn't still stand at Time Inc., taller than ever, between the two departments; it was just that the editors were on the wrong side of it now.

Or so it seemed so long as the acquisition fever raged. Later both the BOMC and its master apparently changed again, and a year or so after the merger, an official of the Club came up to me at a party and murmured almost lasciviously, "You'll be interested to hear that Larry Crutcher is no longer with us"—we got rid of that nasty man. Everything is all right now. We can't imagine what got into us.

The change at Time Inc. was more drastic. All the suits remotely responsible for disconnecting Gloria, Mordecai, and me departed cackling soon afterward, and if we went around to complain today I'm sure we'd find new faces bent over a brand-new game. "You may have a case, Mac—but *what* did you say your name was? I can't seem to find it on the computer."

In such a cool climate, it was presumably the work of a mere idle moment to hire another nasty man to liquidate the judge system altogether. Brigitte and her new team were allowed to go through the motions of judging for exactly two three-year terms, and for a while my friend J. Anthony Lukas kept me abreast of developments—but there *were* no developments (except for an apocalyptic case of blindness that struck poor Kip toward the end). The judges cast their ballots, wisely I'm sure—Lukas and the other additions, Gloria Naylor and Brad Leithauser, were just the kind of people who became judges in the old days, too—and the Party chose the books. Place a businessman in charge of a publishing operation and the first thing he'll try to do is shake all the risk out of it, and the gambling, and eventually the life. And I didn't need a drip-by-drip account of this.

Shortly before the rump court's time was up, a new executioner arrived, one Tracy Brown this time, and he hung around just long enough to feel at home and assume his batting stance, and, slam, off with their heads, Brigitte's and all (except Fadiman's, which stays at least on the masthead); followed by a brief period of adjustment, and then off with Brown's head, too, faster than you can say Danton and Robespierre. So once again there's not a trace of blood on anyone at Time Inc., and its editors seem important again, and in fact it's a pleasure to do business with them.

One thing that would come out of the merger era was a sense of how to conduct these things a little more urbanely without waking up all the customers. Rule number one is, you don't try to throw out a revered institution in one move. It upsets people. First you *reform* it. You make it leaner and meaner, and "position it to meet the demands of the future." *Then* you throw it out. No one will care. Newt Gingrich clearly had the same idea when he talked about "saving Medicare" by trimming it. That which the Gods would destroy, they first make lean and mean. Or, at least, scrawny and resigned. Then you simply blow on it.

Time Inc. had played the whole charade pretty much by the book, and it was all immensely sly, if the object was to shoot oneself in the foot. Although when last heard from, the Club claimed to be doing better than ever (could that be the anonymous spokesman again? at any rate, no figures were given), the BOMC suddenly had no *image* any more that I'm aware of, or even a small place in the national psyche. Nobody drew cartoons about it now, because there wasn't any joke, any handle. It's as if the Old Bailey had been torn down and replaced by a drive-in small claims court. Volume might pick up for a while, but there's nothing like receiving your justice from someone in a wig.

There have been some more serious losses, too, namely a few books and who knows how many readers? To cite just one of the dozens of book-rescues that presumably don't happen anymore: John Keegan's *The Face of Battle* was considered so uncommercial at first that its American publisher printed only 3,500 copies, next thing to not publishing it at all. We thought it was uncommercial, too, but took it on the strength of five convergent hunches, and both it and Keegan have been hot ever since. The easy part of book club judging is simply to tell a good book from a commercial one; the hard part, the art, is to sense when a book might be both. So a good hunch is worth its weight in gold, and each judge had a trophy shelf of titles bagged because he or she guessed right—for example, in my case, Robert Hughes's *The Fatal Shore* and the dual selection of Anne Tyler's *The Accidental Tourist* and Garrison Keillor's *Lake Wobegon Days*. One's pride in these was an exquisite mixture of the crass and the high-minded that faithfully mirrored the place where we worked at its worst and best. But the point is that the publisher mightn't even have gambled on 3,500 copies if the possibility of an off-the-wall book club selection hadn't existed. And how many other marginal titles owed their lives to similar calculations?

As for the lost readers—legend has it that sometime in the early 1980s Stephen King announced, "I've got the Literary Guild audience, now I want the BOMC one." I doubt he'd bother to say this now. Although a number of BOMC members probably stayed put out of inertia, my guess (and it's just a guess) is that the extra ones who once made the BOMC such a great launching pad have either joined the Guild *et al.* or dropped out of book clubs altogether and gone back to borrowing books from friends and libraries and watching a lot more television. Now that the BOMC has gone the way of the British royal family and other preposterous pleasures, I can even imagine the Helen Hokinson woman herself tearing up her last "negative-option" card and joining her semiliterate husband on the golf course. So literature's loss may turn out to be the horse show's gain.

It's also possible that under the combined pressure of the discount bookstores and various electrical boxes, large-scale literary book clubs are doomed anyhow. But I suspect that Harry Scherman would have demanded a little more proof. At the very least he'd have launched a Book of the Internet division by now, and maybe hired a spectacular judge or two, like the aforementioned Stephen King—who seems to have a real writer trapped in there—

and why not Salman Rushdie? (Where will the next meeting be held? Only the Book Club knows.)

But Scherman was a real salesman, with a real love of books, whereas the guys I met from Time Inc. had probably never run a lemonade stand, let alone a bookstore. ("My wife reads a lot" seemed the closest they'd ever come to the actual product.) It was a trademark of the eighties that the big operators knew all about the money of things but not about the things themselves. Which may be okay for the National Biscuit Company, but in a business where a Jane Austen or an E. M. Forster can suddenly catch fire, you need a lover's instincts, not an accountant's—and a friend at the Literary Guild, of all places, tells me that they recently began allowing their resident bookworms to play hunches just the way we used to.

In fact, the next logical step might be to assemble about five of these bookworms around a table, feed them well, and let the mysterious rhythms of talk and digestion do the rest. I can easily imagine something like the following. Fadiman: "I know it's not going to make any money, but I keep going back to that Irish thing, what's its name—*Angela* something or other." Or Highet: "Somehow I can't seem to get that bally Savannah book out of my head." (Richler: "I don't know about the book, but the title could sell a million copies.") Hutchens: "Will any of you gentlemen be watching the World Series this weekend?"

Sometimes it worked like that and sometimes it didn't. But whether this is going on in one head or five, *something* like it has to happen for publishing to work at all. And one only hopes that the trade gets back to it before humanity returns to symbols and hieroglyphs and books have disappeared altogether.

1999